Routledge Revivals

Humanist Essays

First published in 1964, this is a short collection of both literary and philosophical essays. Whilst two essays consider Greek literature written at the point at which the Athenian empire was breaking apart, another group explore the background from which Christianity arose, considering Paganism and religious philosophy at the time of Christ. These, in particular, display Gilbert Murray's 'profound belief in ethics and disbelief in all revelational religions', as well as his conviction that the roots of our society lie within Greek civilization. Finally, there is an interesting discussion of Order and the motives of those who seek to overthrow it.

Humanist Essays

Gilbert Murray

First published in 1964
By George Allen & Unwin Ltd

This edition first published in 2014 by Routledge
2 Park Square, Milton Park, Abingdon, Oxon, OX14 4RN

Simultaneously published in the USA and Canada
by Routledge
711 Third Avenue, New York, NY 10017

Routledge is an imprint of the Taylor & Francis Group, an informa business

© 1964 George Allen & Unwin Ltd

All rights reserved. No part of this book may be reprinted or reproduced or utilised in any form or by any electronic, mechanical, or other means, now known or hereafter invented, including photocopying and recording, or in any information storage or retrieval system, without permission in writing from the publishers.

Publisher's Note
The publisher has gone to great lengths to ensure the quality of this reprint but points out that some imperfections in the original copies may be apparent.

Disclaimer
The publisher has made every effort to trace copyright holders and welcomes correspondence from those they have been unable to contact.

A Library of Congress record exists under LC control number: 64054617

ISBN 13: 978-0-415-73001-3 (hbk)
ISBN 13: 978-1-315-85064-1 (ebk)
ISBN 13: 978-0-415-73002-0 (pbk)

GILBERT MURRAY

HUMANIST ESSAYS

Gilbert Murray

UNWIN BOOKS
GEORGE ALLEN & UNWIN LTD · LONDON
BARNES & NOBLE, INC · NEW YORK

FIRST PUBLISHED IN THIS EDITION 1964

This book is copyright under the Berne Convention. Apart from any fair dealing for the purposes of private study, research, criticism or review, as permitted under the Copyright Act, 1956, no portion may be reproduced by any process without written permission. Enquiry should be made to the publishers.

This edition © George Allen & Unwin Ltd, 1964

UNWIN BOOKS
George Allen & Unwin Ltd
Ruskin House, Museum Street
London, W.C.1

Published in the United States
in 1964
by Barnes & Noble Inc
105 Fifth Avenue New York 3

PRINTED IN GREAT BRITAIN
in 9 point Plantin type
BY C. TINLING & CO. LTD
LIVERPOOL, LONDON AND PRESCOT

CONTENTS

INTRODUCTION, *page* 7

I. LITERARY

I. Religio Grammatici: the Religion of a 'Man of Letters', 13
II. Aristophanes and the War Party, 30
III. The Bacchae of Euripides, 51
IV. Poesis and Mimesis, 78
V. Literature as Revelation, 93

II. PHILOSOPHICAL

VI. Pagan Religion and Philosophy at the Time of Christ, 107
VII. The Stoic Philosophy, 139
VIII. The Conception of Another Life, 154
IX. What is Permanent in Positivism, 169
X. Satanism and the World Order, 188

INTRODUCTION

These essays have been chosen from two previous collections, ESSAYS AND ADDRESSES (1921) *and* STOIC, CHRISTIAN AND HUMANIST (1940). *The occasions for which they were originally written are indicated in footnotes. In his Preface to* ESSAYS AND ADDRESSES *Professor Murray wrote:*

To make a collection even on a small scale of one's occasional writings on popular subjects throughout a long period of years is, I find, a matter of some anxiety. A man has generally little confidence in his past self. There is no knowing what it may have done, or what foolish things it may have thought or written, ten or twenty years ago. I confess that when I began to look through my papers with a view to the present selection I rather expected to find embarrassing self-contradictions or indiscretions of which I should now be ashamed. In this I was agreeably disappointed, but I did find what from the reader's point of view is perhaps worse, a good deal of repetition, or rather a constant attempt, by different means and in different contexts, to say very much the same thing.

Popular essays are normally written upon large and profound subjects about which neither the writer nor the reader can claim exact knowledge. That is inevitable and by no means blameworthy. Yet it does seem fair to ask that one who takes it upon him to advise his neighbours about uncertain and speculative things ought first to possess exact knowledge about something or other. It is not merely that he ought to know some little corner of the world before passing judgements on the world as a whole. He ought also to know the difference between knowing and not knowing; he ought to have mastered, in some one subject, the method by which knowledge is acquired. And whatever his subject is, his experience of it will be an invaluable help to him in understanding matters outside it, and will probably here and there enable him to see some things which people with a different experience have failed to see. Of course it will also to some extent mislead him; that is inevitable. It will, in spite of all vigilance, give a bias or a colour to his conceptions.

Professor Murray goes on to say that he is for good or evil a 'grammaticus', in particular a student of Greek; and that his special form of experience and the point of view to which it leads are given in his first essay, Religio Grammatici. *Starting from some study of "letters" as the record made by the human soul of those moments of life which it has valued most and most longs to preserve, he makes his attempt to understand its present adventures and prospects.*

In his Preface to STOIC, CHRISTIAN AND HUMANIST, *which with one addition makes up the second part of this collection, Professor Murray wrote:*

The essays are in part the results of special reading and study. I have worked a good deal at various times on problems of ancient religion and modern anthropology, and at one time when I was invited to give the Gifford Lectures on Natural Religion I thought of making a systematic attempt at a statement of my *Weltanschauung*, comprising a profound belief in ethics and disbelief in all revelational religions.

In another aspect, however, the essays are merely by-products of a long life in which I have had almost constantly in the back of my mind, as a half-conscious preoccupation, the aspirations, problems and moral compulsions which form part at least of the substance of religion.

I do not know if my experience is at all peculiar. But I believe my reaction toward the traditional religion of the society in which I was born falls into three periods. It began entirely as a moral rebellion in early childhood. Oddly enough, it was the miracle of the Gadarene swine that first shocked me. I cannot be sure of my age at the time, but it was before I left Australia and therefore before my eleventh birthday. It seemed to me so monstrously cruel to drive—or be indirectly responsible for driving—a lot of unoffending pigs over a precipice. It was just the sort of thing I could imagine being done by very wicked boys, the kind of boys that tortured animals and loved bullying. The germ of criticism once admitted, I began in my teens to be uneasy about other elements in the New Testament: the unreasonable cursing of the fig-tree, the doctrine of eternal damnation, and the whole conception of vicarious atonement. What could a schoolboy think of a master who, when offended, made no particular difference between the guilty and the innocent, but insisted on his right to flog somebody?

It seems to me, as I look back, that I was a very innocent and perhaps priggish boy, crudely humanitarian and idealist. The cruelty to animals in my school in the bush almost drove me mad. I had many fights about it. And there were other things I hated almost as much. When first, by mere accident, I came across the writings of

Shelley I was almost dazzled by finding suddenly the expression of my own unspoken dream. This, I felt, was the right thing. This was what I wanted, what I craved for. It was the antidote to all the coarseness and brutality and contempt for weaker creatures which raged round about me.

I do not mean that I was on the whole unhappy at my Australian school. The spirits of the young are mercurial. I liked my masters, enjoyed most of my lessons, and loved cricket. But I began even then to feel that it was no good talking to the authorities, clerical and other, about the scruples or ideals that moved me most. Certainly I was always too shy to think of explaining myself.

The intellectual reasons for disbelief came to me much later. Here I was influenced not so much by the obviously unscientific character of the accounts of the creation and other stories in the Old Testament, as by the discovery that different nations had different religions, and by a subsequent comparative study of religion and anthropology. I found that every successive civilization has had its own explanation of the world. Each has claimed to be, alone and exclusively, the Way, the Truth and the Life. The explanations have varied as the civilizations varied, and passed away as the civilizations passed. It was, for instance, simply due to historical causes that Europe became Christian and Asia Minor Moslem, and that England, for instance, adopted its particular form of Christianity. Consequently it seemed improbable that the particular country and age in which I happened to be born had received an exclusive revelation of the truth.

Besides that, in my later school days and early years as an undergraduate, I continued to feel that the rather conventional clergymen who formed the majority of my teachers were not very inspiring, not people to whom one could talk freely of serious things. The best and most interesting people I knew were Free-thinkers. It was not till I came to know Charles Gore, afterwards Bishop of Oxford, that I discovered that extreme orthodoxy was compatible not merely with great charm and intellectual power but with a most sensitive humanity and generosity of outlook. This strong high-churchman was, I found, quite as good a man as the two or three radical Freethinkers whom I adored and towards whom I still feel a profound affection and gratitude. I ceased forthwith to be anti-clerical, though I did not seriously change my beliefs or disbeliefs.

The World War and events in post-war Europe have revealed a vast and awful gulf between the 'ideologies' or, as I should prefer to say, the fundamental faiths of different kinds of men. The gulf stares us in the face; it is of enormous importance, but it is hard to define. It is certainly not a mere clash between Socialism and capitalism, between Conservatism and a desire for change, between democracy and some other political system. Nor yet is it between Christianity and scepticism. Lenin's Russia is anti-God. Franco's Spain is devoutly Catholic. The German Government is partly Christian, partly Pagan; the Japanese Government Shinto-Buddhist: but much the same foul deeds have been done, and not only done but admired and glorified by all of them. The revolt of the human conscience against such cruelties has been often no doubt Christian versus non-Christian, but much more consistently Liberal versus militarist. If many of us cannot help feeling in the world about us what Coleridge felt in his nightmare:

> A lurid light, a trampling throng,
> Sense of intolerable wrong,
> And what I scorned, that only strong:

it is impossible to identify 'that which we scorn' with any particular orthodoxy or unorthodoxy. One is often reminded of Mr Gladstone's phrase, 'the denial of God erected into a system of Government', and tempted to describe the conflict, in broader terms, as a clash between religion in some sense and an utter denial of the fundamental elements of religion. Yet even this conception is not quite satisfying, because if a certain lowering of standards and an acceptance of money values as more important than moral values may be due to lack of religion, the worst actual abominations of the time are due to various forms of fanaticism, a fanaticism sometimes religious, sometimes political, but strangely similar to that which raged in the Religious Wars. One can perhaps truly say that what is being endangered in Europe is what people call 'the Christian spirit'; but that phrase will mean the Christian spirit as humanized and liberalized in the nineteenth century, a spirit totally different from that of the hell-ridden persecuting Christianities of various past ages. I would just as soon call it 'a humane spirit' or 'a Liberal spirit'. We call it Christian because when our own conscience rejects some action we like to find some authority for our feeling. We say that Jesus or St Francis would condemn it, just as a Chinese would appeal to Confucius or an ancient Roman to the philosophers:

> Chrysippus non dicet idem, nec mite Thaletis
> Ingenium, dulcique senex vicinus Hymetto,
> Qui partem acceptae dura inter vincla cicutae
> Accusatori nollet dare.

INTRODUCTION 11

No doubt the higher moral effort of man in every nation will, for the great majority, express itself in the traditional religious conventions of that nation. Moral idealism in England will be for the most part Protestant, in Austria Catholic, in Turkey Moslem, in China Confucian or Buddhist. But in the more civilized communities, as in ancient Greece, there has always been a minority who, through some speculative urge in their own minds or perhaps through the circumstances of their lives, have felt convinced that the traditional frame of dogmas current about them did not represent the exclusive truth, the necessary truth, or even any exact truth at all about the ultimate mysteries, and have tried to keep their sense of the duty of man towards his neighbour and his own highest powers clear of the confusing and sometimes perverting mythology on which it is traditionally said to be based. Its real basis is the rock of human experience.

What I have written in this little book may, I fear, alienate or at least pain some of the friends with whom I have worked most closely for certain great humane causes. They may ask why I should write such criticism at all. If I cannot positively help the faith of the average man, why can I not at least keep silent? My answer is that, if these subjects are of importance to mankind, as I believe them to be, it is our duty to seek the truth about them.

To complete the outline of Gilbert Murray's life: he was born on January 2, 1866 in Sydney, Australia, and after his early schooldays there came to England to continue his education, at the Merchant Taylors' school and St John's College Oxford, where he had a brilliant career. At the age of twenty-three he became Professor of Greek at Glasgow University, and in the same year married Lady Mary Howard, daughter of the Earl of Carlisle. Between 1904 and 1907 many of the translations of Greek plays for which he is so well known were staged at the Court Theatre under the Vedrenne-Barker management. He was appointed Regius Professor of Greek at Oxford in 1908 and, with one interval in 1926 as Professor of Poetry at Harvard, he held the post until 1936. He was awarded the O.M. in 1941. In public affairs he was a strong advocate of international co-operation, being closely associated with the League of Nations from its inception, and more recently with the United Nations Association. He died at Oxford on May 20, 1957, and his ashes rest in Westminster Abbey.

CHAPTER I

Religio Grammatici:
The Religion of a 'Man of Letters'[1]

It is the general custom of this Association to choose as its President alternately a classical scholar and a man of wide eminence outside the classics. Next year you are to have a man of science, a great physician who is also famous in the world of learning and literature. Last year you had a statesman, though a statesman who is also a great scholar and man of letters, a sage and counsellor in the antique mould, of world-wide fame and unique influence.[2] And since, between these two, you have chosen, in your kindness to me, a professional scholar and teacher, you might well expect from him an address containing practical educational advice in a practical educational crisis. But that, I fear, is just what I cannot give. My experience is too one-sided. I know little of schools and not much even of pass-men. I know little of such material facts as curricula and time-tables and parents and examination papers. I sometimes feel—as all men of fifty should—my ignorance even of boys and girls. Besides that, I have the honour at present to be an official of the Board of Education; and in public discussions of current educational subjects an officer of the Board must in duty be like the poetical heroine—'He cannot argue, he can only feel.'

I believe, therefore, that the best I can do, when the horizon looks somewhat dark not only for the particular studies which we in this Society love most, but for the habits of mind which we connect with those studies, the philosophic temper, the gentle judgement, the interest in knowledge and beauty for their own sake, will be simply, with your assistance, to look inward and try to realize my own confession of faith. I do, as a matter of fact, feel clear that, even if knowledge of Greek, instead of leading to bishoprics as it once did, is in future to be regarded with popular suspicion as a mark of either a reactionary or an unusually feckless temper, I am never-

---

[1] Presidential Address to the Classical Association, January 8, 1918.
[2] Sir William Osler and Lord Bryce.

theless not in the least sorry that I have spent a large part of my life in Greek studies, not in the least penitent that I have been the cause of others doing the same. That is my feeling, and there must be some base for it. There must be such a thing as *Religio Grammatici*, the special religion of a 'Man of Letters'.

The greater part of life, both for man and beast, is rigidly confined in the round of things that happen from hour to hour. It is ἐπὶ συμφοραῖς, exposed for circumstances to beat upon; its stream of consciousness channelled and directed by the events and environments of the moment. Man is imprisoned in the external present; and what we call a man's religion is, to a great extent, the thing that offers him a secret and permanent means of escape from that prison, a breaking of the prison walls which leaves him standing, of course, still in the present, but in a present so enlarged and enfranchised that it is become not a prison but a free world. Religion, even in the narrow sense, is always seeking for *Sotêria*, for escape, for some salvation from the terror to come or some deliverance from the body of this death.

And men find it, of course, in a thousand ways, with different degrees of ease and of certainty. I am not wishing to praise my talisman at the expense of other talismans. Some find it in theology, some in art, in human affection; in the anodyne of constant work; in that permanent exercise of the inquiring intellect which is commonly called the search for Truth; some find it in carefully cultivated illusions of one sort or another, in passionate faiths and undying pugnacities; some, I believe, find a substitute by simply rejoicing in their prison, and living furiously, for good or ill, in the actual moment.

And a scholar, I think, secures his freedom by keeping hold always of the past and treasuring up the best out of the past, so that in a present that may be angry or sordid he can call back memories of calm or of high passion, in a present that requires resignation or courage he can call back the spirit with which brave men long ago faced the same evils. He draws out of the past high thoughts and great emotions; he also draws the strength that comes from communion or brotherhood.

> Blind Thamyris and blind Maeonides,
> And Tiresias and Phineus, prophets old,

come back to comfort another blind poet in his affliction. The Psalms, turned into strange languages, their original meaning often lost, live on as a real influence in human life, a strong and almost always an ennobling influence. I know the figures in the tradition may be unreal, their words may be misinterpreted. But the communion is quite a real fact. And the student, as he realizes it, feels himself one of a long line of torchbearers. He attains that which is the most compelling desire of every human being, a work in life which it is worth living for, and which is not cut short by the accident of his own death.

It is in that sense that I understand *Religio*. And now I would ask you to consider with me the proper meaning of *Grammatikê*, and the true business of the 'Man of Letters' or '*Grammaticus*'.

II

A very very, long time ago—the palaeontologists refuse to give us dates—mankind, trying to escape from his mortality, invented *Grammata* or letters. Instead of being content with his spoken words, ἔπεα πτερόεντα which fly as a bird flies and are past, he struck out the plan of making marks on wood or stone, or bone or leather or some other material, significant marks which should somehow last on, charged with meaning, in place of the word that had perished. Of course the subjects for such perpetuation were severely selected. Infinitely the greater part of man's life, even now, is in the moment, the sort of thing that is lived and passes without causing any particular regret, or rousing any definite action for the purpose of retaining it. And when the whole process of writing or graving was as difficult as it must have been in remote antiquity, the words that were recorded, the moments that were so to speak made imperishable, must have been very rare indeed. One is tempted to think of the end of Faust; was not the graving of a thing on brass or stone, was not even the painting of a reindeer in the depths of a palaeolithic cave, a practical though imperfect method of saying to the moment '*Verweile doch, Du bist so schön*' ('Stay longer, thou art so beautiful')? Of course the choice was, as you would expect, mostly based on material considerations and on miserably wrong considerations at that. I suppose the greater number of very ancient inscriptions or *Grammata* known to the world consist either in magical or religious formulae, supposed to be effective in producing material welfare; or else in titles of kings and honorific records of their achievements; or else in contracts and laws in which the spoken word eminently needed preserving. Either charms or else boasts or else contracts; and it is worth remembering that so far as they have any interest for us now it is an interest quite different from that for which they were engraved. They were all selected for immortality by reason of some present personal urgency. The charm was expected to work; the boast delighted the heart of the boaster; the contract would compel certain slippery or forgetful persons to keep their word. And now we know that the charm did not work. We do not know who the boaster was, and, if we did, would probably not admire him for the thing he boasts about. And the slippery or forgetful persons have long since been incapable of either breaking or fulfilling the contract. We are in each case only interested in some quality in the record which is different from that for which people recorded it. Of course there may be also the mere historical interest in these things as facts; but that again is quite different from the motive for their recording.

In fact one might say to all these records of human life, all these *Grammata* that have come down to us, what Marcus Aurelius teaches us to say to ourselves: ψυχάριον εἶ βαστάζον νέκρον; each one is 'a little soul carrying a corpse'. Each one, besides the material and temporary message it bears, is a record, however imperfect, of human life and character and feeling. In so far as the record can get across the boundary that separates mere record of fact from philosophy or poetry, so far it has a soul and still lives.

This is clearest, of course, in the records to which we can definitely attribute beauty. Take a tragedy of Aeschylus, a dialogue of Plato, take one of the very ancient Babylonian hymns or an oracle of Isaiah. The prophecy of Isaiah referred primarily to a definite set of facts and contained some definite—and generally violent—political advice; but we often do not know what those facts were, nor care one way or another about the advice. We love the prophecy and value it because of some quality of beauty, which subsists when the value of the advice is long dead; because of some soul that is there which does not perish. It is the same with those magnificent Babylonian hymns. Their recorders were doubtless conscious of their beauty, but they thought much more of their religious effectiveness. With the tragedy of Aeschylus or the dialogue of Plato the case is different, but only different in degree. If we ask why they were valued and recorded, the answer must be that it was mainly for their poetic beauty and philosophic truth, the very reasons for which they are read and valued now. But even here it is easy to see that there must have been some causes at work which derived their force simply from the urgency of the present, and therefore died when that present faded away.

And similarly an ancient work may, or indeed must, gather about itself new special environments and points of relevance. Thucydides and Aristophanes' *Knights* and even Jane Austen are different things now from what they were in 1913. I can imagine a translation of the *Knights* which would read like a brand-new topical satire. No need to labour the point. I think it is clear that in any great work of literature there is a soul which lives and a body which perishes; and further, since the soul cannot ever be found naked without any body at all, it is making for itself all the time new bodies, changing with the times.

III

Both soul and body are preserved, imperfectly of course, in *Grammata* or Letters; in a long series of marks scratched, daubed, engraved, written or printed, stretching from the inscribed bone implements and painted rocks of prehistoric man, through the great literatures of the world, down to this morning's newspaper and the MS. from which I am speaking; marks which have their own history also and their own vast varieties. And 'the office of the art *Grammatikē* is so to deal with the Grammata as to recover from them all that can be recovered of that which they have saved from oblivion, to reinstate as far as possible the spoken word in its first impressiveness and musicalness'.[1] That is not a piece of modern sentiment. It is the strict doctrine of the scribes. Dionysius Thrax gives us the definition; ἡ Γραμματική is ἐμπειρία τις ὡς ἐπὶ τὸ πολὺ τῶν παρὰ ποιήταις τε καὶ συγγραφεῦσι λεγομένων; an ἐμπειρία, a skill produced by practice, in the things said in poets and prose-writers; and he goes on to divide it into six parts, of which the first and most essential is Reading Aloud κατὰ προσῳδίαν—with just the accent, the cadences, the expression, with which the words were originally spoken before they were turned from λόγοι to γράμματα, from 'winged' words to permanent Letters. The other five parts are concerned with analysis; interpretation of figures of speech; explanation of obsolete words and customs; etymology; grammar in the narrow modern sense; and lastly κρίσις ποιημάτων, or, roughly, literary criticism. The first part is synthetic and in a sense creative; and most of the others are subservient to it. For I suppose if you had attained by study the power of reading aloud a play of Shakespeare exactly as Shakespeare intended the words to be spoken, you would be pretty sure to have mastered the figures of speech and obsolete

[1] Rutherford, *History of Annotation*, p. 12.

B

words and niceties of grammar. At any rate, whether or no you could manage the etymologies and the literary criticism, you would have done the main thing. You would, subject to the limitations we considered above, have recreated the play.

We intellectuals of the twentieth century, poor things, are so intimately accustomed to the use of Grammata that probably many of us write more than we talk and read far more than we listen. Language has become to us primarily a matter of Grammata. We have largely ceased to demand from the readers of a book any imaginative transliteration into the living voice. But mankind was slow in acquiescing in this renunciation. Isocrates, in a well-known passage (5, 10) of his Letter to Philip, laments that the scroll he sends will not be able to say what he wants it to say. Philip will hand it to a secretary and the secretary, neither knowing nor caring what it is all about, will read it out 'with no persuasiveness, no indication of changes of feeling, as if he were giving a list of items'. The early Arab writers in the same situation used to meet it squarely. The sage wrote his own book and trained his disciples to read it aloud, each sentence exactly right, and generally, to avoid the mistakes of the ordinary untrained reader, he took care that the script should not be intelligible to such persons.

These instances show us in what spirit the first Grammatici, our fathers in the art, conceived their task, and what a duty they have laid upon us. I am not of course overlooking the other and perhaps more extensive side of a scholar's work; the side which regards a piece of ancient or foreign writing as a phenomenon of language to be analysed and placed, not as a thing of beauty to be recreated or kept alive. On that side of his work the Grammaticus is a man of science or *Wissenschaft*, like another. The science of language demands for its successful study the same rigorous exactitude as the other natural sciences, while it has for educational purposes some advantages over most of them. Notably, its subject matter is intimately familiar to the average student, and his ear very sensitive to its varieties. The study of it needs almost no apparatus, and gives great scope for variety and originality of attack. Lastly, its extent is vast and its subtlety almost infinite; for it is a record, and a very fine one, of all the immeasurable varieties and gradations of human consciousness. Indeed, as the Grammata are related to the spoken word, so is the spoken word itself related to the thought or feeling. It is the simplest record, the first precipitation. But I am not dealing now with the Grammaticus as a man of science, or an educator of the young; I am considering that part of his function which belongs specially to *Religio* or *Pietas*.

IV

Proceeding on these lines we see that the scholar's special duty is to turn the written signs in which old poetry or philosophy is now enshrined back into living thought or feeling. He must so understand as to re-live. And here he is met at the present day by a direct frontal criticism. '*Suppose, after great toil and the expenditure of much subtlety of intellect, you succeed in re-living the best works of the past, is that a desirable end? Surely our business is with the future and present, not with the past. If there is any progress in the world or any hope for struggling humanity, does it not lie precisely in shaking off the chains of the past and looking steadily forward?*' How shall we meet this question?

First, we may say, the chains of the mind are not broken by any form of ignorance. The chains of the mind are broken by understanding. And so far as men are unduly enslaved by the past it is by understanding the past that they may hope to be freed. But, secondly, it is never really the past—the true past—that enslaves us; it is always the present. It is not the conventions of the seventeenth or eighteenth century that now make men conventional. It is the conventions of our own age; though of course I would not deny that in any age there are always fragments of the uncomprehended past still floating, like dead things pretending to be alive. What one always needs for freedom is some sort of escape from the thing that now holds him. A man who is the slave of theories must get outside them and see facts; a man who is the slave of his own desires and prejudices must widen the range of his experience and imagination. But the thing that enslaves us most, narrows the range of our thought, cramps our capacities and lowers our standards, is the mere Present—the present that is all round us, accepted and taken for granted, as we in London accept the grit in the air and the dirt on our hands and faces. The material present, the thing that is omnipotent over us, not because it is either good or evil, but just because it happens to be here, is the great Jailer and Imprisoner of man's mind; and the only true method of escape from him is the contemplation of things that are not present. Of the future? Yes; but you cannot study the future. You can only make conjectures about it, and the conjectures will not be much good unless you have in some way studied other places and other ages. There has been hardly any great forward movement of humanity which did not draw inspiration from the knowledge, or the idealization, of the past.

No: to search the past is not to go into prison. It is to escape out of prison, because it compels us to compare the ways of our own age with other ways. And as to Progress, it is no doubt a real fact. To many of us it is a truth that lies somewhere near the roots of our religion. But it is never a straight march forward; it is never a result that happens of its own accord. It is only a name for the mass of accumulated human effort, successful here, baffled there, misdirected and driven astray in a third region, but on the whole and in the main producing some cumulative result. I believe this difficulty about Progress, this fear that in studying the great teachers of the past we are in some sense wantonly sitting at the feet of savages, causes real trouble of mind to many keen students. The full answer to it would take us beyond the limits of this paper and beyond my own range of knowledge. But the main lines of the answer seem to me clear. There are in life two elements, one transitory and progressive, the other comparatively if not absolutely non-progressive and eternal, and the Soul of man is chiefly concerned with the second. Try to compare our inventions, our material civilization, our stores of accumulated knowledge, with those of the age of Aeschylus or Aristotle or St Francis, and the comparison is absurd. Our superiority is beyond question and beyond measure. But compare any chosen poet of our age with Aeschylus, any philosopher with Aristotle, any saintly preacher with St Francis, and the result is totally different. I do not wish to argue that we have fallen below the standard of those past ages; but it is clear that we are not definitely above them. The things of the spirit depend on will, on effort, on aspiration, on the quality of the individual soul; and not on discoveries and material advances which can be accumulated and added up.

As I tried to put the point some ten years ago, in my Inaugural Address at Oxford, 'one might say roughly that material things are superseded but spiritual things not; or that everything considered as an achievement can be superseded, but considered as so much life, not. Neither classification is exact, but let it pass. Our own generation is perhaps unusually conscious of the element of change. We live, since the opening of the great epoch of scientific invention in the nineteenth century, in a world utterly transformed from any that existed before. Yet we know that behind all changes the main web of life is permanent. The joy of an Egyptian child of the First

Dynasty in a clay doll was every bit as keen as the joy of a child now in a number of vastly better dolls. Her grief was as great when it was taken away. These are very simple emotions, but I believe the same holds good of emotions much more complex. The joy and grief of the artist in his art, of the strong man in his fighting, of the seeker after knowledge of righteousness in his many wanderings; these and things like them, all the great terrors and desires and beauties, belong somewhere to the permanent stuff of which daily life consists; they go with hunger and thirst and love and the facing of death. And these it is that make the permanence of literature. There are many elements in the work of Homer or Aeschylus which are obsolete and even worthless, but there is no surpassing their essential poetry. It is there, a permanent power which we can feel or fail to feel, and if we fail the world is poorer. And the same is true, though a little less easy to see, of the essential work of the historian or the philosopher.'

You will say perhaps that I am still denying the essence of human Progress; denying the progress of the human soul, and admitting only the sort of progress that consists in the improvement of tools, the discovery of new facts, the recombining of elements. As to that I can only admit frankly that I am not clear.

I believe we do not know enough to answer. I observe that some recent authorities are arguing that we have all done injustice to our palaeolithic forefathers, when we drew pictures of them with small brain-pans and no chins. They had brains as large and perhaps as exquisitely convoluted as our own; while their achievements against the gigantic beasts of prey that surrounded them show a courage and ingenuity and power of unselfish co-operation which have perhaps never since been surpassed. As to that I can form no opinion; I can quite imagine that, by the standards of the last Judgement, some of our modern philanthropists and military experts may cut rather a poor figure beside some nameless Magdalenian or Mousterian who died to save another, or, naked and almost weaponless, defeated a sabre-toothed tiger or a cave-bear. But I should be more inclined to lay stress on two points. First, on the extreme recentness, by anthropological standards, of the whole of our historic period. Man has been on the earth at least some twenty or thirty thousand years, and it is only the last three thousand that we are much concerned with. To suppose that a modern Englishman must necessarily be at a higher stage of mental development than an ancient Greek is almost the same mistake as to argue that Browning must be a better poet than Wordsworth because he came later. If the soul, or the brain, of man is developing, it is not developing so fast or so steadily as all that.

And next I would observe that the moving force in human progress is not widespread over the world. The uplifting of man has been the work of a chosen few; a few cities, a few races, a few great ages, have scaled the heights for us and made the upward way easy. And the record in the Grammata is precisely the record of these chosen few. Of course the record is redundant. It contains masses of matter that is now dead. Of course, also it is incomplete. There lived brave men before Agamemnon. There have been saints, sages, heroes, lovers, inspired poets in multitudes and multitudes, whose thoughts for one reason or another were never enshrined in the record, or if recorded were soon obliterated. The treasures man has wasted must be infinitely greater than those he has saved. But, such as it is, with all its imperfections the record he has kept is the record of the triumph of the human soul—the Triumph or, in Aristotle's sense of the word, the Tragedy.

It is there. That is my present argument. The soul of man, comprising the forces that have made progress and those that have achieved in themselves the end of progress, the moments of living to which he has said that they are too beautiful to be allowed to pass; the soul of man stands at the door and knocks. It is for each one of us to open or not to open.

For we must not forget the extraordinary frailty of the tenure on which these past moments of glory hold their potential immortality. They only live in so far as we can reach them; and we can only reach them by some labour, some skill, some imaginative effort and some sacrifice. They cannot compel us, and if we do not open to them they die.

V

And here perhaps we should meet another of the objections raised by modernists against our preoccupation with the past. *'Granted, they will say, that the ancient poets and philosophers were all that you say, surely the valuable parts of their thought have been absorbed long since in the common fund of humanity. Archimêdes, we are told, invented the screw; Eratosthenes invented the conception of longitude. Well, now we habitually operate with screws and longitude, both in a greatly improved form. And, when we have recorded the names of those two worthies and put up imaginary statues of them on a few scientific laboratories, we have surely repaid any debt we owe them. We do not go back laboriously with the help of a trained Grammaticus, and read their works in the original. Now admitting—what is far from clear—that Aeschylus and Plato did make contributions to the spiritual wealth of the human race comparable to the inventions of the screw and of longitude, surely those contributions have been absorbed and digested, and have become parts of our ordinary daily life? Why go back and labour over their actual words? We do not most of us want to re-read even Newton's* Principia.'

This argument raises exactly the point of difference between the humane and the physical. The invention of the screw or the telephone is a fine achievement of man; the effort and experience of the inventor make what we have called above a moment of glory. But you and I when using the telephone have no share whatever in that moment or that achievement. The only way in which we could begin in any way to share in them would be by a process which is really artistic or literary; the process of studying the inventor's life, realizing exactly his difficulties and his data and imaginatively trying to live again his triumphant experience. That would mean imaginative effort and literary study. In the meantime we use the telephone without any effort and at the same time without any spiritual gain at all, merely a gain—supposing it is a gain—in practical convenience.

If we take on the other hand the invention, or creation, of *Romeo and Juliet*, it is quite clear that you can in a sense by using it—that is, by reading the play—recapture the moment of glory: but not without effort. It is different in kind from a telephone or a hot-water tap. The only way of utilizing it at all is by the method of Grammatikê; by reading it or hearing it read and at the same time making a definite effort of imaginative understanding so as to re-live, as best one can, the experience of the creator of it. (I do not of course mean his whole actual experience in writing the play, but the relevant and essential part of that experience.) This method, the method of intelligent and loving study, is the only way there is of getting any sort of use out of *Romeo and Juliet*. It is not quite true, but nearly true, to say that the value of *Romeo and Juliet* to any given man is exactly proportionate to the amount of loving effort he has spent in trying to relive it. Certainly, in the absence of such effort *Romeo and Juliet* is without value and must die. It may stand at the door and knock, but its voice is not heard amid the rumble of the drums of Santerre. And the same is true of all great works of art or imagination, especially those which are in any way removed from us by differences of age or of language. We need not repine at this. The fact that so many works whose value and beauty is universally recognized require effort for their understanding is really a great benefit to contemporary and future work, because it accustoms the reader or spectator to the expectation of effort. And the unwillingness to make imaginative effort is the prime cause of almost all decay of art. It is the caterer, the man whose business it is to provide enjoyment with the very minimum of effort, who is in matters of art the real assassin.

VI

I have spoken so far of Grammatikê in the widest sense, as the art of interpreting the Grammata and so re-living the chosen moments of human life wherever they are recorded. But of course that undertaking is too vast for any human brain, and furthermore, as we have noticed above, a great mass of the matter recorded is either badly recorded or badly chosen. There has to be selection, and selection of a very drastic and ruthless kind. It is impossible to say exactly how much of life ought to be put down in Grammata, but it is fairly clear that in very ancient times there was too little and in modern times there is too much. Most of the books in any great library, even a library much frequented by students, lie undisturbed for generations. And yet if you begin what seems like the audacious and impossible task of measuring up the accumulated treasures of the race in the field of letters, it is curious how quickly in its main lines the enterprise becomes possible and even practicable. The period of recorded history is not very long. Eighty generations might well take us back before the beginnings of history-writing in Europe; and though the beginnings of Accad and of Egypt, to say nothing of the cave-drawings of Altamira, might take one almost incalculably further in time, the actual amount of Grammata which they provide is not large. Thus, firstly, the period is not very long; and, again, the extension of literature over the world is not very wide, especially if we confine ourselves to that continuous tradition of literature on which the life of modern Europe and America is built. China and India form, in the main, another tradition, which may stimulate and instruct us, but cannot be said to have formed our thought.

If you take any particular form of literature, the limits of its achievement become quickly visible. Take drama; there are not very many good plays in the world: Greece, France, England, Spain, and for brief periods Russia, Scandinavia, and Germany, have made their contributions; but, apart from the trouble of learning the languages, a man could read all the very good plays in the world in a few months. Take lyric or narrative poetry; philosophy; history:

there is not so much first-rate lyric poetry in the world, nor yet narrative; nor much first-rate philosophy; nor even history. No doubt when you consider the books that have to be read in order to study the history of a particular modern period—say, the time of Napoleon or the French Revolution—the number seems absolutely vast and overwhelming, but when you look for those histories which have the special gift that we are considering, that is the gift of retaining and expressing a very high quality of thought or emotion— the number dwindles at an amazing rate. And in every one of these forms of literature that I have mentioned, as well as many others, we shall find our list of the few selected works of outstanding genius begin with a Greek name.

'That depends,' our modernist may say, 'on the principles on which you make your selection. Of course the average Grammaticus of the present day will begin his selected historians with Herodotus and Thucydides, just as he will begin his poets with Homer, because he has been brought up to think that sort of thing. He is blinded, as usual, with the past. Give us a Greekless generation or two and the superstition will disappear.' How are we to answer this?

With due humility, I think, and yet with a certain degree of confidence. According to Dionysius Thrax the last and highest of the six divisions of Grammatikê was κρίσις ποιημάτων, the judgement or criticism of works of imagination. And the voice of the great mass of trained Grammatici counts for something. Of course they have their faults and prejudices. The tradition constantly needs correcting. But we must use the best criteria that we can get. As a rule any man who reads Herodotus and Thucydides with due care and understanding recognizes their greatness. If a particular person refuses to do so, I think we can fairly ask him to consider the opinions of recognized judges. And the judgement of those who know the Grammata most widely and deeply will certainly put these Greek names very high in their respective lists.

On the ground of pure intellectual merit, therefore, apart from any other considerations, I think any person ambitious of obtaining some central grasp on the Grammata of the human race would always do well to put a good deal of his study into Greek literature. Even if he were fatherless, like Melchizedek, or homeless, like a visitor from Mars, I think this would hold. But if he is a member of our Western civilization, a citizen of Europe or America, the reasons for studying Greek and Latin increase and multiply. Western civilization, especially the soul of it as distinguished from its accidental manifestations, is after all a unity and not a chaos; and it is a unity chiefly because of its ancestry, a unity of descent and of brotherhood. (If any one thinks my word 'brotherhood' too strong in the present state of Europe, I would remind him of the relationship between Cain and Abel.)

VII

The civilization of the Western world is a unity of descent and brotherhood; and when we study the Grammata of bygone men we naturally look to the writings from which our own are descended. Now, I am sometimes astonished at the irrelevant and materialistic way in which this idea is interpreted. People talk as if our thoughts were descended from the fathers of our flesh, and the fountain-head of our present literature and art and feeling was to be sought among the Jutes and Angles.

Paradise Lost and *Prometheus Unbound* are not the children of *Piers Ploughman* and *Beowulf*; they are the children of Vergil and Homer, of Aeschylus and Plato. And *Hamlet* and *Midsummer Night's Dream* come mainly from the same ancestors, though by a less direct descent.

I do not wish to exaggerate. The mere language in which a book is written counts of course for much. It fixes to some extent the forms of the writer's art and thought. *Paradise Lost* is clearly much more English in character than Lucan's *Pharsalia* is Spanish or Augustine's *City of God* African. Let us admit freely that there must of necessity be in all English literature a strain of what one may call vernacular English thought, and that some currents of it, currents of great beauty and freshness, would hardly have been different if all Romance literature had been a sealed book to our tradition. It remains true that from the Renaissance onward, nay, from Chaucer and even from Alfred, the higher and more massive workings of our literature owe more to the Greeks and Romans than to our own un-Romanized ancestors. And the same is true of every country in Europe. Even in Scandinavia, which possesses a really great home literature, in some ways as noble as the Greek or the Hebrew, the main currents of literary thought and feeling, the philosophy and religion and the higher poetry, owe more to the Graeco-Roman world than to that of the Vikings. The movements that from time to time spring up in various countries for reviving the old home tradition and expelling the foreigner have always had an exotic character. The German attempts to worship Odin, to regard the Empire as a gathering of the German tribes, to expel all non-

Germanic words from the language by the help of an instrument called—not very fortunately—a 'Zentralbureau', have surely been symptoms of an error only not ridiculous because it is so deeply tragic. The twisting of the English language by some fine writers, so that a simple Latin word like 'cave' gives place to a recondite old English 'stoney-dark'; the attempts in France to reject the 'Gaulois' and become truly 'Celtique', are more attractive but hardly in essence more defensible. There is room for them as protests, as experiments, as personal adventures, or as reactions against a dominant main stream. They are not a main stream themselves. The main stream is that which runs from Rome and Greece and Palestine, the Christian and classical tradition. We nations of Europe would do well to recognize it and rejoice in it. It is in that stream that we find our unity, unity of origin in the past, unity of movement and imagination in the present; to that stream that we owe our common memories and our power of understanding one another, despite the confusion of tongues that has now fallen upon us and the inflamed sensibilities of modern nationalism. The German Emperor's dictum, that the boys and girls in his Empire must 'grow up little Germans and not little Greeks and Romans', is both intellectually a Philistine policy and politically a gospel of strife.

I trust no one will suppose that I am pleading for a dead orthodoxy, or an enforced uniformity of taste or thought. There is always a place for protests against the main convention, for rebellion, paradox, partisanship, and individuality, and for every personal taste that is sincere. Progress comes by contradiction. Eddies and tossing spray add to the beauty of every stream and keep the water from stagnancy. But the true Grammaticus, while expressing faithfully his personal predilections or special sensitivenesses, will stand in the midst of the Grammata, not as a captious critic, nor yet as a jealous seller of rival wares, but as a returned traveller amid the country and landscape that he loves. He will realize the amount of love and care which has gone to the making of the *Traditio*, the handing down of the intellectual acquisitions of the human race from one generation to another, the constant selection of thoughts and discoveries and feelings and events so precious that they must be made into books, and then of books so precious that they must be copied and recopied and not allowed to die. The *Traditio* itself is a wonderful and august process, full no doubt of abysmal gaps and faults, like all things human, but full also of that strange half baffled and yet not wholly baffled splendour which marks the characteristic works of man. I think the Grammaticus, while not sacrificing his judgement, should accept the *Traditio* and rejoice in it, rejoice to be the intellectual child of his great forefathers, to catch at their spirit, to carry on their work, to live and die for the great unknown purpose which the eternal spirit of man seems to be working out upon the earth. He will work under the guidance of love and faith; not, as so many do, under that of ennui and irritation.

VIII

My subject today has been the faith of a scholar, *Religio Grammatici*. This does not mean any denial or disrespect towards the religions of others. A Grammaticus who cannot understand other people's minds is failing in an essential part of his work. The religion of those who follow physical science is a magnificent and life-giving thing. The *Traditio* would be utterly wrecked without it. It also gives man an escape from the world about him, an escape from the noisy present into a region of facts which are as they are and not as foolish human beings want them to be; an escape from the commonness of daily happenings into the remote world of high and severely trained imagination; an escape from mortality in the service of a growing and durable purpose, the progressive discovery of truth. I can understand also the religion of the artist, the religion of the philanthropist. I can understand the religion of those many people, mostly young, who reject alike books and microscopes and easels and committees, and live rejoicing in an actual concrete present which they can ennoble by merely loving it. And the religion of Democracy? That is just what I am preaching throughout this discourse. For the cardinal doctrine of that religion is the right of every human soul to enter, unhindered except by the limitation of its own powers and desires, into the full spiritual heritage of the race.

All these things are good, and those who pursue them may well be soldiers in one army or pilgrims on the same eternal quest. If we fret and argue and fight one another now, it is mainly because we are so much under the power of the enemy. I sometimes wish that we men of science and letters could all be bound by some vow of renunciation or poverty, like monks of the Middle Age; but of course no renunciation could be so all-embracing as really to save us from that power. The enemy has no definite name, though in a certain degree we all know him. He who puts always the body before the spirit, the dead before the living, the ἀναγκαῖον before the καλόν; who makes things only in order to sell them; who has forgotten that there is such a thing as truth, and measures the world by advertisement or by money; who daily defiles the beauty that surrounds him and makes vulgar the tragedy; whose innermost religion is the worship of the Lie in his Soul. The Philistine, the vulgarian, the Great Sophist, the passer of base coin for true, he is all about us and, worse, he has his outposts inside us, persecuting our peace, spoiling our sight, confusing our values, making a man's self seem greater than the race and the present thing more important than the eternal. From him and his influence we find our escape by means of the Grammata into that calm world of theirs, where stridency and clamour are forgotten in the ancient stillness, and that which was in its essence material and transitory has for the most part perished, while the things of the spirit still shine like stars. Not only the great things are there, seeming to stand out the greater because of their loneliness; there is room also for many that were once in themselves quite little, but now through the *Grammata* have acquired a magic poignancy, echoes of old tenderness or striving or laughter beckoning across gulfs of death and change; the watchwords that our dead leaders and forefathers loved, *viva adhuc et desiderio pulcriora*.[1]

---

[1] 'Living still and more beautiful because of our longing.'

CHAPTER II

Aristophanes and the War Party[1]

THERE is no commoner cause of historical misjudgement than the tendency to read the events of the past too exclusively in the light of the present, and so twist the cold and unconscious record into the burning service of controversial politics. And yet history is inevitably to a great extent a work of the imagination. No good historian is content merely to repeat the record of the past. He has to understand it, to see behind it, to find more in it than it actually says. He cannot understand without the use of his constructive imagination, and he cannot imagine effectively without the use of his experience. I believe it is one of the marks of a great historian, such as he in whose honour this annual lecture was established, such as he who now does us the honour of occupying the chair,[2] to see both present and past, as it were, with the same unclouded eye; to realize the past story as if it were now proceeding before him, and to envisage the present much in the same perspective as it will bear when it is one chapter, or so many pages, in the great volume of the past.

We know in Gibbon's case how much the historian of the Roman Empire learnt from the Captain of the Hampshire Grenadiers. And it would surely be folly to tell a man who had lived through the French or the Russian Revolution to forget his own experience when he came to treat of similar events in history. To do so is to fall into that great delusion that haunts the hopes of so many savants, the delusion of supposing that in these matters man can attain truth by some sure mechanical process without ever committing himself to the fallible engine of his own personality.

Greek history has been, for reasons not difficult to unravel, constantly reinterpreted according to the political experiences and preferences of its writers. Cleon in particular, the most vivid figure of the Peloponnesian War, plays in the history books many varied parts. Heeren and Passow, writing under the influence of the French Revolution, treat him as a 'bloodthirsty sans-culotte' who established

[1] The Creighton Lecture, London School of Economics, 1918.
[2] Dr Mandell Creighton and Lord Bryce.

a reign of terror. (Busolt, iii. 988 ff.) Mitford, a good English Tory reeling under the horror of the first Reform Bill, took him as a shocking example of what democracy really is and must be. Grote, on the contrary, saw him as a vigorous and much-abused Radical, and justified his war-policy for the sake of his democratic ardour at home. In our own day Mr Grundy and Mr Walker somewhat reinforce the position of Mitford, while Mr Zimmern, following Beloch and Ferrero, sees in Cleon little more than the figurehead of a great social and economic movement. For my own part I would fain go back to the actual language of Thucydides and regard Cleon simply as 'the most violent of the citizens, and at that time most persuasive to the multitude'. We need bring in no nicknames of modern parties; that phrase tells us essentially what we need to know.

I propose today to consider the impression made on Athenian society by that long and tremendous conflict between Athens and Sparta which is called the Peloponnesian War, using the light thrown by our own recent experience. That war was in many respects curiously similar to the present war. It was, as far as the Hellenic peoples were concerned, a world-war. No part of the Greek race was unaffected. It was the greatest war there had ever been. Arising suddenly among civilized nations, accustomed to comparatively decent and half-hearted wars, it startled the world by its uncompromising ferocity. Again, it was a struggle between Sea-power and Land-power; though Athens, like ourselves, was far from despicable on land, and Sparta, like Germany, had a formidable fleet, and adopted the same terrorist policy of sinking all craft whatsoever, enemy or neutral, which they found at sea. (*Thucydides* ii. 67.) It was a struggle between the principles of democracy and military monarchy; and in consequence throughout the Hellenic world there was a violent dissidence of sympathy, the military and aristocratic parties everywhere being pro-Spartan, and the democratic parties pro-Athenian. From the point of view of military geography, again, the democratic sea-empire of Athens suffered much from its lack of cohesion and its dependence on sea-borne resources, while the military land empire of the Peloponnesians gained from its compact and central position. It would perhaps be fanciful to go further and suggest that the Thracian hordes played something the same part in the mind of the Athenians as the Russians with some of us. And, when they failed, alas, there was no America to make sure that the right side won!

Again, in the commonplaces of political argument, we find in that part of the Peloponnesian War about which we have adequate information, a division of parties curiously similar to our own. There were no pro-Spartans in Athens, just as there are no pro-Germans in the proper sense of the word with us. There was roughly a Peace by Negotiation party, led by Nicias, and a Knock-out-Blow party, led by Cleon. The latter emphasized the delusiveness of an 'inconclusive Peace' and the impossibility of ever trusting the word of a Spartan; the former maintained that a war to the bitter end would only result in the exhaustion of both sets of combatants and the ruin of Greece as a whole. And Providence, unusually indulgent, vouchsafed to both parties the opportunity of proving that they were right. After ten years of war Nicias succeeded in making a peace treaty, which, however, the firebrands on both sides proceeded at once to violate; war broke out again, as the war party had always said it would, and after continuing altogether twenty-seven years left Athens wrecked and Sparta bleeding to death, just as the peace party had always prophesied!

Of course such parallels must only be allowed to amuse our reflections, not to distort our judgements. It would be easy to note a thousand points of difference between the two great contests. But I must notice in closing one last similarity between the atmospheres of the two wars which is profoundly pathetic, if not actually disquieting. The more the cities of Greece were ruined by the havoc of war, the more the lives of men and women were poisoned by the fear and hate and suspicion which it engendered, the more was Athens haunted by shining dreams of the future reconstruction of human life. Not only in the speculations of philosophers like Protagoras and Plato, or town-planners like Hippodamus, but in comedy after comedy of Aristophanes and his compeers—the names are too many to mention—we find plans for a new life; a great dream-city in which the desolate and oppressed come by their own again, where rich and poor, man and woman, Athenian and Spartan are all equal and all at peace, where there are no false accusers and—sometimes—where men have wings. This Utopia begins as a world-city full of glory and generous hope; it ends, in Plato's Laws, as one little hard-living asylum of the righteous on a remote Cretan hill-top, from which all infection of the outer world is rigorously excluded, where no religious heretics may live, where every man is a spiritual soldier, and even every woman must be ready to 'fight for her young, as birds do'. The great hope had dwindled to be very like despair; and even in that form it was not fulfilled.

The war broke out in 432 BC between the Athenian Empire,

comprising nearly all the maritime states of Greece, on the one hand, and on the other the Peloponnesian Alliance led by Sparta. The first war lasted till 421; then followed the Peace of Nicias, interrupted by desultory encroachments and conflicts not amounting to open war till 418 when the full flood recommenced and lasted till the destruction of Athens in 404.

I wish to note first a few of the obvious results arising from so long and serious a war. The most obvious was the over-crowding of Athens due to the influx of refugees from the districts exposed to invasion. They lived, says Thucydides, in stuffy huts or slept in temples and public buildings and the gates of the city wall, as best they could (*Thucydides* ii. 52). 'You love the people?' says the Sausage-monger in Aristophanes' *Knights* to Cleon, 'but here they are for seven years living in casks and holes and gateways. And much you care! You just shut them up and milk them.' As every one knows, this over-crowding resulted in the great outbreak of a plague, similar to the Black Death, in 430, a point emphasized by Thucydides but not, if I remember rightly, ever mentioned by Aristophanes. I suppose there are some things which, even to a comic genius, are not funny.

There was great scarcity of food, of oil for lighting, and of charcoal for burning. 'No oil left,' says a slave in the *Clouds*: 'Confound it,' answers his master; 'why did you light that drunkard of a lamp?' (*Clouds* 56.) 'What are you poking the wick for,' says an Old Man to his son in the *Wasps*, 'when oil is so scarce, silly? Any one can see *you* don't have to pay for it!' (*Wasps* 252 ff.) But food was dearer still. 'Good boy,' says the same Old Man a little later, 'I'll buy you something nice. You would like some knuckle-bones, I suppose?'

Boy. I'd sooner have figs, papa.

OLD MAN. Figs? I'd see you all hanged first. Out of this beggarly pay I have to buy meal and wood and some bit of meat or fish for three. And you ask for figs!' And the Boy bursts into tears.

I think the passage in the *Acharnians* where the hero, parodying a scene in a tragedy, threatens to murder a sack of charcoal, and the Chorus of charcoal-burners are broken-hearted at the thought, is perhaps more intelligible to us this winter than it was before the war.

The scarcity of food is dwelt upon again and again. It is treated almost always as a joke, but it is a joke with a grim background. Many places suffered far more than Athens. Melos had been reduced by famine (*Birds* 186). The much-ravaged Megara, an enemy so contemptibly weak and yet, for geographical reasons, so maddeningly inconvenient to the Athenians, was absolutely starving.

Farce comes near to the border of tears in the scene of the *Acharnians* where the Megarian comes to sell his children in a sack, as pigs, and we hear how the fashionable amusement in Megara is to have starving-matches round a fire (*Acharnians* 750-752).

In Athens itself prices were high, as we saw in the scene from the *Wasps*. Everybody was in debt, like Strepsiades in the *Clouds*, like Peithetairos and Euelpides in the *Birds*. The King of the Birds, we hear, 'had once been a human being, like you and me; and owed money, like you and me; and was thankful not to pay it, like you and me'. (*Birds* 114 ff.). That was one of the reasons why, though Athens was certainly 'a great and prosperous city and open to every one to spend money in', the heroes of that play determined to seek another home.

But the liveliest description of the general lack of food is in the *Knights*, in a scene of which the point has often been missed. Cleon is addressing the Council, thundering accusations of conspiracy and 'the hidden hand', when the Sausage-monger resolves to interrupt him and bursts—quite illegally—in with the news that a shoal of sprats has come into the Piraeus and can be had cheap, extraordinarily cheap. The hungry and anxious faces suddenly clear. They vote a crown to the bringer of good tidings, and prepare to rush off. Cleon, to regain his ascendancy, proposes a vast sacrifice of kids, as a thank-offering. The Sausage-monger at once doubles the number, and proposes a still further extravagance of public feasting next day if sprats fall to a hundred the obol. The councillors accept the proposal without discussion and stream out. Cleon shrieks for them to wait: a herald has come from the Spartans to propose terms of peace! At another time that would have held them. But now there are cries of derision. 'Peace? Yes, of course. When they know that we have cheap fish. We don't want peace! Let the war rip!' Cleon had taught them their lesson only too well. (*Knights* 625-680).

Another effect of the war was the absence of men of military age from Athens. The place was full of women and *Gerontes*—technically, men over sixty. And the young men were being killed out. That explains such phrases, for example, as the remark that Argos was now powerful because she had plenty of young men (Contrast *Hdt*. vi. 83). It explains too why the plots of three of our eleven extant comedies, and quite a number of those only known from fragments, are based on suppositions of what the women might do if they held together. In the *Lysistrata*—the name means Dismisser of Armies—the heroine, determined on compelling both sides to make peace, organizes a general strike of all wives and mistresses, both in Athens and Sparta. They seize the Acropolis, and dress themselves in their most bewitching clothes, but will not say a word to any husband or lover till peace is made. And when the authorities are summoned to put the revolt down, alas, they amount to nothing but a crowd of scolding old gentlemen. It is much the same in the *Ecclesiazusae*, or Women in Parliament, only there they pack the Assembly disguised as men, carry a measure transferring the voting power from men to women and then introduce a socialist Utopia. The third woman-play, the *Thesmophoriazusae*, turns on literature, not on politics.

The evidence is not sufficient to show whether there really was any general movement for peace among the women, or yet for socialism. At the present time women probably feel the pinch of scarcity and the difficulties of housekeeping more than men do; and possibly they feel the deaths of the young men more than the old men do. But these are only two factors among an enormous number that are operating.

The third material result which seems worth specially mentioning was the dearth of servants, though this was due to a different cause from those which produce the same effect among us. It was that the slaves, who of course had no patriotism towards the city of their owners, deserted in vast numbers. At a certain moment we are told that more than 20,000 had escaped from Athens. Life no doubt was extra hard, and escape was easy. The master, if he was under sixty, was apt to be away on duty; and if you once got outside the town into the open country, where the enemy was in force, there was a good chance of not being pursued.

The slaves thus correspond to what is called the 'international proletariate', or would correspond if such a class really existed. They were a class without rights, without interests, without preference for one country or one set of masters over another. In modern Europe it seems as a rule to take an extraordinary amount of prolonged misery before an oppressed class loses its national feeling.

Now let us turn from the material effects of the war to a more interesting side of the subject, the effects upon political opinion. I think that on this point, owing to the exceptional vividness and richness of our sources, quite a good deal can be made out. We have not only the direct narrative of Thucydides, who writes at first hand of what he has himself observed and felt, and several speeches of contemporary orators, concerned with public or private suits. We have also the eleven comedies of Aristophanes, representing the political opposition, and treating of public affairs with unusual freedom of speech and also, amid the wildest exaggerations, with a singularly acute perception of his opponent's point of view. The Greeks were not politicians and dramatists for nothing.

The first simple fact to realize is that the war was a long, hard, and evenly balanced war. Consequently each side, as usual, thought its own successes much greater than they really were, though of course much less than they ought to be. They could not understand why, considering their own moral and intellectual superiority to the enemy, they did not succeed sooner in completely crushing him. There arose a demand for energy, energy at any price, and then more energy. But why, even with energy, did things continue to go wrong? The mob became hysterical. Evidently there was a hidden hand; there were traitors in our midst! This was dreadful enough; but the fact that with the utmost vigilance it was impossible to discover any traitors, made it infinitely exasperating. Athens swarmed with informers and false accusers. The old comedy is full of hits at these public nuisances, and they have left their mark on the historians and even the non-political writers. In tragedy, for example, references to contemporary affairs are extremely rare, but Euripides in the *Ion*, written in 415, alludes passingly to Athens as 'a city full of terror'. (*Ion* 601.)

In this state of things it became of course extremely difficult, if not dangerous, to work for peace. Nicias no doubt wished for a peace on reasonable terms, to be followed by an alliance with Sparta and a loyal co-operation between the two chief states of Greece. And there was, as far as we can see, no particular reason to regard Sparta as in any special sense an outcast from Greek civilization, or congenitally incapable of loyal action. But though all our authorities agree in praising both the character and abilities of Nicias, there is a constant complaint of his slowness, his lack of dash, and his reluctance to face, or to encourage, the howls of the patriotic mob. When he was commander-in-chief, Plutarch tells us, he lost popularity by spending all his day working at the Stratêgion, or War Office, and then going straight home, instead of making himself agreeable to the orators and disseminators of news, or making speeches to 'ginger' the Assembly.

As an offset to this rather gloomy picture, it is worth noting that Athenian civilization was hard to destroy. There were very few executions of citizens and no judicial murders even when passions ran most fiercely. And *pari passu* there were no assassinations. And though Aristophanes and the other comedians speak a good deal of the danger they run in attacking Cleon, they seem to have exercised during the first ten years or so of the war a degree of freedom of speech which is almost without a parallel in history. If you can with impunity, in public, refer to the leading statesman of the day as 'a whale that keeps a public-house and has a voice like a pig with its bristles on fire', you are somewhat debarred from denouncing the rigours of the censorship. (*Wasps* 35 ff.) In other Greek states, of which Corcyra is the standing example, there were civil wars, political proscriptions, and massacres. But it took a long time even for a war so deep-rooted and corrupting as the Peloponnesian to destroy the high civilization that had been built up in the Athens of Pericles. The only really atrocious acts which can be laid to the account of the war party at Athens are acts of ferocity to enemies or quasi-enemies, like the treatment of Megara and Mêlos; monstrous severity to those parts of the Empire which showed disloyalty during the war, like the massacres of Mitylênê and Skiônê; and thirdly, unless I am mistaken, a pretty constant practice of harsh and unscrupulous exploitation of subject-allies, which at times amounted to absolute tyranny and extortion.

After these general considerations, let us proceed to reconstruct the definite political criticism passed by the moderates or 'pacifists' on the government of Cleon. Of course such reconstruction is not quite easy. The criticism is hardly ever both directly and seriously expressed. In Thucydides it is serious but seldom direct; it has mostly to be gathered from implications. In the orators it is allusive and powerfully affected by the necessities of the particular cause which the speaker is pleading. In Aristophanes it is abundant and in one sense direct enough to satisfy the most exacting critic; but it is confused first by the wild and farcical atmosphere of the old comedy, which attains its end sometimes by exaggeration and sometimes, on the contrary, by paradox—I mean, by representing a public man in a character exactly the opposite to that for which he is notorious; and secondly, a point which is apt to be forgotten, by the subtle tact with which the poet has always to be handling his audience. To allow for these distorting media is not a question of scientific method; it is a question of familiarity with the subject and the language, of humour and of common sense. And it follows that one's interpretation can never be absolutely certain.

However, to take first the attitude of the opposition towards the enemy. It is plain enough how the average Athenian citizen under the influence of war-fever regarded him. It was folly to speak of ever making any treaty with a Spartan, 'who was no more to be trusted than a hungry wolf with its mouth open'. (*Lysistrata* 629.) The Spartans are to blame for everything, everything that has gone wrong; they are creatures 'for whom there exists no altar and no honour and no oath!' (*Acharnians* 308, 311.) The clergy, that is to say, the prophets and oracle-dealers are represented in Greek comedy, just as they are later by Erasmus and Voltaire, as more ferocious in their war-passions than the average layman. For example, in the *Peace*, when that buried goddess has been recovered from the bowels of the earth and all the nations are rejoicing, the soothsayer Hierocles comes to interrupt the peace-libations with his oracles: 'O miserable creatures and blind, not knowing the mind of the gods! Behold, men have made covenants with angry-eyed apes. Trembling gulls have put their trust in the children of foxes.' And again, 'Behold, it is not the pleasure of the blessed gods that ye cease from war until the wolf weds the lamb.' Again, 'Never shall ye make the crab walk straight; never shall ye make the sea-urchin smooth.' (*Peace* 1049–1120.)

These prophets are never sympathetically treated by Aristophanes. Sometimes they are simply kicked or beaten at sight. Sometimes they are argued with, as in this scene. 'Are we never to stop fighting?' asks the hero of the play. 'Are we to draw lots for which goes to the Devil deepest, when we might simply make peace and together be the leaders of Hellas?' And a little later he retorts on the oracles which Hierocles quotes from the prophet Bakis with a better oracle from Homer: 'Without kindred or law or hearthstone is the man who loves war among his people.' (*Peace* 1096 ff.)

In the *Acharnians* the hero deliberately undertakes to argue that the Spartans—whom he duly hates, and hopes that an earthquake may destroy them, for he too has had his vineyard ravaged—were, after all, not to blame in everything; on the contrary, they have in some points been treated unjustly. It is a bold undertaking. In very few great wars can it have been possible for a man on the public stage to argue such a thesis on behalf of the enemy; and Dicaeopolis has to do it with a block ready for cutting his head off if he does not prove his point. His argument is that the cause of the war was the Athenians' tariff-war against Megara—a small Dorian state under the protection of Sparta. There was a deliberately injurious tariff against Megarian goods; and then, instead of letting the tariff work in the casual happy-go-lucky way that was usual in antiquity, 'a lot of wicked little pinch-beck creatures, degraded, falsely stamped and falsely born', made a trade of informing against Megarian woollen goods. And if ever they saw a pumpkin or a hare or a young pig or a head of garlic or some stray lumps of salt, 'that's from Megara!' they shouted, and it was confiscated before nightfall. This led naturally enough to troubles on the frontier. Drunken young Athenians began making outrages across the Megarian border—the current form of outrage was to carry off a female slave; angry young Megarians made reprisals, till

> At last in wrath the Olympian Pericles
> Broke into thunder, lightning and damnation
> On Greece; passed laws written like drinking-songs,
> That no Megarian by land or sea
> Or sky or market should be left alive!

(The allusion is to a drinking-song beginning 'Would that not by land or sea,' etc.) The Megarians were reduced to starvation; Sparta, intervening, made a petition on behalf of Megara to have the decree rescinded. They pleaded many times and Athens refused; and then came the rattling of shields. 'They ought not to have rattled their shields, you say? Well, what ought they to have done? Suppose a Spartan had sailed out in a skiff and confiscated a puppy-dog belonging to the smallest islander in your League, would you have sat still? God bless us, no. In a moment you would have had three hundred ships of war on the water,' and so on, and so on.

The Chorus who listen to this bold pleading are shaken by it. Half go with the speaker, and half not. (*Acharnians* 496–561.)

Much the same account is given a few years later in the *Peace* (*Peace* 603–656). The hostile tariff against Megara was the first cause of the war; but the speaker here is more interested in what happened after. 'Your dependencies, or subject-allies,' he says, 'saw that you and the Spartans were snarling at each other; so, in fear of the tribute you made them pay, they moved heaven and earth to induce the chief men in Sparta to fight for their independence. And they, like the covetous curs and deceivers of strangers that they are, drove peace with shame out of the world and grabbed at war.' He goes on to show how most of the suffering fell on the tillers of the soil.

I will not discuss the truth of this account further than to observe that to my mind the only question is a question of proportion. The cruel tariff-war against Megara is a *vera causa*. It did exist, and it did act, as such tyrannies always act, as a cause of war. But how much weight it should be given among all the other causes is a question it would be futile at present to discuss. The object of Pericles' policy was, as far as we can judge, to compel Megara by sheer coercion to join the Athenian alliance, to which it seemed naturally to belong by geography and commercial interest, and give up the Spartan alliance, to which it belonged by race and sympathy.

The next point at issue between Aristophanes and Cleon is an interesting one. It is the treatment of the dependencies. Athens was the head of a great league, originally formed for defence against the Persians, and consisting chiefly of the Ionian islands and maritime states which had been under the Persian yoke. This league of equals had gradually transformed itself into an Empire, in which Athens provided most of the military and naval force and dictated the foreign policy, while the dependencies paid tribute for their protection.

These Ionian cities had been outstripped in power and wealth by Athens and the larger commercial units. But they had a tradition of ancient culture and refinement. Their language was still the authorized dialect of poetry and the higher prose. And, though most of them were now democratically governed, their old families had still much influence and wealth. Aristophanes, like Sophocles and other Athenian writers, had strong links of sympathy with Ionia. His policy would doubtless have been that of Aristides, whose arrangement of the tribute payable by the dependencies was accepted as a model of justice. The democratic war party took just the opposite view. There were remnants of the old aristocratic families still in the islands; they must be taught a lesson. There was money: it must be extorted to provide pay for the Athenian populace. There was secret disaffection: it must be rooted out. There was occasionally an open rebellion: it must be met by wholesale executions. The islanders were all traitors at heart, and the worst they got was better than their deserts!

In the year 426, just before the earliest of his comedies that has come down to us entire, Aristophanes produced a play of extraordinary daring, called the *Babylonians*, in which he represented all the dependencies as slaves on a treadmill, watched by a flogging gaoler called Demos. One fragment describes soldiers demanding billets. Another shows some extortioner saying, 'We need 200 drachmae.' 'How am I to get them?' asks the unhappy islander. 'In this quart pot!' is the answer. There is mention of some soldier ordering a yoke of plough-oxen to be killed because he wanted beef. To make the insult to the Athenian Government greater, the play was produced at the Great Dionysia, in the summer, when visitors from the Ionian cities were present in large numbers in Athens. One can imagine their passionate delight at finding such a champion.

It was a little too much. Cleon brought a series of prosecutions against the poet, who remarks in a subsequent comedy (*Acharnians* 377 ff.):

> And how Cleon made me pay—
> I've not forgotten—for my last year's play!
> Dragged me before the Council, brought his spies
> To slander me, gargled his throat with lies,
> Niagaraed me and slooshed me, till—almost—
> With so much sewage I gave up the ghost!

His spirit was not quenched, however. His next play, the *Acharnians*, was a definite plea for peace, and his next, the *Knights*, a perfectly exuberant and uncompromising attack on Cleon, now at the very height of his power.

It is noteworthy that in the *Knights* there is clear evidence of the terror that Cleon inspired. The character who represents him was not made up to look like him, and was not called by his name—at least not till the play was more than half finished, and it was clear how the audience would take it. Furthermore, though I think the most burning cause of quarrel that Aristophanes had against Cleon was his treatment of the dependencies, or allies, these are not once mentioned by name till the last word of the last line of the play, when Cleon is removed from office and borne off to pursue his true vocation of selling cat's meat at the city gates, and exchanging 'Billingsgate' with the fish-sellers and prostitutes.

> Carry him high
> And show him to the Allies whom he wronged.

There are plenty of general references to extortion, however. Cleon stands on the Council rock watching the sea, like the look-out man watching for herrings or tunnies, ready to harpoon the tribute as it comes (313). He knows all the rich and harmless men who have held any office and are consequently open to prosecution and blackmail (260 ff.). He saves money by not paying the sailors, but letting them live on the islanders instead (*Knights* 1366 f.; *Acharnians* 161–163). In any strait he demands war-ships for collecting arrears—there were probably always arrears of tribute due from some place or other—and sends them out to collect—with no questions asked (1070–1078). An informer in another play, the *Birds*, mentions with glee his own method, which is to go to an island and summon a rich islander to trial in Athens. Then, in the scarcity of ships, the islander cannot get a passage to Athens, while the informer is allowed to go in a man-of-war. The trial is brought on at once and the islander condemned in his absence (*Birds* 1410–1468).

Cleon's defence of his own policy is illuminating. The war meant vast expenditure and crippled production. The country population were driven for safety into the towns and ceased to produce wealth, while of course they had to be fed. Wealth and food must be got from somewhere, and Cleon undertook to get it. 'When I was on the Council, O Demos,' he says, 'I produced a huge balance in the treasury. I racked these men and squeezed those and blackmailed the others. I cared not a jot for any private person as long as I could make you happy.' As Lysias, the respectable democratic orator, puts it, 'When the Council has sufficient revenue it commits no offences; but when it is in difficulties it is compelled to accept impeachments and confiscations of property, and to follow the proposals of the most unprincipled speakers.' (*Lysias* 30, 22.) Of course the art of popular extortion lies in choosing your victims. Rich Ionians could be robbed without the Athenian mob turning a hair; and when that supply failed it was fairly safe to attack a rich Athenian suspected of 'moderatism'. 'What will you do,' asks the Sausage-monger of the reformed and converted Demos at the end of the *Knights*, 'if some low lawyer argues to the jury that there will be no feed for them unless they find the defendant guilty?' 'Lift him up and fling him into the Pit,' cries the indignant Demos, 'with the fattest of the informers as a millstone round his neck.' (*Knights* 1358–1363.) Such arguments were heard in the French Revolution, and are mentioned also by Lysias (27, 1).

Cleon's policy was to win, to win completely, at any cost and by any means. And, as in the French Revolution, such a policy became more and more repulsive to decent men. Nicias, the leader of Cleon's opponents, wanted a peace of reconciliation, but he seldom faced the Assembly. He was a good soldier, a good organizer, a skilful engineer; he devoted himself to his military work and increasingly stood out from politics. Our witnesses are unanimous in saying that from the time of Pericles onward there was a rapid and progressive deterioration in the class of man who acquired ascendancy in Athens. In part no doubt this alleged deterioration merely represented a change in social class; the traders or business men, the 'mongers' as Aristophanes derisively calls them, came to the front in place of the landed classes and the families of ancient culture. But I hardly see how we can doubt that there really was a moral and spiritual degradation as well, from Pericles and Cimon to Hyperbolus and his successors.

The *locus classicus* is, of course, the scene in the *Knights* where the Sausage-man or Offal-monger is introduced as the only possible rival for Cleon, the tanner or Leather-monger. In this scene the Paphlagonian slave, i.e. Cleon, has fallen asleep, and two of his fellow-slaves, representing Cleon's honest and disgraced rivals, Nicias and Demosthenes succeed in stealing a book of oracles which he keeps under his pillow.

The two-thousand-year-old jests may strike us as sometimes coarse and sometimes frigid; and my translation is a rough one. But there is a passion in the scene that keeps it alive and significant. Demosthenes, I should explain, is a little drunk from the start (*Knights* 125–225). He holds the book of oracles.

DEMOSTHENES. You gory Paphlagonian, you did well
To keep this close! You feared the oracle
About yourself.
    NICIAS.   About himself? Eh, what?
    DEMOSTHENES. It's written here, man, how he goes to pot.
    NICIAS. How?
    DEMOSTHENES. How? This book quite plainly prophesies
How first a Rope-monger must needs arise
The fortunes of all Athens to control. . . .
    NICIAS. Monger the first! What follows in the roll?
    DEMOSTHENES. A Mutton-monger next our lord shall be. . . .
    NICIAS. Monger the second! What's his destiny?
    DEMOSTHENES. To reign in pride until some dirtier soul
Rise than himself. That hour his knell shall toll.
For close behind a Leather-monger reels,
—Our Paphlagonian—lunging at his heels,
Niagara-voiced, a roaring beast of prey.
    NICIAS. The Mutton-monger runs, and fades away
Before him?
    DEMOSTHENES. Yes.
    NICIAS.   And that's the end? The store
Is finished? Oh, for just one monger more!
    DEMOSTHENES. There is one more, and one you'd never guess.
    NICIAS. There is! What is he?
    DEMOSTHENES.   Shall I tell you?
    NICIAS.   Yes!
    DEMOSTHENES. His fall is by an Offal-monger made.
    NICIAS. An Offal-monger? Glory, what a trade! . . .
Up, and to work! That monger must be found!
    DEMOSTHENES. We'll seek him out. [*They proceed to go seeking, when they see a man with a pieman's tray hanging round his neck, selling offal.*]

NICIAS. See! On this very ground,
By Providence!
DEMOSTHENES. O blessing without end!
O Offal-monger, friend and more than friend!
To us, to Athens, saviour evermore! . . .
This way!
OFFAL-MONGER. What's up? What are you shouting for?
DEMOSTHENES. Come here: come forward, and be taught by me
Your splendid fate, your rich felicity!
NICIAS. Here! Take his tray off! Pour into his head
The blessed oracles and all they've said.
I'll go and keep my eye on Paphlagon. [*Exit* NICIAS.]
DEMOSTHENES. Come, my good man, put all these gadgets down. Kiss
Earth thy Mother and the gods adore.
OFFAL-MONGER. There. What's it all about?
DEMOSTHENES. O blest and more!
Now nothing but tomorrow, Lord of All!
O Prince of Athens the majestical . . .
OFFAL-MONGER. Look here, gents, can't you let me wash my stuff
And sell the puddings? I've had mor'n enough.
DEMOSTHENES. Puddings, deluded being? Just look up.
You see those rows and rows of people?
OFFAL-MONGER. Yup.
DEMOSTHENES. Y o u are their Lord and Master! Y o u, heaven-sent.
To people, market, harbour, parliament,
To kick the Council, break the High Command,
Send men to gaol, get drunk in the Grand Stand. . . .
OFFAL-MONGER. Not me?
DEMOSTHENES. Yes—and you don't yet see it—you!
Get up on . . . here, your own old tray will do.
See all the islands dotted round the scene?
OFFAL-MONGER. Yes.
DEMOSTHENES. The great ports, the mercantile marine?
OFFAL-MONGER. Yes.
DEMOSTHENES. Yes! And then the man denies he's blest!
Now cast one eye towards Carthage in the west,
One round to Caria—take the whole imprint.
OFFAL-MONGER. Shall I be any happier with a squint?
DEMOSTHENES. Tut, tut, man! All you see is yours to sell.
You shall become, so all the stars foretell,
A great, great man.
OFFAL-MONGER. But do explain: how can
A poor little Offal-monger be a man?
DEMOSTHENES. That's just the reason why you are bound to grow.
Because you are street-bred, brazen-faced and low.
OFFAL-MONGER. You know, I don't know quite as I deserve . . .

DEMOSTHENES. You don't know quite? What means this shaken nerve?
Some secret virtue? No?—Don't say you came
Of honest parents!
    OFFAL-MONGER. Honest? Lord, not them!
Both pretty queer!
    DEMOSTHENES.   Oh, happy man and wife!
To start your son so well for public life.
    OFFAL-MONGER. Just think of the eddication I ain't had,
Bar letters: and I mostly learnt them bad!
    DEMOSTHENES. The pity is you learnt such things at all.
'Tis not for learning now the people call,
Nor thoughtfulness, nor men of generous make.
'Tis brute beasts without conscience. Come and take
The prize that gods and prophets offer you.

    .   .   .   .   .   .

    OFFAL-MONGER. Of course I like them. But I can't see yet
How ever I shall learn to rule a state.
    DEMOSTHENES. Easy as lying! Do as now you do,
Turn every question to a public stew;
Hash things, and cook things. Win the common herd
By sweet strong sauces in your every word.
For other gifts, you have half the catalogue
Already, for the perfect demagogue,
A blood-shot voice, low breeding, huckster's tricks—
What more can man require for politics?
The prophets and Apollo's word concur.
Up! To all Sleeping Snakes libation pour,
And crown your brow, and fight him!
    OFFAL-MONGER.   Who will fight
Beside me? All the rich are in a fright
Before him, and the poor folk of the town
Turn green and vomit if they see him frown.

    You feel the tone. The bitter contempt, in part the contempt of the beaten aristocrat for the conquering plebeian, of the partisan for his opponent, of the educated man for the uneducated, but in part, I think, genuinely the contempt of the man of honest traditions in manners and morals for the self-seeker with no traditions at all. It recurs again and again, in all mentions of Cleon and his successor Hyperbolus, or their flatterers and hangers-on; priests and prophets, shirkers of military service, rich profiteers with a pull on the government, and above all of course the informers, or false-accusers.
    The informers rose into prominence for several causes. First, the war-fever and the spy-mania of the time; next, the general

exasperation of nerves, leading to quarrels and litigation; next, the general poverty and the difficulty of earning a living. An informer if he won his case received a large percentage of the penalty imposed. By the time of the *Birds* (414 BC) and the *Ecclesiazusae* (389 BC) Aristophanes implies jestingly that it was the only way left of making a living, and every one was in it (*Ecclesiazusae* 562). In the *Plutus* an informer bursts into tears because, in the New World introduced by the *dénouement* of that play, a good man and a patriot, like himself, is reduced to suffering. 'You a good man and a patriot?' 'If ever there was one.' . . . 'Are you a tiller of the soil?' 'Do you think I am mad?' 'A merchant?' 'H'm, that is how I describe myself when I have to sign a paper.' 'Have you learnt any profession?' 'Rather not.' 'Then how do you live?' 'I am a general supervisor of the affairs of the City and of all private persons.' 'What is your qualification?' 'I like it.' The informer scores a point later on. 'Can't you leave these trials and accusations to the proper officials?' they say to him. 'The City appoints paid judges to settle these things.' 'And who brings the accusation?' says the informer. 'Any one who likes.' 'Just so. I am a person who likes.' (*Plutus* 901–919.)

In the *Acharnians* (860–950), when the Boeotian farmer comes to market with his abundance of good things, there arises a difficulty about any export adequate to repay such imports. He wants something that is abundant in Athens but scarce in Boeotia. Fish and pottery are suggested, but do not satisfy him: when the brilliant idea occurs, give him a live informer! At this moment an informer enters; his name by the way is Nikarchos, 'Beat-the-Government'—a name formed like Nikoboulos, 'Beat-the-Council'—and suggests that if Cleon on the whole encouraged and utilized the false accusers for the purpose of keeping his rivals out of power, they were sometimes too strong for him himself. 'He is rather small,' says the Boeotian doubtfully. 'But all of him bad,' is the comforting retort. Nikarchos immediately denounces the Boeotian wares as contraband, and finding lamp-wicks among them, detects a pro-Spartan plot for setting the docks on fire. He is still speaking when he is seized from behind, tied with ropes, wrapped carefully in matting wrong side up, so as not to break—and carried off.

Besides the συκοφάνται and blackmailers, we hear a good deal about κόλακες, or flatterers of those in power, and a good deal about profiteers. There are the ambassadors and people on government missions with their handsome maintenance allowances, young officers with 'cushy jobs' (*Acharnians* 61–90, 135–137, 595–619), the people who profit by confiscations (*Wasps* 663–718), the various trades that gain by war (*Peace* 1210–1255): the armourers, crest-makers, helmet-makers, trumpet-makers; the prophets and priests, who gain by the boom in superstition; the geometers or surveyors, who survey annexed territory (*Birds* 960–1020), together with other colonially-minded profiteers. In the *Peace*, when that goddess is discovered buried out of human sight in a deep pit, all the Greeks start to drag her out, but some hinder more than help. There are soldiers who want promotion, politicians who want to be generals, slaves who want to desert, and of course there are munition-workers. As the work goes on it appears that the Boeotians, who have plenty to eat, are not pulling; the jingo General, Lamachus, is not pulling; the Argives, being neutral, have never pulled at all; they only grinned and got profit from both sides; and the unhappy Megarians, though they are doing their best, are too weak with famine to have any effect. Eventually all these people are warned off; so are the chief combatants, the Spartans and Athenians, because they do nothing but quarrel and make accusations against each other. Only the tillers of the soil are left to pull, the peasants and farmers of all nations alike. They are not politicians, and they know what it is to suffer (*Peace* 441–510). So the goddess is hoisted up, and the various cities, in spite of their wounds and bandages and black-eyes and crutches, fall to dancing and laughing together for very joy.

It is a permanent count against Cleon that he has repeatedly refused peace. 'Archeptolemus brought us peace, and you spilt it on the ground. You insulted every embassy from every city that invited us to treat, and kicked them out of town.'(*Knights* 795 ff.) 'And why?' answers Cleon. 'Because I mean to give the Athenian Demos universal Empire over Hellas.' 'Bosh,' answers the Sausage-man: 'it is because the whole atmosphere of war suits you! The general darkness and ignorance, the absence of financial control, the nervous terror of the populace, and even their very poverty and hunger, which make them more and more dependent on you.'

In the *Peace*, the god Hermes makes a speech to the Athenians. 'Whenever the Spartans had a slight advantage,' he says (211 ff.), 'it was "Now by God, we've got the little Attic beasts on the run!" And when you Athenians had the best of it and the Spartans came with peace proposals, "It is a cheat," you cried. "Don't trust a word they say. They'll come again later, if we stick to our gains."' 'I recognize the style,' says the Athenian who listens. No one in Athens dared to propose peace. In a whimsical scene at the opening of the

Acharnians an archangel or demi-god walks into the Assembly explaining that he is an Immortal Being, but the authorities will not give him a passport. 'Why does he want one?' 'The gods have commissioned him to go to Sparta and make peace.' Immediately there is a cry for the police, and the archangel is taught that there are certain subjects that even an immortal must not meddle with (*Acharnians* 45-54). And yet if peace is not made—one would imagine that one heard the voice of a present-day moderate speaking —it means the destruction not of Athens or Sparta alone but of all Hellas. God is sweeping Hellas with the broom of destruction (*Peace* 59). The devil of war has the cities in a mortar and is only looking for a pestle to pound them into dust (*Peace* 228-287). By good luck it happens that the Athenian pestle is just broken—Cleon killed in Thrace—and when war looks for the Spartan pestle it is lost too—Brasidas, the Spartan general, also killed. So comes the chance for peace, and for the policy of Nicias, which comprised an alliance between Athens and Sparta and a pan-Hellenic patriotism. It is noticeable in the *Knights* that the pacifist Offal-monger retorts on Cleon the accusation of not possessing an 'imperial mind'. Cleon, in his war-hysteria, is for making Athens a mean city; making it hated by the allies, hated by the rest of Hellas, thriving on the misfortunes of others, and full of hatred against a great part—not to say the best part—of its own citizens (*Knights* 817 f.). And when Cleon finally falls the cry is raised 'Hellânie Zeu!—Zeus of all Hellas —thine is the prize of victory!' The Offal-monger, like Aristophanes himself, was 'a good European'.

The peace of Nicias failed. The impetus of the war was too great. The natural drift of affairs was in Cleon's direction, and the farther Athens was carried the harder it became for any human wisdom or authority to check the rush of the infuriated herd. And since Nicias was too moderate and high-minded and law-abiding to fight Cleon with his own weapons, he lost hold on the more extreme spirits of his own party; so that at the end of the war the informers had created the very thing they had dreamed about and had turned their own lies into truth. There was at last an actual pro-Spartan group; there were real secret societies, real conspiracies; and a party that was ready to join hands with the enemy in order to be delivered from the corrupted and war-maddened mob that governed them.

One is tempted in a case like this to pass no judgement on men or policies, but merely record the actual course of history and try to understand the conflicting policies and ideals; instead of judgement, taking refuge in the *lacrimae rerum*—the eternal pity that springs from the eternal tragedy of human endeavour. When the soldiers of Nicias in Sicily, mad with thirst, pressed on to drink the water, thick with blood and mire, of the little stream where the enemy archers shot them down at leisure, it was not only an army that perished but a nation, and a nation that held the hopes of the world. When we read that immortal praise of Athens which our historian puts into the mouth of Pericles, the city of law and freedom, of simplicity and beauty, the beloved city in whose service men live and die rejoicing as a lover in his mistress, we should notice that the words are spoken in a Funeral Speech. The thing so praised, so beloved, is dead; and the haunting beauty of the words is in part merely the well-known magic of memory and of longing. For Thucydides the dream of a regenerated life for mankind has vanished out of the future, and he rebuilds it in his memory of the past. The Peloponnesian war has ended wrong; and whatever the end might have been, it had already wrecked Hellas.

Our war has at least ended right: and, one may hope, not too late for the recovery of civilization. In spite of the vast material destruction, in spite of the blotting out from the book of life of practically one whole generation of men, in spite of the unmeasured misery which has reigned and reigns still over the greater part of Europe, in spite of the gigantic difficulties of the task before us; in spite of the great war-harvest of evil and the exhaustion of brain and spirit in most of the victorious nations as well as in the vanquished, our war has ended right; and we have such an opportunity as no generation of mankind has ever had of building out of these ruins a better international life and concomitantly a better life within each nation. I know not which thought is the more solemn, the more awful in its responsibility: the thought of the sacrifice we survivors have asked or exacted from our fellow-men; or the thought of the task that now lies upon us if we are not to make that sacrifice a crime and a mockery. Blood and tears to which we had some right, for we loved those who suffered and they loved us; blood and tears to which we had no right, for those who suffered knew nothing of us, nor we of them; misery of the innocent beyond measure or understanding and hitherto without recompense; that is the price that has been paid, and it lies on us, who live, to see to it that the price is not paid in vain. By some spirit of co-operation instead of strife, by sobriety instead of madness, by resolute sincerity in public and private things, and surely by some self-consecration to the great hope for which those who loved us gave their lives.

'A city where rich and poor, man and woman, Athenian and Spartan, are all equal and all free; where there are no false accusers and where men'—or at least the souls of men—'have wings'. That was the old dream that failed. Is it to fail always and for ever?

November 7, 1918.

CHAPTER III

The Bacchae in relation to Certain Currents of Thought in the Fifth Century[1]

OF the two dramas that make up the main part of this volume, the *Hippolytus* can be left to speak for itself. Its two thousand five hundred years have left little mark upon it. It has something of the stateliness of age, no doubt, but none of the staleness or lack of sympathy. With all the severe lines of its beauty, it is tender, subtle, quick with human feeling. Even its religious conceptions, if we will but take them simply, forgetting the false mythology we have learned from handbooks, are easily understood and full of truth. One of the earliest, if not the very earliest, of love tragedies, it deals with a theme that might easily be made ugly. It is made ugly by later writers, especially by the commentators whom we can see always at work from the times of the ancient scholia down to our own days. Even Racine, who wished to be kind to his Phèdre, has let her suffer by contact with certain deadly and misleading suggestions. But the Phaedra of Euripides was quite another woman, and the quality of her love, apart from its circumstances, is entirely fragrant and clear. The *Hippolytus*, like most works that come from a strong personality, has its mannerisms and, no doubt, its flaws. But in the main it is a singularly satisfying and complete work of art, a thing of beauty, to contemplate and give thanks for, surrounded by an atmosphere of haunting purity.

If we turn to *The Bacchae*, we find a curious difference. As an effort of genius it is perhaps greater than the *Hippolytus*, at any rate more unusual and rare in quality. But it is unsatisfying, inhuman. There is an impression of coldness and even of prolixity amid its amazing thrill, a strange unearthliness, something that bewilders. Most readers, I believe, tend to ask what it means, and to feel, by implication, that it means something.

[1] Originally an introduction to a volume of translations of the *Hippolytus*, *Bacchae* and *Frogs* (vol. III of *The Athenian Drama*). Geo. Allen and Unwin, Ltd., 1902.

Now this problem, what *The Bacchae* means and how Euripides came to write it, is not only of real interest in itself; it is also, I think, of importance with regard to certain movements in fifth-century Athens, and certain currents of thought in later Greek philosophy.

The remark has been made, that, if Aristotle could have seen through some magic glass the course of human development and decay for the thousand years following his death, the disappointment would have broken his heart. A disappointment of the same sort, but more sharp and stinging, inasmuch as men's hopes were both higher and cruder, did, as a matter of fact, break the hearts of many men two or three generations earlier. It is the reflection of that disappointment on the work of Euripides, the first hopefulness, the embitterment, the despair, followed at last by a final half-prophetic vision of the truths or possibilities beyond that despair, that will, I think, supply us with an explanation of a large part of *The Bacchae*, and with a clue to a great deal of the poet's other work.

There has been, perhaps, no period in the world's history, not even the openings of the French Revolution, when the prospects of the human race can have appeared so brilliant as they did to the highest minds of Eastern Greece about the years 470–445 BC. To us, looking critically back upon that time, it is as though the tree of human life had burst suddenly into flower, into that exquisite and short-lived bloom which seems so disturbing among the ordinary processes of historical growth. One wonders how it must have felt to the men who lived in it. We have but little direct testimony. There is the tone of solemn exaltation that pervades most of Aeschylus, the high confidence of the *Persae*, the *Prometheus*, the *Eumenides*. There is the harassed and half-reluctant splendour of certain parts of Pindar, like the Dithyramb to Athens and the fourth Nemean Ode. But in the main the men of that day were too busy, one would fain think too happy, to write books.

There is an interesting witness, however, of a rather younger generation. Herodotus finished his Histories when the glory was already gone, and the future seemed about equally balanced between good and evil. But he had lived as a boy in the great time. And the peculiar charm of his work often seems to lie mainly in a certain strong and kindly joyousness, persistent even amid his most grisly stories, which must be the spirit of the first Athenian Confederation not yet strangled by the spirit of the Peloponnesian war.

What was the object of this enthusiasm, the ground of this high hopefulness? It would, of course, take us far beyond our limits to attempt any full answer to such a question.[1] But for one thing, there was the extraordinary swiftness of the advances made; and, for another, there was a circumstance that has rarely been repeated in history—the fact that all the different advances appeared to help one another. The ideals of freedom, law, and progress; of truth and beauty, of knowledge and virtue, of humanity and religion; high things, the conflicts between which have caused most of the disruptions and despondencies of human societies, seemed for a generation or two at this time to lie all in the same direction. And in that direction, on the whole, a great part of Greece was with extraordinary swiftness moving. Of course, there were backwaters and reactionary forces. There was Sparta and even Aetolia; Pythagoras and the Oracle at Delphi. But in the main, all good things went hand in hand. The poets and the men of science, the moral teachers and the hardy speculators, the great traders and the political reformers—all found their centre of life and aspiration in the same 'School of Hellas', Athens. The final seal of success was set upon the movement by the defeat of the Persian invasion and the formation of the Athenian League. The higher hopes and ideals had clashed against the lower under conditions in which the victory of the lower seemed beforehand certain; and somehow, miraculously, ununderstandably, that which was high had shown that it was also strong. Athens stood out as the chief power of the Mediterranean.

Let us recall briefly a few well-known passages of Herodotus to illustrate the tone of the time.

Athens represented Hellenism (Hdt. i. 60). 'The Greek race was distinguished of old from the barbarian as nimbler of intellect and further removed from primitive savagery (or stupidity). . . . And of all Greeks the Athenians were counted the first for wisdom.'

She represented the triumph of Democracy (Hdt. v. 78). 'So Athens grew. It is clear not in one thing alone, but wherever you test it, what a good thing is equality among men. Even in war, Athens, when under the tyrants, was no better than her neighbours; when freed from the tyrants, she was far the first of all.'

And Democracy was at this time a thing which stirred enthusiasm. A speaker says in Herodotus (iii. 80): 'A tyrant disturbs ancient laws, violates women, kills men without trial. But a people ruling—first, the very name of it is beautiful. Isonomiê (Equality in law); and, secondly, a people does none of these things.'

'The very name of it is beautiful!' It was some twenty-five years

[1] A magnificent text for such a discussion would be found in the great lyric on the Rise of Man in Sophocles' *Antigone* (v. 332 ff.).

later that an Athenian statesman, of moderate or rather popular antecedents, said in a speech at Sparta (Thuc. vi. 89): 'Of course, all sensible men know what Democracy is, and I better than most, having suffered; but there is nothing new to be said about acknowledged insanity!'

That, however, is looking ahead. We must note that this Democracy, this Freedom, represented by Greece, and especially by Athens, was always the Rule of Law. There is a story told by Aeschylus of the Athenians, by Herodotus of the Spartans, contrasting either with the barbarians and their lawless absolute monarchies. Xerxes, learning the small number of his Greek adversaries, asks, 'How can they possibly stand against us, especially when, as you tell me, they are all free, and there is no one to compel them?' And the Spartan Demarâtus answers (Hdt. vii. 104): 'Free are they, O King, yet not free to do everything; for there is a master over them, even Law, whom they fear more than thy servants fear thee. At least they obey whatever he commands, and his voice is always the same.' In Aeschylus (*Persae* 241 *seqq.*) the speakers present are both Persians, so the point about Law cannot be explained. It is left a mystery, how and why the free Greeks face their death.

It would be easy to assemble many passages to show that Athens represented freedom (*e.g.* Hdt. viii. 142) and the enfranchisement of the oppressed; but what is even more characteristic than the insistence on Freedom is the insistence on A r e t ê, Virtue—the demand made upon each Greek, and especially each Athenian, to be a better man than the ordinary. It comes out markedly from a quarter where we should scarcely expect it. Herodotus gives an abstract of the words spoken by the much-maligned Themistocles before the battle of Salamis—a brief, grudging résumé of a speech so celebrated that it could not in decency be entirely passed over (Hdt. viii. 83): 'The argument of it was that in all things that are possible to man's nature and situation, there is always a higher and a lower'; and that *they* must stand for the higher. We should have liked to hear more of that speech. It certainly achieved its end.

There was insistence on A r e t ê in another sense, the sense of generosity and kindliness. A true Athenian must know how to give way. When the various states were contending for the leadership before the battle of Artemisium, the Athenians, contributing much the largest and finest fighting force, 'thought', we are told (Hdt. viii. 3), 'that the great thing was that Greece should be saved, and gave up their claims'. In the similar dispute for the post of honour and danger before the battle of Plataea, the Athenians did plead their cause, and easily won it (Hdt. ix. 27). But we may notice not only the moderate and disciplined spirit in which they promise to abide by Sparta's decision, and to show no resentment if their claim is rejected, but also the grounds upon which they claim honour—apart from certain obvious points, such as the size of their contingent. Their claims are that in recent years they alone have met the Persians single-handed on behalf of all Greece; that in old times it was they who gave refuge to the Children of Heracles when hunted through Greece by the overmastering tyrant, Eurystheus; it was they who championed the wives and mothers of the Argives slain at Thebes, and made war upon that conquering power to prevent wrong-doing against the helpless dead.

These passages, which could easily be reinforced by a score of others, illustrate, not of course what Athens as a matter of hard fact *was*—no state has ever been one compact mass of noble qualities —but the kind of ideal that Athens in her own mind had formed of herself. They help us to see what she appeared to the imaginations of Aeschylus and young Euripides, and that 'Band of Lovers' which Pericles gathered to adore his Princess of Cities.[1] She represented Freedom and Law, Hellenism and Intellect, Humanity, Chivalry, the championship of the helpless and oppressed.

Did Euripides feel all this? one may ask. The answer to that doubt is best to be found, perhaps, in the two plays which he wrote upon the two traditional feats of generosity mentioned above—the reception of the Children of Heracles, and the championing of the Argive Suppliants. The former, beautiful as it is, is seriously mutilated, so the *Suppliants* will suit our purpose best. It is, I think, an early play rewritten at the time of the Peace of Nicias (421 BC), about the beginning of the poet's middle period,[2] a poor play in many respects, youthful, obvious, and crude, but all aflame with this chivalrous and confident spirit.

The situation is as follows: Adrastus, King of Argos, has led the ill-fated expedition of the Seven Chieftains against Thebes, and been utterly defeated. The Thebans have brutally refused to allow the Argives to bury their dead. The bodies are lying upon the field.

[1] Thuc. 2, 43. 'Fix your eyes on what she might be, and make yourselves her Lovers.'
[2] Some critics consider that it was first written at this time. If so, we must attribute the apparent marks of earliness to deliberate archaism. There is no doubt that the reception of Suppliants was a very old stage subject, and had acquired a certain traditional stiffness of form, seen at its acme in the *Suppliants* of Aeschylus.

Adrastus, accompanied by the mothers and wives of the slain chieftains, has come to Attica, and appealed to Theseus for intercession. That hero, like his son Demophon in *The Children of Heracles*, like his ancestor Cecrops in certain older poetry, is a sort of personification of Athens.

He explains that he always disapproved of Adrastus's expedition; that he can take no responsibility, and certainly not risk a war on the Argives' account.

He is turning away when one of the bereaved women, lifting her suppliant wreaths and branches, cries out to him:

> What is this thing thou doest? Wilt despise
> All these, and cast us from thee beggar-wise,
> Grey women, with not one thing of all we crave?
> Nay, the wild beast for refuge hath his cave,
> The slave God's altar; surely in the deep
> Of fortune City may call to City, and creep,
> A wounded thing, to shelter.

Observe the conception of the duty of one state to protect and help another.—Theseus is still obdurate. He has responsibilities. The recklessness of Athens in foreign policy has become a reproach. At last Aethra, his mother, can keep silence no more. Can he really allow such things to be done? Can Athens really put considerations of prudence before generosity and religion?

> Thou shalt not suffer it, thou being my child!
> Thou hast heard men scorn thy city, call her wild
> Of counsel, mad; thou hast seen the fire of morn
> Flash from her eyes in answer to their scorn!
> Come toil on toil, 'tis this that makes her grand,
> Peril on peril! And common states that stand
> In caution, twilight cities, dimly wise—
> Ye know them; for no light is in their eyes!
> Go forth, my son, and help.—My fear is fled.
> Women in sorrow call thee and men dead!

To help the helpless was a necessary part of what we call chivalry, what the Greeks called religion. Theseus agrees to consult the people on the matter. Meantime there arrives a Theban herald, asking arrogantly, 'Who is Master of the land?' Theseus, although a king, is too thorough a personification of democratic Athens to let such an expression pass:

> Nay, peace, Sir Stranger! Ill hast thou begun,
> Seeking a Master here. No will of one
> Holdeth this land; it is a city and free.
> The whole folk year by year, in parity
> Of service, is our King. Nor yet to gold
> Give we high seats, but in one honour hold
> The poor man and the rich.

The herald replies that he is delighted to hear that Athens has such a silly constitution, and warns Theseus not to interfere with Thebes for the sake of a beaten cause. Eventually Theseus gives his ultimatum:

> Let the slain be given
> To us, who seek to obey the will of Heaven.
> Else, know for sure, I come to seek these dead
> Myself, for burial.—It shall not be said
> An ancient ordinance of God, that cried
> To Athens and her King, was cast aside!

A clear issue comes in the conversation that follows:

> HERALD
> Art thou so strong? Wilt stand against all Greece?
>
> THESEUS
> Against all tyrants! With the rest be peace.
>
> HERALD
> She takes too much upon her, this thy state!
>
> THESEUS
> Takes, aye, and bears it; therefore is she great!

We know that spirit elsewhere in the history of the world. How delightful it is, and green and fresh and thrilling; and how often it has paid in blood and ashes the penalty of dreaming and of τὸ μὴ θνητὰ φρονεῖν!

There is one other small point that calls for notice before we leave this curious play. Theseus represents not only chivalry and freedom and law, but also a certain delicacy of feeling. He is the civilized man as contrasted with the less civilized. It was a custom in many parts of Greece to make the very most of mourning and burial rites, to feel the wounds of the slain, and vow vengeance with wild outbursts of grief. Athenian feeling disapproved of this.

> THESEUS
>
>   This task
> Is mine. Advance the burden of the dead!
>   [*The attendants bring forward the bodies.*]
>
> ADRASTUS
> Up, ye sad mothers, where your sons are laid!
>
> THESEUS
> Nay, call them not, Adrastus.
>
> ADRASTUS
>   That were strange!
> Shall they not touch their children's wounds?
>
> THESEUS
>   The change
> In that dead flesh would torture them.
>
> ADRASTUS
>   'Tis pain
> Alway, to count the gashes of the slain.
>
> THESEUS
> And wouldst thou add pain to the pain of these?
>
> ADRASTUS (*after a pause*)
> So be it!—Ye women, wait in your degrees:
> Theseus says well.

This particular trait, this civilization or delicacy of feeling, is well illustrated in a much finer drama, the *Heracles*. The hero of that tragedy, the rudely noble Dorian chief, has in a fit of madness killed his own children. In the scene to be cited he has recovered his senses and is sitting dumb and motionless, veiled by his mantle. He is, by all ordinary notions, accursed. The sight of his face will pollute the sun. A touch from him or even a spoken word will spread to another the contagion of his horrible blood-stainedness. To him comes his old comrade Theseus (*Heracles* 1214 ff.):

> THESEUS
> O thou that sittest in the shade of Death,
> Unveil thy brow! 'Tis a friend summoneth,
> And never darkness bore so black a cloud
> In all this world, as from mine eyes could shroud

The wreck of thee. . . . What wouldst thou with that arm
That shakes, and shows me blood? Dost fear to harm
Me with thy words' contagion? Have no fear;
What is it if I suffer with thee here?
We have had great joys together.—Call back now
That time the Dead had hold of me, and how
Thou camest conquering! Can that joy grow old,
Or friends once linked in sunshine, when the cold
Storm falleth, not together meet the sea?—
Oh, rise, and bare thy brow, and turn to me
Thine eyes! A brave man faces his own fall
And takes it to him, as God sends withal.

Heracles
Theseus, thou seest my children?

Theseus
       Surely I see
All, and I knew it ere I came to thee.

Heracles
Oh, why hast bared to the Sun this head of mine?

Theseus
How can thy human sin stain things divine?

Heracles
Leave me! I am all blood. The curse thereof
Crawls. . . .

Theseus
No curse cometh between love and love!

Heracles
I thank thee. . . . Yes; I served thee long ago.

Heracles is calmed and his self-respect partially restored. But he still cannot bear to live. Notice the attitude of Theseus towards his suicide—an attitude more striking in ancient literature than it would be in modern.

Heracles
Therefore is all made ready for my death.

Theseus
Thinkest thou God feareth what thy fury saith?

HERACLES (*rising*)
Oh, God is hard; and I hard against God!

THESEUS
What wilt thou? And whither on thine angry road?

HERACLES
Back to the darkness whence my race began!

THESEUS
These be the words of any common man!

HERACLES (*taken aback*)
Aye, thou art scathless. Chide me at thine ease!

THESEUS
Is this He of the Labours, Heracles?

HERACLES
Of none like this, if one dare measure pain!

THESEUS
The Helper of the World, the Friend of Man?

HERACLES (*with a movement*)
Crushed by Her hate! How can the past assuage
This horror....

THESEUS
Thou shalt not perish in thy rage!
Greece will not suffer it.

The passage illustrates not only nobility of feeling in Theseus, but, in a way very characteristic of Euripides, the fact that this nobility is based on religious reflection, on genuinely 'free' thought. Theseus dares the contagion for the sake of his friendship. He also does not believe in the contagion. He does not really think for a moment that he will become guilty of a crime because he has touched some one who committed it. He is in every sense, as Herodotus puts it, 'further removed from primitive savagery'.

But this play also shows, and it is probably the very last of Euripides' plays which does show it, a strong serenity of mind. The loss of this serenity is one of the most significant marks of the later plays of Euripides as contrasted with the earlier. We must not overstate the antithesis. There was always in Euripides a vein of tonic bitterness, a hint of satire or criticism, a questioning of established things. It is markedly present even in the *Alcestis*, in the scene where Admêtus is denounced by his old father; it is present in a graver form in the *Hippolytus*. Yet the general impression produced by those two plays when compared, for instance, with the *Electra* and the *Troades*, is undoubtedly one of serenity as against fever, beauty as against horror. And the same will nearly always hold for the comparison of any of his early plays with any later one. Of course not quite always. If we take the *Troades*, in the year 415, as marking the turning-point, we shall find the *Hecuba* very bitter among the early plays, the *Helena* bright and light-hearted, though a little harsh, among the later. This is only natural. There is always something fitful and irregular in the gathering of clouds, however persistent.

There is one cloud even in the *Suppliants*, possibly a mark of the later retouching of that play. The Theban herald is an unsympathetic character, whose business is to say hard, sinister things, and be confuted by Theseus. These unsympathetic heralds are common stage characters. They stalk in with insulting messages and 'tyrannical' sentiments, are surrounded by howling indignation from the virtuous populace, stand their ground motionless, defying any one to touch their sacred persons, and go off with a scornful menace. But this particular herald has some lines put in his mouth which nobody confutes, and which are rather too strongly expressed for the situation.

Theseus is prepared for his chivalrous war, and the people clamour for it. The herald says (v. 484):

>   Oh, it were well
> The death men shout for could stand visible
> Above the urns! Then never Greece had reeled
> Blood-mad to ruin o'er many a stricken field.
> Great Heaven, set both out plain and all can tell
> The False word from the True, and Ill from Well,
> And how much Peace is better! Dear is Peace
> To every Muse; she walks her ways and sees
> No haunting Spirit of Judgment. Glad is she
> With noise of happy children, running free
> With corn and oil. And we, so vile we are,
> Forget, and cast her off, and call for War,
> City on city, man on man, to break
> Weak things to obey us for our greatness' sake!

If it is true that the *Suppliants* was rewritten, that must be one of the later passages. Athens had had ten years of bitter war by the time the lines were actually spoken.

Let us again take a few typical passages from the historians to see the form in which the clouds gathered over Athens.

The first and most obvious will be from that curious chapter in which Herodotus, towards the end of his life, is summing up his conclusions about the Persian war, of which Athens was so indisputably the heroine. He observes (vii. 139): 'Here I am compelled by necessity to express an opinion which will be offensive to most of mankind. But I cannot refrain from putting it in the way that I believe to be true. . . . The Athenians in the Persian wars were the saviours of Hellas.' By the time that passage was written, apologies were necessary if you wished to say a good word for Athens!

The Athenian League, that great instrument of freedom, had grown into an Empire or Archê. Various allies had tried to secede and failed; had been conquered and made into subjects. The greater part of Greece was seething with timorous ill-feeling against what they called 'The Tyrant City'. And by the opening of the Peloponnesian war, Athens herself had practically ceased to protest against the name. It is strange to recall such words as, for instance, the Spartans had used in 479, when it was rumoured, falsely, that Athens thought of making terms with Persia (Hdt. viii. 142): 'It is intolerable to imagine that Athens should ever be a party to the subjection of any Greek state; always from the earliest times you have been known as the Liberators of Many Men.' It is strange to compare those words with the language attributed to Pericles in 430 in attacking the 'philosophic radicals' of that day (Thuc. ii. 63)[1]:

'Do not imagine that you are fighting about a simple issue, the subjection or independence of certain cities. You have an empire to lose, and a danger to face from those whom your imperial rule has made to hate you. And it is impossible for you to resign your power—if at this crisis some timorous and inactive spirits are hankering after righteousness even at that price! For by this time your empire has become a Despotism ("Tyrannis"), a thing which in the opinion of mankind is unjust to acquire, but which at any rate cannot be safely surrendered. The men of whom I was speaking, if they could find followers, would soon ruin the city. If they were to go and found a state of their own, they would soon ruin that!'

It would not be relevant here to appraise this policy of Pericles, to discuss how far events had really made it inevitable, or when the

[1] These speeches were revised as late as 403, and may well be coloured by subsequent experience. But this particular point is one on which Thucydides may be absolutely trusted. He would not attribute the odious sentiments of Cleon to his hero Pericles without cause.

first false step was taken. Our business, at the moment, is merely to notice the extraordinary change of tone. It comes out even more strongly in a speech made by Cleon, the successor of Pericles, in the debate about the punishment of rebel Mitylênê—a debate remarkable as being the very last in which the side of clemency gained the day (Thuc. iii. 37):

'I have remarked again and again that a Democracy cannot govern an empire; and never more clearly than now, when I see you regretting your sentence upon the Mitylenaeans. Living without fear and suspicion among yourselves, you deal with your allies upon the same principle; and you do not realize that whenever you make a concession to them out of pity, or are misled by their specious reports, you are guilty of a weakness dangerous to yourselves, and you receive no gratitude from them. You must remember that your empire is a Despotism exercised over unwilling subjects who are a l w a y s conspiring against you. They do not obey in return for any kindness you do them; they obey just so far as you show yourselves their masters.'

'Do not be misled,' he adds a little later (iii. 40), 'by the three most deadly enemies of empire, Pity and the Charm of Words and the Generosity of Strength!'

It is a change indeed! A change which the common run of low men, no doubt, accepted as inevitable, or even as a matter of course; which the merely clever and practical men insisted upon, and the more brutal 'patriots' delighted in. They had never loved or understood the old ideals!

Some great political changes can take place without much effect upon men's private lives. But this change was a blight that worked upon daily conduct, upon the roots of character. Thucydides, writing after the end of the war, has two celebrated and terrible chapters (iii. 82, 83) on that side of the question. Every word is apposite to our point; but we may content ourselves with a few sentences here and there.

'In peace and prosperity both states and men,' he says, 'are free to act upon higher motives. They are not caught up by coils of circumstance which drive them without their own volition. But War, taking away the margin in daily life, is a teacher who educates by violence; and he makes men's characters fit their conditions. . . .'

The later actors in the war 'determined to outdo the report of those who had gone before them by the ingenuity of their enterprises and the enormity of their reprisals. . . .' The meaning of words, he notices, changed in relation to things. Thoughtfulness, prudence, moderation, generosity were scouted and called by the names of various vices: recklessness and treachery were prized. 'Frantic energy was the true quality of a man....'

'Neither side cared for religion, but both used it with enthusiasm as a pretext for various odious purposes....'

'The cause of all these evils was the lust of empire, originating in avarice and ambition, and the party spirit which is engendered from such circumstances when men settle themselves down to a contest.'

'Thus Revolution gave birth to every kind of wickedness in Hellas. The simplicity which is so large an element in a noble nature disappeared in a burst of derision. An attitude of mistrustful antagonism prevailed everywhere. No power existed to soften it, no cogency of reason, no bond of religion.' . . . 'Inferior characters succeeded best. The higher kinds of men were too thoughtful, and were swept aside.'

Men caught up in coils of circumstance that drive them without their own volition; ingenious enterprises; enormous revenges; mad ambition; mistrust; frantic energy; the abuse of religion; simplicity laughed out of the world: it is a terrible picture, and it is exactly the picture that meets us in the later tragedies of Euripides. Those plays all, as Dr Verrall has acutely remarked, have an extraordinary air of referring to the present and not the past, of dealing with things that 'matter', not things made up or dreamed about. And it is in this spirit that they deal with them. Different plays may be despairing like the *Troades*, cynical like the *Ion*, deliberately hateful like the *Electra*, frantic and fierce like the *Orestes*; they are nearly all violent, nearly all misanthropic. Amid all their poetical beauty there sounds from time to time a cry of nerves frayed to the snapping point, a jarring note of fury against something personal to the poet and not always relevant to the play. Their very splendours, the lines that come back most vividly to a reader's mind, consist often in the expression of some vice. There are analyses or self-revelations, like the famous outburst of the usurping Prince Eteoclês in the *Phoenissae*:

> These words that thou wilt praise
> The Equal and the Just,—in all men's ways
> I have not found them! These be names, not things.
>   Mother, I will unveil to thee the springs
> That well within me. I would break the bars
> Of Heaven, and past the risings of the stars
> Climb, aye, or sink beneath dark Earth and Sea,
> To clasp my goddess-bride, my Sovranty!

This is my good, which never by mine own
Will shall man touch, save Eteoclês alone!

There are flashes of cruel hate like the first words of old Tyndareus to the doomed and agonized Orestes, whose appearance has been greeted by Menelaus with the words:

Who cometh ghastly as the grave? ...

TYNDAREUS
                              Ah God,
The snake! The snake, that drank his mother's blood,
Doth hiss and flash before the gates, and bow
The pestilence-ridden glimmer of his brow.
I sicken at him!—Wilt thou stain thy soul
With speech, Menelaus, of a thing so foul?

Above all, there is what I will not venture to illustrate, the celebrated Euripidean 'pathos', that power of insight into the cruelty of suffering: the weakness and sensitiveness of the creatures that rend one another; that piteousness in the badness of things which makes them half lovable. This is the one characteristic of Euripides' world which is not present in that of Thucydides. The grimly reticent historian seldom speaks of human suffering; the tragedian keeps it always before our eyes.

This gradual embitterment and exacerbation of thought in Euripides, as shown by the later plays compared with the earlier, is, I believe, generally recognized. I will choose in illustration of it a scene from the *Hecuba*, a tragedy early in date, but in tone and spirit really the first of the late series.[1]

The *Hecuba* deals with the taking of Troy, the great achievement in war of the heroic age of Greece. And the point in it that interests Euripides is, as often, the reverse of the picture—the baseness and, what is worse, the uninterestingness of the conquerors; the monstrous wrongs of the conquered; the moral degradation of both parties, culminating in the transformation of Hecuba from a grave oriental queen into a kind of she-devil. Among the heroes who took Troy were, as every Athenian knew, the two sons of Theseus. The Athenian public would, of course, insist on their being men-

[1] I am the more moved to select this particular scene because I find that the text and punctuation of my edition, which I owe to a remark of Dr Verrall's, confirmed by a re-examination of the Paris MSS., has caused difficulties to some scholars.

E

tioned. And they are mentioned—once! A young princess is to be cruelly murdered by a vote of the Greek host. One wishes to know what these high Athenians had to say when the villain Odysseus consented to her death. And we are told. 'The sons of Theseus, the branches of Athens, made orations contradicting each other'—so like them at their worst!—'but both were in favour of the murder!' Small wonder that Euripides' plays were awarded only four first prizes in fifty years!

In the scene which I select (vv. 795 ff.), the body of Hecuba's one remaining son, Polydôrus, has just been washed up by the sea. He, being very young, had been sent away to the keeping of a Thracian chieftain, an old friend, till the war should be over. And now it proves that the Thracian, as soon as he saw that the Trojan cause was definitely lost, had murdered his charge! Hecuba appeals to her enemy Agamemnon for help to avenge the murder. The 'King of Men' is, as usual in Euripides, a poor creature, a brave soldier and kindly enough amid the havoc he makes, but morally a coward and a sensualist. The scene is outside Agamemnon's tent. Inside the tent is Hecuba's one remaining daughter Cassandra, a prophetess vowed to virginity or to union only with the God; she is now Agamemnon's concubine!

Observe how the nobler part of the appeal fails, the baser succeeds. Hecuba shows Agamemnon her son's body, and tells how the Thracian slew him:

> And by a plot
> Slew him; and when he slew him, could he not
> Throw earth upon his bones, if he must be
> A murderer? Cast him naked to the sea?
> O King, I am but one amid thy throng
> Of servants; I am weak, but God is strong,
> God, and that King that standeth over God,
> Law; who makes gods and unmakes, by whose rod
> We live dividing the Unjust from the Just;
> Whom now before thee standing if thou thrust
> Away—if men that murder guests, and tear
> God's house down, meet from thee no vengeance, where
> Is Justice left in the world? Forbid it, thou!
> Have mercy! Dost not *fear* to wrong me now?...
> Hate me no more. Stand like an arbiter
> Apart, and count the weight of woes I bear.
> I was a Queen once, now I am thy slave;
> I had children once; but not now. And my grave
> Near; very old, broken and homeless.... Stay;

> [*Agamemnon, painfully embarrassed, has moved towards his tent.*]
>
> God help me, whither dost thou shrink away? ...
> It seems he does not listen! ...
> .... So, 'tis plain
> Now. I must never think of hope again. ...
> Those that are left me are dead; dead all save one;
> One lives, a slave, in shame. ... Ah, I am gone! ...
> The smoke! Troy is on fire! The smoke all round!
> > [*She swoons. Agamemnon comes back. Her fellow-slaves tend her. ... She rises again with a sudden thought.*]
>
> What? ... Yes, I might! ... Oh, what a hollow sound,
> Love, here! But I can say it! ... Let me be! ...
> King, King, there sleepeth side by side with thee
> My child, my priestess, whom they call in Troy
> Cassandra. Wilt thou pay not for thy joy?
> Nothing to her for all the mystery,
> And soft words of the dark? Nothing to me
> For her? Nay, mark me; look on these dead eyes!
> This is her brother; surely thine likewise!
> Thou wilt avenge him?

This desperate and horrible appeal stirs him. He is much occupied with Cassandra for the moment. But he is afraid. 'The King of Thrace is an ally of the Greeks, the slain boy was after all an enemy. People will say he is influenced by Cassandra. If it were not for that. ... She answers him in words which might stand as a motto over most of the plays of this period—as they might over much of Tolstoy:

> Faugh! There is no man free in all this world!
> Slaves of possessions, slaves of fortune, hurled
> This way and that. Or else the multitude
> Hath hold on him; or laws of stone and wood
> Constrain, and will not let him use the soul
> Within him! ... So thou durst not? And thine whole
> Thought hangs on what thy herd will say? Nay, then,
> My master, I will set thee free again.

She arranges a plan which shall not implicate him. The Thracian chieftain is allowed to visit her. On the pretence of explaining to him where a treasure is hidden, she entices him and his two children—'it is more prudent to have them present, in case he should die!'—inside the tent of the captive Trojan women. The barbarian women make much of the children, and gradually separate them from their father. They show interest in his Thracian javelins and the texture of his cloak, and so form a group round him. At a given signal they cling to him and hold him fast, murder his children before his face, and then tear his eyes out. Agamemnon, who knew that something would happen, but had never expected this, is horrified and impotent. The blinded Thracian comes back on to the stage, crawling, unable to stand. He gropes for the bodies of his children; for someone to help him; for someone to tear and kill. He shrieks like a wild beast, and the horrible scene ends.

We will not go farther into this type of play. More illustrations would, of course, prove nothing. It is the business of a tragedian to be harrowing. It is a dangerous and a somewhat vulgar course to deduce from a poet's works direct conclusions about his real life; but there is on the one hand the fact of progressive bitterness in Euripides' plays, and, on the other, as we have noticed above, there is the peculiar impression which they make of dealing with living and concrete things. But it is not really anything positive that chiefly illustrates the later tone of Euripides. It is not his denunciations of nearly all the institutions of human society—of the rich, the poor, men, women, slaves, masters, above all, of democracies and demagogues; it is not even the mass of sordid and unbalanced characters that he brings upon the scene—trembling slaves of ambition like Agamemnon; unscrupulous and heartless schemers like Odysseus; unstable compounds of chivalry and vanity like Achilles in the second *Iphigenia*; shallow women like Helen and terrible women like Electra in the *Orestes*—a play of which the scholiast naïvely remarks that 'the characters are all bad except Pylades', the one exception being a reckless murderer who was at least faithful to his friends. It is not points like these that are most significant. It is the gradual dying off of serenity and hope. I think most students of Euripides will agree that almost the only remnant of the spirit of the *Alcestis* or the *Hippolytus*, the only region of clear beauty, that can still be found in the later tragedies, lies in the lyrical element. There are one or two plays, like the *Andromeda*, which seem to have escaped from reality to the country of Aristophanes' *Birds*, and read like mere romance; and even in the *Electra* there are the songs. Euripides had prayed some twenty years before his death: 'May I not live if the Muses leave me!' And that prayer was heard. The world had turned dark, sordid, angry, under his eyes, but poetry remained to the end radiant and stainless.

It is in this state of mind and a natural development from it which afford in my judgement the best key to the understanding of *The Bacchae*, his last play, not quite finished at his death. It was written under peculiar circumstances.

We have seen from Thucydides what Athenian society had become in these last years of the death-struggle. If to Thucydides, as is possible, things seemed worse than they were, we must remember that to the more impulsive nature and equally disappointed hopes of Euripides they are not likely to have seemed better. We know that he had become in these last years increasingly unpopular in Athens; and it is not hard, if we examine the groups and parties in Athens at the time, to understand his isolation.

Most of the high-minded and thoughtful men of the time were to some extent isolated, and many retired quietly from public notice. But Euripides was not the man to be quiet in his rejected state. He was not conciliatory, not silent, not callous. At last something occurred to make his life in Athens finally intolerable. We do not know exactly what it was. It cannot have been the destruction of his estate; that had been destroyed long before. It cannot have been his alleged desertion by his wife; she was either dead or over seventy. It may have been something connected with his prosecution for impiety, the charge on which Socrates was put to death a few years after. All that we know is one fragmentary sentence in the ancient *Life of Euripides*: 'He had to leave Athens because of the malicious exultation over him of nearly all the city.'

Archelaüs, King of Macedon, had long been inviting him. The poet had among his papers a play called *Archelaüs*, written to celebrate this king's legendary ancestor, so he may before this have been thinking of Macedonia as a possible refuge. He went now, and seems to have lived in some wild retreat on the northern slopes of Mount Olympus, in the Muses' country, as he phrases it:

> In the elm-woods and the oaken,
>   There where Orpheus harped of old,
> And the trees awoke and knew him,
> And the wild things gathered to him,
>   As he sang amid the broken
>   Glens his music manifold.

The spirit of the place passed into his writings. He had produced the *Orestes* in 408. He produced nothing, so far as has been made out, in 407. He died in 406. And after his death there appeared in Athens, under the management of his son, a play that held the

Greek stage for five centuries, a strange and thrilling tragedy, enigmatical, inhuman, at times actually repellent, yet as strong and as full of beauty as the finest work of his prime.

Two other plays were produced with it. Of one, *Alcmaeon in Corinth*, we know nothing characteristic; the second, *Iphigenîa in Aulis*, is in many ways remarkable. The groundwork of it is powerful and bitter; in style it approaches the New Comedy; but it is interspersed with passages and scenes of most romantic beauty; and, finally, it was left at the poet's death half finished. One could imagine that he had begun it in Athens, or at least before the bitter taste of Athens had worn off; that he tried afterwards to change the tone of it to something kindlier and more beautiful; that finally he threw it aside and began a quite new play in a different style to express the new spirit that he had found.

For *The Bacchae* is somehow different in spirit from any of his other works, late or early. The old poet chose a severely traditional subject, the primitive ritual-play of Dionysus from which Greek tragedy is said to have sprung. The young god born of Zeus and the Theban princess, Semelê, travelling through the world to announce his godhead, comes to his own people of Thebes, and—his own receive him not. They will not worship him simply and willingly; he constrains them to worship him with the enthusiasm of madness. The King, Pentheus, insults and imprisons the god, spies on his mystic worship, is discovered by the frenzied saints and torn limb from limb, his own mother, Agâvê, being the first to rend him.

Now it is no use pretending that this is a moral and sympathetic tale, or that Euripides palliates the atrocity of it, and tries to justify Dionysus. Euripides never palliates things. He leaves this savage story as savage as he found it. The sympathy of the audience is with Dionysus while he is persecuted; doubtful while he is just taking his vengeance; utterly against him at the end of the play. Note how Agâvê, when restored to her right mind, refuses even to think of him and his miserable injured pride:

AGÂVÊ
'Tis Dionyse hath done it. Now I see.

CADMUS
Ye wronged him! Ye denied his deity.

AGÂVÊ
Show me the body of the son I love!

Note how Dionysus is left answerless when Agâvê rebukes him:

> DIONYSUS
> Ye mocked me being God. This is your wage.
>
> AGÂVÊ
> Should God be like a proud man in his rage?
>
> DIONYSUS
> 'Tis as my sire, Zeus, willed it long ago.

A helpless, fatalistic answer, abandoning the moral standpoint.

But the most significant point against Dionysus is the change of tone—the conversion, one might almost call it—of his own inspired *Wild Beasts*, the Chorus of Asiatic Bacchanals, after the return of Agâvê with her son's severed head. The change is clearly visible in that marvellous scene itself. It is emphasized in the sequel. Those wild singers, who raged so loudly in praises of the god's vengeance before they saw what it was, fall, when once they have seen it, into dead silence. True, there is a lacuna in the MS. at one point, so it is possible that they may have spoken; but as the play stands, their Leader speaks only one couplet addressed to Cadmus, whom the god has wronged:

> Lo, I weep with thee. 'Twas but due reward
> God sent on Pentheus; but for thee... 'tis hard!

And they go off at the end with no remark, good or evil, about their triumphant and hateful Dionysus, uttering only those lines of brooding resignation with which Euripides closed so many of his tragedies.

Such silence in such a situation is significant. Euripides is, as usual, critical or even hostile towards the moral tone of the myth that he celebrates. There is nothing in that to surprise us.

Some critics have even tried to imagine that Pentheus is a 'sympathetic' hero; that he is right in his crusade against this bad god, as much as Hippolytus was right. But the case will not bear examination. Euripides might easily have made Pentheus 'sympathetic' if he had chosen. And he certainly has not chosen. No. As regards the conflict between Dionysus and Pentheus, Euripides has merely followed a method very usual with him, the method, for instance, of the *Electra*. He has given a careful objective representation of the facts as alleged in the myth: 'If the story is true,' he says, 'then it must have been like this.' We have the ordinary hot-tempered and narrow-minded tyrant—not very carefully studied, by the way, and apparently not very interesting to the poet; we have a well-attested god and suitable miracles; we have a most poignant and unshrinking picture of the possibilities of religious madness. That may be taken as the groundwork of the play. It is quite probable that Euripides had seen some glimpses of Dionysus-worship on the Macedonian mountains which gave a fresh reality in his mind to the legends of ravening and wonder-working Maenads.

But when all this is admitted, there remains a fact of cardinal importance, which was seen by the older critics, and misled them so greatly that modern writers are often tempted to deny its existence. There is in *The Bacchae* real and heartfelt glorification of Dionysus.

The 'objectivity' is not kept up. Again and again in the lyrics you feel that the Maenads are no longer merely observed and analysed. The poet has entered into them, and they into him. Again and again the words that fall from the lips of the Chorus or its Leader are not the words of a raving Bacchante, but of a gentle and deeply musing philosopher.

Probably all dramatists who possess strong personal beliefs yield at times to the temptation of using one of their characters as a mouthpiece for their own feelings. And the Greek Chorus, a half-dramatic, half-lyrical creation, both was and was felt to be particularly suitable for such use. Of course a writer does not—or at least should not—use the drama to express his mere 'views' on ordinary and commonplace questions, to announce his side in politics or his sect in religion. But it is a method wonderfully contrived for expressing those vaguer faiths and aspirations which a man feels haunting him and calling to him, but which he cannot state in plain language or uphold with a full acceptance of responsibility. You can say the thing that wishes to be said; you 'give it its chance'; you relieve your mind of it. And if it proves to be all nonsense, well, it is not you that said it. It is only a character in one of your plays.

The religion of Dionysus as Euripides found it, already mysticized and made spiritual, half-reformed and half-petrified in sacerdotalism, by the Orphic movement, was exactly the kind of mingled mass which lends itself to dramatic and indirect expression. It was gross as it stood; yet it could be so easily and so wonderfully idealized! Euripides seems to have felt a peculiar and almost enthusiastic interest in a further sublimation of its doctrines, a philosophic or prophet-like interpretation of the spirit that a man might see in it if he would. And meantime he did not bind himself. He let his

Bacchanals rave from time to time, as they were bound to rave. He had said his say, and he was not responsible for the whole of Dionysus-worship nor yet of Orphism.

Dionysus, as Euripides takes him from the current conceptions of his day, is the God of spring and youth: and thus of all high emotion, inspiration, intoxication. He is the patron of poetry, especially of dramatic poetry. He has given man Wine, which is his Blood and a religious symbol. He is the clean New Year, uncontaminated by the decay of the past, and as such he purifies from Sin. It is unmeaning, surely, to talk of a 'merely ritual' purification as opposed to something real. Ritual, as long as it fully lives, is charged with spiritual meaning, and can often express just those transcendent things which words fail to utter—much as a look or the clasp of a hand can at times express more than a verbal greeting. Dionysus purified as spiritually as the worshipper's mind required. And he gave to the Purified a mystic Joy, surpassing in intensity that of man, the Joy of a god or a free wild animal. The Bacchanals in this play worshipped him by his many names (vv. 725 ff.):

> 'Iacchos, Bromios, Lord,
> God of God born'; and all the mountain felt
> And worshipped with them, and the wild things knelt,
> And ramped and gloried, and the wilderness
> Was filled with moving voices and dim stress.

That is the kind of god he celebrates.

Euripides had lived most of his life in a great town, among highly educated people; amid restless ambitions and fierce rivalries; amid general scepticism, originally caused, no doubt, in most cases, by higher religious aspirations than those of the common man, but ending largely in arid irreligion; in an ultra political community, led of late years by the kind of men of whom Plato said that if you looked into the soul of one of them you could see 'its bad little eye glittering with sharpness'; in a community now hardened to the condition described in the long passage quoted above from Thucydides. Euripides had lived all his life in this society; for many years he had led it, at least in matters of art and intellect; for many years he had fought with it. And now he was free from it!

He felt like a hunted animal escaped from its pursuers; like a fawn fled to the forest, says one lyric, in which the personal note is surely audible as a ringing undertone (vv. 862 ff.):

> Oh, feet of a fawn to the greenwood fled

> Alone in the grass and the loveliness,
> Leap of the Hunted, no more in dread . . .

But there is still a terror in the distance behind him; he must go onward yet, to lonely regions where no voice of either man or hound may reach. 'What else is wisdom?' he asks, in a marvellous passage:

> What else is wisdom? What of man's endeavour
> Or God's high grace so lovely and so great?
> To stand from fear set free, to breathe and wait;
> To hold a hand uplifted over Hate;
> And shall not loveliness be loved for ever?

He was escaped and happy; he was beyond the reach of Hate. Nay, he was safe, and those who hated him were suffering. A judgement seemed to be upon them, these men who had resolved to have no dealings with 'the three deadly enemies of empire, Pity and the Charm of Words and the Generosity of Strength'; who lived, as Thucydides says in another passage (vi. 90), in dreams of wider and wider conquest, the conquest of Sicily, of South Italy, of Carthage and all her empire, of every country that touched the sea. They had forgotten the essence of religion, forgotten the eternal laws, and the judgement in wait for those who 'worship the Ruthless Will'; who dream

> Dreams of the proud man, making great
>   And greater ever
> Things that are not of God. (vv. 885 ff.)

It is against the essential irreligion implied in these dreams that he appeals in the same song:

> And is thy faith so much to give?
> Is it so hard a thing to see,
> That the Spirit of God, whate'er it be,
> The Law that abides and falters not, ages long,
> The Eternal and Nature-born—these things be strong?

In the epode of the same chorus, taking the ritual words of certain old Bacchic hymns and slightly changing them, he expresses his own positive doctrine more clearly:

> Happy he, On the weary sea,
>   Who hath fled the tempest and won the haven;

> Happy, whoso hath risen, free,
> Above his strivings!

Men strive with many ambitions, seethe with divers hopes, mostly conflicting, mostly of inherent worthlessness; even if they are achieved, no one is a whit the better.

> But whoe'er can know, As the long days go,
> That to *live is happy*, hath found his Heaven!

Could not the wise men of Athens understand what a child feels, what a wild beast feels, what a poet feels, that to live—to live in the presence of nature, of dawn and sunset, of eternal mysteries and discoveries and wonders—is in itself a joyous thing?

'Love thou the day and the night,' he says in another place. It is only so that Life can be made what it really is, a Joy: by loving not only your neighbour—he is so vivid an element in life that, unless you do love him, he will spoil all the rest—but the actual details and processes of living. Life becomes like the voyage of Dionysus himself over magic seas, or rather, perhaps, like the more chequered voyage of Shelley's lovers:

> While Night,
> And Day, and Storm and Calm pursue their flight,
> Our ministers across the boundless sea,
> Treading each other's heels unheededly—

the alternations and pains being only 'ministers' to the great composite joy.

It seemed to Euripides, in that favourite metaphor of his, which was always a little more than a metaphor, that a God had been rejected by the world that he came from. Those haggard, striving, suspicious men, full of ambition and the pride of intellect, almost destitute of emotion, unless political hatreds can be called emotion, were hurrying through Life in the presence of august things which they never recognized, of joy and beauty which they never dreamed of. Thus it is that 'the world's wise are not wise' (v. 395). The poet may have his special paradise, away from the chosen places of ordinary men, better than the sweetness of Cyprus or Paphos:

> The high still dell Where the Muses dwell,
> Fairest of all things fair—

it is there that he will find the things truly desired of his heart, and the power to worship in peace his guiding Fire of inspiration. But

Dionysus gives his Wine to all men, not to poets alone. Only by 'spurning joy' can men harden his heart against them. For the rest

> The simple nameless herd of Humanity
> Hath deeds and faith that are truth enough for me!

It is a mysticism which includes democracy as it includes the love of your neighbour. They are both necessary details in the inclusive end. It implies that trust in the 'simple man' which is so characteristic of most idealists and most reformers. It implies the doctrine of Equality—a doctrine essentially religious and mystical, continually disproved in every fresh sense in which it can be formulated, and yet remaining one of the living faiths of men.

It is at first sight strange, this belittling of 'the Wise' and all their learning. Euripides had been all his life the poet militant of knowledge, the apostle of progress and enlightenment. Yet there is no real contradiction. It is only that the Wise are not wise enough, that the Knowledge which a man has attained is such a poor and narrow thing compared with the Knowledge that he dreamed of. In one difficult and beautiful passage Euripides seems[1] to give us his own apology (vv. 1005 ff.):

> Knowledge, we are not foes!
> I seek thee diligently;
> But the world with a great wind blows,
> Shining, and not from thee;
> Blowing to beautiful things,
> On amid dark and light,
> Till Life through the trammellings
> Of Laws that are not the Right,
> Breaks, clean and pure, and sings
> Glorying to God in the height!

One feels grateful for that voice from the old Euripides amid the strange new tones of *The Bacchae*.

It is not for us to consider at present how far this doctrine is true, nor even how far it is good or bad. We need only see what the essence of it is. That the end of life is not in the future, not in external objects, not a thing to be won by success or good fortune, nor to be deprived of by the actions of others. Live according to Nature, and Life itself is happiness. The Kingdom of Heaven is

---

[1] I say 'seems', because the reading is conjectural. I suggest ἀέντων (= 'let them blow') in place of the MS. ἀεὶ τῶν. The passage is generally abandoned as hopelessly corrupt.

within you—here and now. You have but to accept it and live with it—not obscure it by striving and hating and looking in the wrong place.

On one side this is a very practical and lowly doctrine—the doctrine of contentment, the doctrine of making things better by liking and helping them. On the other side, it is an appeal to the almost mystical faith of the poet or artist who dwells in all of us. Probably most people have had the momentary experience—it may come to one on Swiss mountains, on Surrey commons, in crowded streets, on the tops of omnibuses, inside London houses—of being, as it seems, surrounded by an incomprehensible and almost intolerable vastness of beauty and delight and interest—if only one could grasp it or enter into it! That is just the rub, a critic may say. It is no use telling all the world to find happiness by living permanently at the level of these fugitive moments—moments which in high poets and prophets may extend to days. It is simpler and quite as practical to advise them all to have ten thousand a year.

It is not necessary to struggle with that objection. But it is worth while to remark in closing that historically the line here suggested by Euripides was followed by almost all the higher minds of antiquity and early Christianity. Excepting Aristotle, who clung characteristically to the concrete city and the dutiful tax-paying citizen, all the great leaders of Greek thought turned away from the world and took refuge in the Soul. The words used accidentally above—Live according to Nature—formed the very foundation of moral doctrine not only for the Stoics, but for all the schools of philosophy. The Platonists sought for the Good, the Stoics for Virtue, the Epicureans for Pleasure; but the various names are names for the same End; and it is always an End, not future, but existing—not without or afar, but inside each man's self.

The old devotion to Fifth Century Athens, to that Princess of Cities, who had so fearfully fallen and dragged her lovers through such bloodstained dust, lived on with a kind of fascination as a symbol in the minds of these deeply individual philosophers of later Hellenism and early Christianity. But it was no longer a city on earth that they sought, not one to be served by military conquests, nor efficient police, nor taxes, and public education. It was 'the one great city in which all are free', or it was the city of Man's Soul. 'The poet has said,' writes a late Stoic, who had an exceptionally large and difficult city of his own to look after, 'The poet has said: O Beloved City of Cecrops: canst' though not say: O Beloved City of God?'

CHAPTER IV

Poesis and Mimesis[1]

A DISTINGUISHED woman of letters, long resident abroad, came lately to a friend of mine in London and explained her wish to learn how 'the young' in England were now thinking. She herself had always been advanced in thought, if not revolutionary, and was steeled against possible shocks. My friend dauntlessly collected a bevy of young and representative lions, and the parties met. Unfortunately I know only the barest outline of what took place. The elderly revolutionary fixed on the most attractive and audacious-looking of the group and asked him what author had now most influence with the rising generation of intellectuals. He said without hesitation, 'Aristotle'; and the chief reason he gave for Aristotle's supreme value was that, in his greatest philosophical and æsthetic effects, he never relied on the element of wonder. I believe the evening was not on the whole a success.

However, the story sent me back to the first chapter of the *Poetics* as a subject for this lecture, which your kindness has called upon me to deliver in memory of the honoured and beloved name of Henry Sidgwick. I always felt, if I may say so, the presence of something akin to Aristotle in Professor Sidgwick's mind, the same variety of interest yet the same undistracted and unwavering pursuit of what was true, and I think also the same high disdain, where truth was the object sought, of arousing the stimulant of wonder.

Aristotle, as we all know, lays it down at the very opening of his work that: 'Epic poetry and tragedy, comedy also and dithyrambic poetry, and the music of the flute and the lyre in most of their forms, are all in their general conception modes of imitation.' The statement, I venture to think, appears to most English readers almost meaningless; and so far as it has any meaning, I believe most of them will think it untrue. And both impressions will be deepened when a page or two later the philosopher explains that 'tragedy is an imitation of good men' and comedy 'of bad men'.

[1] The Henry Sidgwick Lecture, Cambridge, 1920.

Let us try the experiment which is so frequently helpful in dealing with the classics when they puzzle us: let us be literal and exact, and entirely disregard elegance. And let us remember to begin with that *poein* means 'to make' and *poêsis* 'making'. The passage then becomes:

'Epos-making and the making of tragedy, also comedy and dithyramb-making and most fluting and harping, in their general conception, are as a matter of fact (not makings but) imitations.'

The thought seems to me to become much clearer. A poet, or maker, who makes a Sack of Troy or a Marriage of Peleus does not make a real Sack or a real Marriage, he makes an imitation Sack or Marriage, just as a painter when he 'paints Pericles' does not make a real Pericles but an imitation or picture of Pericles. It perhaps troubles us for a moment when Aristotle says the painter 'imitates Pericles' or the poet 'imitates the Sack of Troy' instead of saying that he 'makes imitations'. But that is a mere matter of idiom: a maker of toy soldiers would be said in Greek 'to imitate soldiers with tin'. The point is that the artist being a 'maker' does make something, but that something is always an imitation.

Let me illustrate this point of view by two or three examples. You may say that the poet, or maker, does make one perfectly definite and real thing; he makes his poem, or, to put it more concretely, his verses. Quite true. In Greek you can say equally that Homer 'makes hexameters' or 'makes the wrath of Achilles'. But it is significant that Aristotle objects to what he calls the current habit of classing poets according to the verses they make. To call them 'hexameter-makers' or 'iambic-makers' is a shallow and unimportant statement; they must, according to him, be classed as 'makers' by the kind of thing they imitate, or the kind of imitation they make.

Again, why does Aristotle repeatedly and emphatically say that the most imitative of all Arts is Music, and (*Pol.* 1340a 18) that the *homoiomata* or likenesses produced by music are most exactly like the originals, for example the imitations of anger or mercy or courage? It seems very odd to us to say that a tune is more like anger than a good portrait of Pericles is like Pericles. But if we think of the musician as a 'maker' making imitation 'anger' or imitation 'love', surely that imitation anger or love which he makes in a sensitive listener is most extraordinarily like the real emotion—more closely like than any imitation produced by another art? Again, following this clue we can see why Aristotle, though living in a great architectural age, never classes architecture among the imitative arts which with him are equivalent to the 'fine arts'. The architect makes real houses or real temples; he does not make imitations.

I hope we see also a more important point: that it is a mere error, an error born from operating with imperfectly understood tests, when critics blame Aristotle for not appreciating the 'creative power' of art. So far from ignoring it, he starts with it. He begins by calling it *poesis*, 'making' or 'creation', and then goes on to observe that it is not quite like ordinary creation. Nor is it. It is a making of imitations.

Let us follow him a little further. What objects does his poet imitate or make imitations of? 'Characters, emotions, and *praxeis*'—how shall we translate the last word? Most scholars translate 'actions', as if from πράττω, 'to act'. But I cannot help thinking that Professor Margoliouth is right in taking it from the intransitive πράττω, 'to fare', though in that case we have no exact noun to translate it by. Poetry shows the 'farings' of people, how they fare well or ill. It is not confined to showing 'actions'.

Poetry differs from history in that history makes imitations of what did happen, and poetry of what might happen. Which difference makes poetry deeper and more philosophic than history. And lastly there is a great difference between tragedy, epic and high poetry on the one hand, and comedy, satire and low poetry on the other, that 'makers' in the high style make better people than ourselves, and makers in the low style make worse people. This causes a difficulty to some readers. They do not admit that Milton's Satan, Shakespeare's Macbeth, Aeschylus's Clytemnestra are 'better' than the average man. For my own part I feel no difficulty in regarding them all as my betters. If I met them I should certainly feel small and respectful. But it seems as if in our language the word for 'good' had become more sharply moralized than its Greek equivalents, and perhaps one ought to say instead of 'better', 'higher' or 'greater'.

Poetry, then, creates a sort of imitation world, a world of characters, passions and 'ways of faring', which may be indefinitely 'better' than those we know, as well as worse; its details need not be imitations of any particular things that ever existed, but are so far limited by the existing world that they ought to present 'things that might exist' or, as Aristotle explains it in another passage, 'things that look as if they might exist'. (We might add, if it were necessary, that for psychological reasons the subjects of poetry must be in some sense taken from the real world, because there is no other place from which to take them.) And the value to us of this imitation world according to Aristotle is simply that we contemplate it with delight; though almost every other Greek writer lays more stress on a further claim, that this contemplation makes us better men.

If I have made clear this Aristotelian conception of poetry I should like to compare it with the famous claim made by Matthew Arnold in his Essay on the Study of Poetry, published in 1880 as a general introduction to Ward's English Poets. He there argues that the chief function of poetry is the criticism of life.

'Our religion,' he says, 'parading evidences such as those on which the popular mind relies now; our philosophy, pluming itself on its reasonings about causation and finite and infinite being: what are they but the shadows and dreams and false show of knowledge? The day will come when we shall wonder at ourselves for having trusted to them, for having taken them seriously; and the more we perceive their hollowness, the more we shall prize the "breath and finer spirit of knowledge offered to us by poetry." . . . "More and more mankind will discover that we have to turn to poetry to interpret life for us, to console us, to sustain us." ' And a little further on, 'The consolation and the stay will be of power in proportion to the power of the criticism of life.'

Poetry as the creation of an imitation world and poetry as the criticism of life: how are the two conceptions related to one another? Are they contradictory or compatible? They are quite compatible, I think. They differ only in their points of emphasis or their angle of vision. For to make an imitation of 'characters, passions and ways of faring' necessarily implies a criticism upon life, inasmuch as the imitator must select the things that strike him as most interesting and characteristic and must say something about them. The chief difference between Aristotle and Matthew Arnold is a difference about the true purpose of poetry, and curiously enough in this controversy almost all our Greek authorities are on the side of Matthew Arnold and almost all our modern critics loudly agree with Aristotle. Aristotle says the aim of poetry is to give delight; Arnold says it is to help us to live better. I will not dwell on this difference. It too is only a difference of emphasis, for Arnold expressly admits the element of mere delight as one of the aims of poetry, and Aristotle's own Hymn to Virtue might have been written to illustrate Arnold's doctrine. It is a lyric of considerable beauty and charm, but the whole weight of its effort is in the direction that Arnold requires. It seeks to draw from the world of poetry help for mankind in the heavy task of living. If I had to suggest in a few words the reason why Arnold demands so much from poetry and Aristotle so little, I would point out that the modern writer expressly begins by saying that our religion and philosophy have failed us, and therefore we must go to poetry for the things which they have promised but not provided, while Aristotle was remarkably well furnished both with Ethics and with Metaphysics. If Aristotle ever felt 'weary of himself and sick of asking', he never thought of going to Homer and Hesiod for his answer. He went to them for poetry and for story-telling. Arnold's generation, being poorly off for religious belief and almost beggared in philosophy, tended to put on to poetry all the work that ought to be done by those defaulting Muses; while on the other hand Aristotle, being almost destitute of prose fiction, where we roll and roll in inexhaustible and stifling abundance, makes poetry take the place of the novel. The result is that Aristotle treats poetry as the natural vehicle for story-telling, while we are always demanding of it doctrines about psychology and the art of life. And consequently we are establishing a new conventional canon of what is poetical and what not. It is very significant, for instance, that when Aristotle wants to give an instance of a work in metre which is so essentially prosaic in character that it cannot be called poetry, he chooses the philosophic poem of Empedocles; whereas almost every English reader who comes across Empedocles feels his breath catch at the sheer beauty of the poetry. On the other hand there were probably many narrative poems which entirely pleased Aristotle but would instantly strike a modern critic as the sort of thing that would be better in prose. Every generation has its blind spots.

Let us notice how the elements of criticism and mimesis vary in degree in different poems. And first of all let us consider whether a perfectly direct practical criticism of life can be poetry. Some people deny it, but I think they are clearly wrong. It has certainly been felt as poetry in past ages. The Psalms are full of it. So are the Greek anthologies; and the passages quoted from poets in antiquity are *gnômæ*, or direct criticisms of life, more often than anything else. If you take the Essay to which I have referred you will find that Matthew Arnold takes a number of lines from Homer, Milton, Dante and Shakespeare as typical of the very highest poetry and capable of acting as touchstones of criticism. Nearly all of them are direct criticisms of life, and suggestions for living. But let us clinch the matter. Take one of the greatest and best known of modern sonnets:

POESIS AND MIMESIS

> The World is too much with us; late and soon,
>   Getting and spending, we lay waste our powers:
>   Little we see in nature that is ours;
> We have given our hearts away, a sordid boon.
> This sea that bares her bosom to the moon,
>   The winds that will be howling at all hours
>   And are upgathered now, like sleeping flowers,
> For this, for everything, we are out of tune.
> It moves us not. Great God, I'd rather be
>   A Pagan, suckled in a creed outworn,
>   So might I, standing on this pleasant lea,
>   Have glimpses that would make me less forlorn,
> Catch sight of Proteus rising from the sea,
>   Or hear old Triton blow his wreathèd horn!

Perfectly direct criticism and advice, yet undoubtedly poetry.—I wonder if doubt will be felt about another passage of criticism, in a style now out of fashion:

> Know then thyself, presume not God to scan:
> The proper study of mankind is man;
> Placed on this isthmus of the middle state,
> A being darkly wise and rudely great,
> With too much knowledge for the sceptic side,
> With too much weakness for the Stoic's pride,
> He hangs between in doubt to move or rest,
> In doubt to deem himself a God or beast,
> In doubt his mind or body to prefer,
> Born but to die, and reasoning but to err;
> Alike in ignorance, his nature such,
> Whether he thinks too little or too much;
> Chaos of thought and feeling all confused,
> Still by himself abused—and disabused,
> Created half to rise and half to fall,
> Great Lord of all things, yet a prey to all:
> Sole judge of truth, through endless error hurled,
> The glory, jest, and riddle of the world!

Unless we are to interpret the word 'poetry' in some esoteric sense of our own, I do not see how we can doubt that this too is poetry. If people now are bored by it, or see nothing in it, I do not think I should draw the moral that this is not poetry; I should prefer to conclude, with all deference, that the Lord had made the heart of this people fat and made their ears heavy, and shut their eyes lest they turn again and be healed. However, if people do reject it from the range of poetry, it will not be because it is criticism. It is criticism just as much as the Wordsworth sonnet and no more. But the burden of its criticism is different. Wordsworth criticizes life for not being more permeated by the spiritual imagination; Pope criticizes man as being such a frail thing, contradictory and uncertain. Wordsworth's remedy is to live with more imagination and reverie; Pope's remedy is prudence and moderation, Sophrosyne and $M\eta\delta\grave{\epsilon}\nu\ \check{a}\gamma a\nu$, that rule which seemed to the ancients to lie near the heart of poetry and to most people now appears only suitable to prose.

Next, in this poetry of direct criticism, is there any imaginative creation? Do these two poems, in Aristotle's phrase, 'imitate' anything at all? I think they do. Pope's man is a real picture. We can ask, 'Is that like the men we know?' And Wordsworth's world, and his life that would be so different if the world did not interrupt it, are imitations in the Greek sense. Still these two poems seem to give a maximum of criticism and a minimum of mimesis.

Direct criticism is one pole and mere mimesis the opposite pole; poetry ranges from one to the other, while some of the greatest poetry combines both. Some of the greatest creators are also the most vehement critics. Among the moderns Shelley in his larger efforts lives habitually in a world of vision and can scarcely breathe at peace except in its atmosphere; yet he is always bringing it into competition with the real world; insisting that it is in fact what this actual world ought to be and is trying to be, and is, perhaps, even now on the verge of becoming. Among the ancients Aeschylus and Euripides are both magical creators and earnest critics. I can hardly imagine a more profound criticism of life than the Oresteia or one more poignant than the Trojan Women. Yet both move in the realms of inspired lyrical mimesis. The Homeric poets make a world extraordinarily consistent and alive; people may differ about the amount of deliberate criticism of this world which it contains, but for my own part I agree with the common Greek opinion that it is a great deal. About Milton I am less clear. The power of creative mimesis is tremendous; and we know from the rest of Milton's work that he was a copious and somewhat opinionated critic. But my own feeling is that, in the main, his imagined world is almost nothing to him but a place of beauty, a sanctuary and an escape. Virgil is a great and profound critic. His consummate poetical power is curiously little dependent on any gift of mere mimesis. If we seek examples of almost unmixed mimesis we shall look to those poets who have created great imitation worlds with a coherence and a character of their own. I think we must also say, with a wide range of territory and a large population. William Morris and Spenser and Chaucer among modern English writers are the names that occur at once; creators of large worlds of fantasy with very little element of criticism, except that which is implicit in every act of selection.

But the type and prophet of this uncritical mimesis, I would almost call him the martyr of this faith; a man who seems hardly to have lived at all except in the world of his imagination; who tells us that even as a boy he could scarcely speak without falling into verse; who sprang straight to a perfection of form which remained the unchallenged model of all similar poetry for centuries after; who poured forth his imaginative creations, his 'copies of life', with such copiousness that the poets of the middle ages and the renaissance went to him as to an inexhaustible quarry from which to build their houses and streets and cities; a man of unexampled popularity in his own day and of almost unexampled influence afterwards; Ovid is one towards whom the present generation has resolutely turned its blind spot. If he were archaic, or uncouth, or earnest, or nobly striving after ideals he cannot reach; if he were even difficult or eccentric, so as to make some claim upon us; we should doubtless be attracted to him and read him with our imaginations alert. But he does his work too well, he asks no indulgence; he is neat and swift and witty and does not need our help; consequently we have no use for him. I suspect we are wrong. 'My work is done,' he writes at the end of the *Metamorphoses*:

> My work is done: which not the All Father's ire
> Shall sweep to nothingness, not steel, nor fire,
> Nor eating Time.—Come when thou wilt, O Hour,
> Which save upon my body hast no power,
> And bring to its end this frail uncertainty
> That men call life. A better part of me
> Above the stars eternal shall, like flame,
> Live, and no death prevail against my name.

He was a poet utterly in love with poetry: not perhaps with the soul of poetry—to be in love with souls is a feeble and somewhat morbid condition—but with the real face and voice and body and clothes and accessories of poetry. He loved the actual technique of the verse, but of that later. He loved most the whole world of mimesis which he made. We hear that he was apprenticed to the law, but wrote verses instead of speeches. He married wives and they ran away or died and he married others. He had a daughter and adored her, and taught her verses. He was always in love and never with anyone in particular. He strikes one as having been rather innocent and almost entirely useless in this dull world which he had not made and for which he was not responsible, while he moved triumphant and effective through his own inexhaustible realm of legend. He came somehow under the displeasure of the government, and by a peculiar piece of cruelty was sent with all his helpless sweetness and sensuousness and none of the gifts of a colonist, to live in exile in that dreadful region

> Where slow Maeotis crawls, and scarcely flows
> The frozen Tanais through a waste of snows.

Where, like an anodyne for a gnawing pain, he tried to forget himself in verses and yet more verses, until he died.

What a world it is that he has created in the *Metamorphoses*! It draws its denizens from all the boundless resources of Greek mythology, a world of live forests and mountains and rivers, in which every plant and flower has a story, and nearly always a love story; where the moon is indeed not a moon but an orbèd maiden, and the Sunrise weeps because she is still young and her belovèd is old; and the stars are human souls; and the Sun sees human virgins in the depths of forests and almost swoons at their beauty and pursues them; and other virgins, who feel in the same way about him, commit great sins from jealousy and then fling themselves on the ground in grief and fix their eyes on him, weeping and weeping till they waste away and turn into flowers; and all the youths and maidens are indescribably beautiful and adventurous and passionate, though not well brought up, and, I fear, somewhat lacking in the first elements of self-control; and they all fall in love with each other, or, failing that, with fountains or stars or trees; and are always met by enormous obstacles, and are liable to commit crimes and cause tragedies, but always forgive each other, or else die. A world of wonderful children where nobody is really cross or wicked except the grown-ups; Juno, for instance, and people's parents, and of course a certain number of Furies and Witches. I think among all the poets who take rank merely as storytellers and creators of mimic worlds, Ovid still stands supreme. His criticism of life is very slight; it is the criticism passed by a child, playing alone and peopling the summer evening with delightful shapes, upon the stupid nurse who drags it off to bed. And that too is a criticism that deserves attention.

We have spoken of one side of Poetry; the side particularly meant by Aristotle when he says that poets are only makers 'by imitation'; makers, that is, of imitation persons and imitation worlds, which may or may not involve criticism upon our existing life. He dissented, we remember, from the view of those who thought that a poet was principally a maker because he made verses. But after all there is obviously something in their view, and in a later part of the *Poetics* Aristotle pays a good deal of attention to them. There is something which a poet really makes as much as a weaver makes his cloth. He makes the actual texture of his verses. He makes his own poems.

Here again we find our vision full of blind spots. Some people would say our ears deaf to particular qualities of sound. Of course we can all see that poetical style develops and decays in various countries. In England the eighteenth-century poets learnt to write much smoother heroic couplets than Shakespeare or Ben Jonson could write, while they lost much of the art of writing blank verse; Dryden in the *Ode on St Cecilia's Day* achieved effects which were thought remarkable at the time but would have argued mere incompetence in any writer later than 1820. We have seen many changes of technique in our own day. That is all obvious. But the point that I wish now to illustrate is the extraordinary diversity of style and of aim which results naturally from the use of different languages. Words are the bricks or stones with which you build. And Latin words, Greek words, French words, English words, have to be used in very different ways, and each language has its own special effects. The English can do trisyllabic and even quadrisyllabic metres, it seems to me, incomparably better than other modern nations. A poem like Swinburne's *Dolores* is probably impossible in any European language but its own; still more so the extraordinary beauty and exactitude of 'By the waters of Babylon we sat down and wept'. I think the cause of this great advantage is twofold; first, we have a very marked and clear system of stress accents, and secondly, our culture has been largely in the hands of people who knew and even wrote Latin and Greek verse. French has no system of stress accents except the slightly iambic rhythm which pervades every sentence, whatever the words may be. Consequently French is almost incapable of any purely metrical beauty. German has a stress accent like ours, but, if my ear is to be trusted, it has scarcely attempted the finest lyrical effects of English verse. On the other hand we cannot approach the effects produced in French verse by their wonderful diphthongs and nasals and long syllables. Our wretched indeterminate vowel, our tendency to pronounce clearly only one syllable in every polysyllabic word or word-group, cuts us off from such effects as

> Comme c'est triste voir s'enfuir les hirondelles:

or

> Puisque j'ai vu tomber dans l'onde de ma vie
> Une feuille de rose arrachée à tes jours.

A language which talks of 'Jezebel' as 'Jessuble' cannot produce the same effects as one which says 'Jé-za-bel' with each syllable distinct: Et venger Athalie Achab et Jézabel.

But the point which I wish specially to illustrate is, I think, another of our blind spots: the special style produced in Latin poetry—it is less marked in Greek—by the necessities of the language and the metre. I assume that today nearly all intelligent young men and women despise Latin poetry and think of its characteristics as somewhat odious and markedly unpoetical. And I would begin by recalling that all through the middle ages and the renaissance, down to the later part of the eighteenth century, Latin poetry was the central type and model of all poetry. When you spoke of poetry you meant first and foremost the Latin poets. It gives us a shock when Marlow (whom we respect) in the most tragic moment of Dr Faustus makes his hero quote Ovid (whom we despise), and we hardly notice the passionate beauty of the line—slightly altered—which he quotes:

> O lente lente currite, noctis equi!

But Marlow was doing the natural thing. Ovid was to him what he was to his predecessors and contemporaries and followers. It is we who are odd.

Let me, if I can, try to describe the beauty which our ancestors found in the conventional Latin style. It is a beauty entirely dependent on the influential character of the language; we speakers of an uninflected language are shut off from it. We express the relations of our words to one another not by inflections but by their order in the sentence. Consequently we are tied up to one everlasting cast-iron order of words, and all those innumerable delicate beauties which Latin and Greek find in the order of their words in the sentence are debarred to us. The difference is heightened by the respective treatment of metre in ancient and modern tongues. Their metres were very marked. They were a delight in themselves and had rules which a poet never broke. Our metres are mostly inconspicuous: as a rule they are only types to which we approximate with as much or as little exactitude as we find convenient. Our poetry is apt to slip out like a stream of wet mud or concrete; theirs was built and fitted, chip by chip, block by block, of hard marble.

Take an average Ovidian couplet: the first two lines of one of the *Heroides*, imaginary letters written by legendary damsels to absent lovers. This is Phyllis, a princess of the wild Thracian mountains, writing to Demophoon of Athens:

> Hospita, Demophoôn, tua te Rhodopêia Phyllis,
> Ultra promissum tempus abesse queror.

'I, Phyllis of Rhodopê, O Demophoon, your late hostess, complain that you are absent beyond the time promised.' That I flatter myself is a blameless translation. Not a single iota of poetry or of character either is left in it.

Now let us try to see what we have left out, and to conceive the effect of the order of the words in Latin. 'Hospita' first: it is the feminine of 'stranger', 'strange woman'. Demophoon opens the letter and the first word is 'The strange woman'. What strange woman will it be? The next word is merely the vocative 'O Demophoon'; then 'tua te', 'thine to thee' or strictly 'thine thee', the 'thee' being object to the verb. Why cannot we say, 'thine to thee?' Are not the words sudden and poignant? Then follows the name, Rhodopeia Phyllis; Phyllis, 'She of the Phylla or waving leaves,' Rhodopeia, from the mountains of Rhodope; all the magic of old Greek romance and much of the music comes with those two words. The mountains and the forest leaves and she who is his own: How does the sentence go on? Ultra promissum—long syllable after long syllable, quite naturally and not with any strain, adding to the words 'beyond the promised time' a slow ache and a sense of long waiting. Then simply 'abesse queror', 'you are absent, and I complain'.

> Hospita, Demophoôn, tua te Rhodopêia Phyllis,
> Ultra promissum tempus abesse queror.

That is *Poesis*. That is the way to build your line if you work in an inflected language.

It seems then as if this theory, not explicitly Aristotle's but implicit in his language and based upon it, will practically work as a description of the function of Poetry, and of the other arts which Aristotle groups with poetry. It is Poêsis, a Making, but in one large respect the Poêsis is Mimêsis, so that poetry is *Poesis* plus *Mimesis*, a making or manufacture based upon an imitation. And it can be judged in two ways: either by the skill shown in the making, the beauty of texture, the quality and shape of the stones chosen and the way in which they are laid together in the architecture; or else by the sort of things which the poet has selected out of the infinite and all-coloured world in order to make his imitation. Of course the two proceed quickly to run together in practice. The subject of any poem is very hard to separate from its style; for every change of a word or phrase, which is a change in style, alters in some degree the whole mimesis, which is the subject; and suggestions that you can express a noble thought in ignoble language or *vice versa* are open to the same difficulties as the idea that you can express a clear thought in muddled language or a confused thought in lucid language. I do not wish to raise these speculative questions. But I do venture to suggest that the conception of Art as mimesis, though rejected by almost all recent critics, has a justification and may even show a real profundity of insight. Mimesis is, I suspect, not only an essential element in all art, but also our greatest weapon both for explaining and for understanding the world.

For these purposes the choice lies between mimesis and definition; on the one hand the instinctive comprehensive method of art, the attempt to understand a thing by making it, to learn a thing by doing it, and on the other the more exact but much narrower method of intellectual analysis, definition and proposition. Each has its proper sphere. Mimesis is not much use in mathematics or scientific discovery, except in the form of diagrams. But if a mere 'grammaticus' may learn by looking on at the august battles of philosophers, I observe that some of these are now saying that the greatest advance made during the last century has been the discovery that there are degrees in truth. Others of course maintain that any given proposition is either true or false and that there are no degrees possible. It is not a bit 'more true' to say that $7 \times 7 = 48$ than to say that it equals a million. Now I speak under correction, but it seems probable that the belief in degrees of truth implies a belief in mimesis rather than definition or assertion as the best method for expressing, and doubtless also for reaching, truth. The mimesis is never exact; it is always more or less adequate, more or less complete. It is essentially a thing of degrees. And its advantage over the intellectual method of definition or proposition is merely that it is much more fruitful and solid and adequate and easily transmitted; its disadvantage that it is more elusive, deceptive and incapable of verification. But I think it is true of all art and of all human conduct, though not true of purely scientific facts, that the best way to understand them is in some sense or other to go and do likewise.

My friend and colleague Dr Geoffrey Smith, killed on the Somme, held a view about human progress which I wish he had lived to express with the exactitude and great knowledge which belonged to him. It was, as I understood him, that in the biological or physiological sense Man had not made any advance worth speaking of since the earliest times known to us; but that our ancestors, from their arboreal days onward, stood out from all other animals by their extraordinary power of mimesis. When they met with a sort of conduct which they liked, they had the power of imitating it, and of course also the power of selecting for imitation the particular elements in it that appealed to them most. Sometimes they imitated badly and chose the wrong things; sometimes they seem, like our poor relations in the Zoological Gardens today, to have imitated without any coherent plan or choice at all. But on the whole there has been a coherence in the main stream of human mimesis; we have imitated the things we admired, and our admirations have developed further on more or less similar lines. We have formed ideals, and our ideals have guided us. It is this power of idealism, this curious power of seeing what we like or admire and then trying to imitate it; seeing things that were beautiful and trying to make others like them; seeing things that roused interest or curiosity and trying by the mimetic imagination to get inside them and understand them; that has been the great guiding force in the upward movement of humanity. The direction we take depends on the things we choose to imitate; and the choice depends on the sort of persons we really are: and what we are, again, depends on what we choose to imitate. By mimesis we make both ourselves and the world. The whole art of behaviour, or conduct itself, is a poesis which is also a mimesis. For every act we perform is a new thing made, a new creation, which has never been seen on earth before; and yet each one is an imitation of some model and an effort after some aim. And thus we proceed, so far as our life is voluntary and not mechanical, towards an end which can never be attained and is always changing as we change, but which is in its essence the thing which at each successive moment we most want to be. We cannot define it more. 'Infinite beauty in art, infinite understanding in knowledge, infinite righteousness in conduct' ... such words all ring false because they are premature or obsolete attempts to define, and even to direct, wants that are often still subconscious, still unformed, still secret, and which are bearing us in directions and towards ends of aspiration which will doubtless be susceptible of analysis and classification when we and they are things of the past, but which for the present are all to a large extent experiment, exploration, and even mystery. But we can be sure with Plato that the two things that determine the way of life for each one of us are, as he puts it, 'The road of our longing and the quality of our soul' (*Laws* X., p. 904c). That is our Mimesis and our Poesis, our choice of subject and our execution.

CHAPTER V

Literature as Revelation[1]

THE first time I met Dr Spence Watson and heard him speak was at a great meeting in the St James's Hall, London, held to congratulate the Irish leader, Parnell, on the collapse of the criminal charges made against him by *The Times* newspaper. Some of you will remember the occasion. The charges were based on certain letters which *The Times* published in facsimile and scattered broadcast over England. These were shown to be forgeries which *The Times* had bought at a very high price; the forger himself, a man called Pigott, was discovered and convicted; he confessed and fled and blew his brains out. The whole situation was intensely dramatic—as well as extremely instructive. The meeting, addressed by Parnell himself and by two famous Newcastle men, Dr Spence Watson and Mr John Morley, was one of the most thrilling I have ever attended. And I remember still how Dr Spence Watson's short speech ended in a ringing call of 'God save Ireland'.

There are some people to whom politics seem a kind of magnificent game, a game of much skill and of not much scruple. There are some again who regard political life as a kind of arena in which different parties and different classes and different trading corporations struggle and intrigue for their respective interests. But to those two men I have mentioned politics formed neither a pleasant game nor an exciting intrigue, far less an indirect way of pursuing your own interest. To them politics came as a revelation and a duty. They saw, or believed they saw, one or two fundamental truths on which the whole life and *moral* of the nation depended; and, those truths once seen, it became an unquestioned duty, through fair weather or foul, through good report or evil report, to pursue them and to live for them. I always felt with Dr Spence Watson that his political principles had much of the quality of a religion. They threw light all round them upon the non-political parts of life; and, though

[1] The Robert Spence Watson Lecture, delivered to the Literary and Philosophical Society of Newcastle-upon-Tyne, October 1, 1917.

he was a vigorous fighter, I believe that, like most good religions, his strong principles rather increased than lessened his general human charity.

It was the thought of Dr Spence Watson's attitude towards politics that suggested to me the subject of this lecture. For, though the parallel is not exact in detail, there are among lovers of literature, as among lovers of politics, some who like it for all sorts of other reasons, and some who demand of it nothing less than a kind of revelation. Most people of culture, I believe, belong to the first class. They like literature because they like to be amused, or because the technique of expression interests them and rouses their strongest faculties, or because a book stands to them for society and conversation, or because they just happen to like the smell and feel of a book and the gentle exercise of cutting pages with a paperknife. Or they like to study the varieties of human nature as shown in books, and to amass the curious information that is to be found there. Those are the really cultured people. You will find that they like Lamb's *Essays* and *Lavengro*, and Burton's *Anatomy*, and Evelyn's *Diary*, and the *Religio Medici*, and the *Literary Supplement*. And the other class—to which I certainly belonged all through my youth and perhaps on the whole still belong—does not really much like the process of reading, but reads because it wants to get somewhere, to discover something, to find a light which will somehow illumine for them either some question of the moment or the great riddles of existence. I believe this is the spirit in which most people in their youth read books; and, considering their disappointments, it is remarkable, and perhaps not altogether discreditable, how often they cling to this hope far on into the region of grey hairs or worse than grey hairs.

Now, in putting before you the case for these over-sanguine or over-youthful people, I believe, as I have said, that I shall have the persons of culture and the connoisseurs against me; but the artists and writers themselves will be really on my side. Almost all the writers—and they are pretty numerous—whom I have known intimately are, I believe, subject to a secret sadness when they are praised for being amusing or entertaining or readable or the like. What really delights them, especially the novelists and writers of light comedy, is to be treated as teachers and profound thinkers. Nobody is quite content to think that the serious business of his own life makes merely the fringe and pastime of other people's. There is a well-known story of an essay written on the poet Keats by a stern young Nonconformist at a certain university, in which he said that after all the important question to ask was whether Keats had ever saved a soul. He answered it, I regret to say, in the negative, and condemned Keats accordingly. Now this essayist is generally ridiculed by persons of culture for having set up for the poor poet a perfectly absurd and irrelevant test. 'Keats,' says the man of culture, 'was no more trying to save souls than to improve railway locomotives. He was simply trying to write beautiful poetry, which is an entirely different thing.'

Now I do not believe that the man of culture is right. I suspect that the young Nonconformist was perfectly correct in the test he applied; that a really great poet ought to save souls and does save souls; and, furthermore, that he will not be at all grateful to you if you tell him that souls are not his business, and he can leave them to the parson. I think, if the essayist went wrong—and if he concluded that Keats was a bad poet I take it as certain that he did go wrong—it was partly that he took the saving of a soul in too narrow and theological a sense, and partly that he had not really sunk himself deep enough into Keats's thought to know whether he could save a soul or not. That is, in the first place I would have asked him to consider whether it is not in some sense 'saving a soul' to enable a living man to rise up above himself and his personal desires, and to see beauty and wonder in places where hitherto he had seen nothing; in the second place, I would have asked him whether, before condemning Keats, he had really considered and really understood what Keats meant when, for example, in the climax of one of his greatest poems, he sums up the message to mankind of the Grecian Urn:

> 'Beauty is truth, truth beauty,'—that is all
> Ye know on earth, and all ye need to know.

I do not say that that message is true. I do not myself fully understand what Keats meant by it. But I am sure that to him, and to many people who learnt it from him, that thought has come as a revelation.

Let me speak of another case in my own experience. I remember when I was a boy of fifteen in Paris, sitting down on a bench in the garden of the Tuileries with a copy of Rousseau's book on the *Contrat Social*, which I had just bought for twopence-halfpenny. I knew it was a celebrated book, and sat down in a sober mood to read it, partly from a sense of duty. And the first sentence of the first chapter ran: 'Man was born free, and he is everywhere in chains.'

'Man was born free, and he is everywhere in chains.' I remember the thrill with which I read and re-read those words. As a matter of fact, I quite misunderstood their place in Rousseau's argument. But so did other people, and I can realize now the thrill with which, when they were first published, they ran through Europe, awakening, unforgettable, stirring the seeds of fire that blazed out in the Great Revolution.

Take a third instance, the passage in Milton's great pamphlet pleading for the freedom of the Press, where Milton seems gradually, with increasing intensity, to realize what a book really at its best is, something greater than a living man: how to kill a man is, of course, a sin. It is to slay God's image; but to kill a good book is to kill the very essence of a man's thought, 'to slay God's image, as it were, in the eye'. For the particular man is but human and will in any case die before long; 'but a good book is the precious life-blood of a master-spirit, treasured up for a life beyond life'. When you take in your hand some of the great immortal books of the past, how that sentence comes back to your mind and illumines them! My thoughts turn naturally to some of those Greek tragedies on which I especially work; the *Agamemnon* of Aeschylus, say, or the *Trojan Women* of Euripides. What is it, that one should read it and re-read it now, two thousand odd years after it was written? What is it, that it should still have the power to stir one's whole being? That is the answer: it is simply what Milton has said, nothing more and nothing less, 'the precious life-blood of a master-spirit, treasured up for a life beyond life'.

I have taken three instances of the kind of writing that has an element of what I venture to call 'revelation', but before going further I will stop to answer some criticisms about them. In the first place, the person of culture, to whom we were a little disagreeable at the beginning of this lecture, will interpose. 'You appear,' he will say, 'to be basing your admiration of Keats on the truth of one exceedingly obscure and questionable proposition about Beauty being the same as Truth. Personally, I do not care a straw whether it is true or not; I only care whether it is suitable in its place in the poem; but even supposing it is true, it is only one tiny fragment of Keats's work. What about all the rest of his work, which, to his credit be it said, contains hardly any of these dogmatic sentences which you choose to describe as revelation? Is Keats's greatness to rest on the very few apophthegms about life which his work contains—they are far more numerous and probably more true in Martin Tupper or Ella Wheeler Wilcox—or is it to rest frankly on the sheer beauty of the mass of his work? You know quite well it must rest on the latter.'

How are we to answer this? Well, in the first place we must explain that I only chose those isolated sentences for convenience' sake. It was easier to explain what I meant by revelation if I could find it expressed in a single sentence. But as a rule the writers who have most of the element of revelation about them do not crystallize their revelation into formulae. It is something that radiates from all their work, as in practical life there is generally far more inspiration radiating from the example of a man's whole activity than from the moral precepts that he happens to utter. Shelley is simply bursting with this power of revelation. To a man who has once read himself into Shelley, the world never looks the same again. The same is true of Goethe, the same is emphatically true of certain Greek poets, like Aeschylus and Euripides. But it would be hard to select any particular sentences from their works as summing up the essence of their doctrine. Even Tolstoy, who has this power of revelation to an extraordinary degree, and who was always trying, trying consciously and intensely, to put into clear words the message that was burning inside him, even Tolstoy never really gets it expressed. He lays down, in his religious books, lots and lots of rules, some of them sensible, some of them less so, some of them hopelessly dogmatic and inhuman, many of them thrilling and magnificent, but never, never getting near to the full expression of the main truth he had discovered about the world and was trying to teach. The message of Keats, whatever it is, lies in all Keats, though by accident a great part of it may be summed up in a particular sentence. The message of Plato is in all Plato, the message of Tolstoy in all Tolstoy. There is a beautiful passage in Renan's *Life of Jesus* where he points out that when Jesus Himself was asked what His doctrine was, what exact new dogmatic truth He had to declare, He could give no direct answer. He certainly could not produce a series of doctrinal texts; He could only say 'Follow me'. The message a man has to give radiates from him; it is never summed up in a sentence or two.

So, if we go back to Keats and the person of culture, we will say to him not in the least that the greatness of Keats depends on the truth or importance of one or two statements he made; but that it does depend very greatly on a certain intense power of vision and feeling which runs through the whole of his work and which happens to express itself almost in the form of a religious dogma in one or two places—say in the opening passage of *Endymion* and the last stanza of the *Ode to a Grecian Urn*.

Now let me notice another curious thing about these revelations in literature. They are never statements of fact. They are never accurately measured. I am not sure that you might not safely go further and say they are never really discoveries; they are nearly all of them as old as the hills, or at least as old as the Greek philosophers and the Book of Job. Their value is not in conveying a new piece of information; their value lies in their power of suddenly directing your attention, and the whole focus of your will and imagination, towards a particular part of life. 'Man was born free, and he is everywhere in chains.' That is only true to a limited extent; and so far as it is true it is not in the least new. Everybody knew it, as a bare fact. But Rousseau expressed it more vividly, perhaps felt it more keenly, believed it to be more important, than other people had. What is more, he meant to draw conclusions from it; and I think what thrills one especially in reading or thinking of the words is the thought of those conclusions that are to be drawn. They are not defined; they are left vague; that makes them all the more tremendous.

Think of life as a vast picture gallery, or museum; or better, perhaps, as a vast engineering workshop. It is all those things, among others. Then think of oneself walking through it. You know how the average man walks through a museum or a workshop when he knows nothing particular about it. You try hard to be intelligent; failing in that you try to conceal your lack of intelligence. You would like to be interested, but you do not know what is interesting and what is not. Some of the specimens strike you as pretty; some of the engines seem to you very powerful; you are dazzled and amused by the blaze of the fires, you are secretly interested in the men and wish you could talk to them. But in the main you come out at the other end tired and rather dispirited and having got remarkably little out of it. That is the way a stupid and uneducated man, with no one to help him, goes through life.

Next, suppose you go through the same museum, or the same workshop, with a thoroughly competent guide. In the museum he knows what all the specimens are, which are rare and which ordinary, and why they are interesting; he makes you look at things; makes you understand things; makes you see a hundred details, every one of them significant, that you would never have noticed by yourself. In the workshop, he shows how the various machines work, tells how they were invented and what difference their invention made; he takes you to see a particularly skilled workman and makes you realize where his skill comes in; he makes you feel the cleverness and the beauty of the machinery. That is like going through life with the help and guidance of a proper average educator, what one calls a person of culture.

Now thirdly, suppose on the day of your visit the ordinary guide is not available. Instead you are taken by a man who is not a regular guide to the institution but is working, so they tell you, at certain parts of it. And you find very likely as you go with him that there are large parts that he does not know or at least has nothing to say about, but when you get to his particular subject he tells you not only what the other guide told, but also various things which the other guide thought not worth mentioning, but which, as now explained to you, seem searching and deep and new; and you gradually realize that you are talking to a man who has made, or is on the point of making, a great discovery. In the museum he takes specimens that seemed to have nothing to do with each other and shows that when you put them together there comes a sudden flood of suggestion, a stream of questions never yet asked, but when once asked sure to find an answer. And you go away not so much filled with knowledge, but all alive with interest and the sense of movement; feeling that your feet have been set on a road into the future. You have seen some one thing or set of things with an intensity that has revealed what was before unsuspected and made, as it were, an illumination in one part of life. That, I think, is like going through under the guidance of the sort of literature that gives inspiration.

The great difference, intellectually speaking, between one man and another is simply the number of things they can see in a given cubic yard of world. Do you remember Huxley's famous lecture on *A Piece of Chalk*, delivered to the working men of Norwich in 1868, and how the piece of chalk told him secrets of the infinite past, secrets of the unfathomed depths of the sea? The same thing happens with a book. I remember once picking up a copy of *Macbeth* belonging to the great Shakespearian scholar, Andrew Bradley, and reading casually his pencilled notes in the margin. The scene was one which I knew by heart and thought I understood; but his notes showed me that I had missed about half a dozen points on every page. It seems to me that the writers who have the power of revelation are just those who, in some particular part of life, have seen or felt considerably more than the average run of intelligent human beings. It is this specific power of seeing or feeling more things to the cubic yard in some part of the world that makes a writer's work really inspiring.

To have felt and seen more than other people in some particular region of life: does that give us any sort of guarantee that the judgements which a man passes are likely to be true? Not in the least. Suppose a man has seen and experienced some particular corner of, say, the Battle of the Somme and can give you a thrilling and terrific account of it, that is no particular reason for expecting that his views about the war as a whole will be true. It is on the whole likely that he will see things in a wrong proportion. The point in his favour is only that he does really know *something*, and, whatever his general views are, he can help you to know something. I will confess my own private belief, which I do not wish anyone to share, that of all the books and all the famous sayings that have come as a revelation to human beings, not one is strictly true or has any chance of being true. Nor, if you press me, do I really think it is their business to be strictly true. They are not meant to be statements of fact. They are cries of distress, calls of encouragement, signals flashing in the darkness; they seem to be statements in the indicative mood, but they are really in the imperative or the optative—the moods of command or prayer or longing; they often make their effect not by what they say but by the tone in which they say it, or even by the things they leave unsaid.

Do you remember Garibaldi's speech to his men when his defence of Rome had proved fruitless, and the question was whether to make terms with the Austrians or to follow him? 'Let those who wish to continue the War against the stranger come with me. I offer neither pay nor quarters nor provisions. I offer hunger, thirst, forced marches, battles and death.'[1] The force of that appeal was in what he did not say. He obviously offered them something else too; something so glorious that as a matter of fact most of them followed him; but he did not mention it.

Sometimes the word of revelation is a metaphor; the speaker knows he cannot attain exact truth, he can only, as it were, signal in the direction of it. There is a wonderful story in a little-read Saxon historian, who wrote in Latin, the Venerable Bede, about the conversion of the Saxons to Christianity. The King was debating whether or no to accept the new religion, and consulted his counsellors. And one old Pagan warrior said: 'Do you remember how last midwinter King Edwin held festival in the great hall, with brands burning and two huge fires on the hearths, while outside there was storm and utter darkness? And the windows by the roof being open, a bird flew suddenly from the darkness outside into the

[1] *Garibaldi's Defence of Rome*, G. M. Trevelyan, p. 231.

warm and lighted place and out on the other side into the outer darkness. Like that bird is the life of man.'[1]

Or what again shall we say of the following? A message sent many years ago by the famous Russian revolutionary, Katherine Breshlovsky—the grandmother of the Revolution as she is called; a message smuggled out of prison and sent to her friends and followers bidding them not to despair or to think that nothing was being accomplished. 'Day and night we labour; instead of meat, drink and sleep we have dreams of Freedom. It is youth calling to youth through prison walls and across the world.' It seems like a series of statements, statements which it is hard to describe as either true or not true. Yet I doubt if it is really a statement; it is more like a call in the night.

Or take the saying of one of the ancient rabbis after the fall of Jerusalem, when the heathen had conquered the holy places and to a pious Jew the very roots of life seemed to be cut: 'Zion is taken from us; nothing is left save the Holy One and His Law.' Nothing is left save the Holy One and His Law. Does it not seem at the same time to say two things: that nothing is left, and that everything is left that really matters? All is lost, and nothing that matters is lost. The message has just that quality of self-contradiction which shows that it is not saying all it means, that it is pointing to something beyond itself, calling the hearer's attention not to a fact but to a mystery.

Or take one of the greatest and simplest of all these burning words, the word of a Greek philosopher of a late and decadent period, who has nevertheless made a great stir in the world: 'Though I speak with the tongues of men and of angels, and have not charity, I am but a sounding brass or a tinkling cymbal. Though I give my body to be burned, and have not charity, it profiteth me nothing.' Who can analyse that into a statement of fact?

By now, I think, we have reached a point where we can formulate a further conclusion about these words of inspiration or revelation. They never are concerned with direct scientific fact or even with that part of experience which is capable of being expressed in exact statement. They are concerned not with that part of our voyage which is already down in the Admiralty charts. They are concerned with the part that is uncharted; the part that is beyond the mist, whither no one has travelled, or at least whence no one has brought back a clear account. They are all in the nature of the guess that goes before scientific knowledge; the impassioned counsel of one who

[1] *Bede's Chronicle*, Bk. 2, chap. 14.

feels strongly but cannot, in the nature of things, prove his case. This fact explains three things about them: their emotional value, their importance, and their weakness. Their weakness is that they are never exactly true, because they are never based on exact knowledge. Their importance is that they are dealing with the part of the journey that is just ahead of us, the hidden ground beyond the next ridge which matters to us now more than all the rest of the road. Their emotional value is intense just because they are speaking of the thing we most long to know, and in which the edge of the emotion is not dulled by exact calculations. A good Moslem believes in Mohammed far more passionately than any one believes in the multiplication table. That is just because in the case of the multiplication table he *knows* and is done with it; in the case of Mohammed he does not *know*, and makes up for his lack of knowledge by passionate feeling.

The same consideration explains why young people in each generation are so specially fond of the writers who have this quality of revelation about them. Young people, if they are normally ambitious and full of vitality, as one expects them to be, are always on the look out for a revelation. For purely physical or biological reasons, they are hopeful; they expect that the time coming, which will be their own time, is sure to be much better than the present, in which they hardly count, or the past, in which they did not count at all. (It is amusing to note in passing that, when there is a difference of opinion between young and old, each tends to reject the other for the same reason—because he seems to represent the superseded past. The young man listens impatiently to the old, thinking: Yes, of course; that is what they thought when people wore whiskers, in the time of Queen Victoria. And the old man listens impatiently to the young, thinking: Yes, of course; that is just the sort of nonsense I used to talk when my whiskers were just sprouting, in the reign of Queen Victoria.) I am inclined to think in general that the typical attitude of a young man—a fairly modest and reasonable young man—towards his elders is to feel that they evidently know a great deal and have read a surprising quantity of books, but how strangely they have contrived to miss the one thing that matters! And the one thing that matters, where will he find it? Clearly in some teacher whom his elders have not heard, or have not listened to. It may be a personal acquaintance whose conversation inspires him. It may be a new writer with a message, or an older writer whom his elders might have read but did not. It may even be some quite ancient writer, in whom a new message has been discovered. There are two requirements only for the prophet—or rather for entrance to the competition for rank as a prophet. You must have been neglected by the last generation, and you must have the prophetic style. You must have some strong conviction, however vague and however disproportionate, about those parts of life which are imperfectly charted and immediately interesting, and you must represent something unknown or at least untaught by our uncles and our schoolmasters.

I do not think that there has been any general failure in Europe, or indeed in America, to appreciate what I have called the literature of revelation. Quite the contrary. The last century has been particularly fruitful in that sort of writing, both the genuine sort and the various popular imitations. The demand has been enormous and has naturally created a supply. The demand has been uncritical and the supply consequently indiscriminate.

If you ask the cause why this demand and supply have been so great of late years, as compared for example with the eighteenth century, when there was probably more actual originality of thought, I would suggest two main causes. First, the spread of education and the rise of democracy. The reading public, formerly very restricted, has been constantly reinforced by new social classes with new demands and new expectations. Secondly, the change in our treatment of the young, the much greater stress laid on encouragement and the general avoidance of repression in education. We have trained—or at least permitted—the young to be far more self-confident and adventurous, and naturally they have gone forth in quest of new ideas and new prophets. One should also notice that, apart from any change in quality, the mere size of the present reading public has had an effect on literature. In old days a book in order to succeed had to please a majority of its readers. Now it need not. It is calculated that if an English writer of the present day was hated and despised or utterly ignored by 90 per cent. of his possible readers in the English-speaking world, tolerated but not read or bought by another 5 per cent., rather liked but still not bought by $2\frac{1}{2}$ per cent., and bought by only the remaining $2\frac{1}{2}$, his circulation would be something hitherto unparalleled and he would be one of the richest and most brutally successful men in the country. It is exactly like a picture in a too large gallery competing with several thousand other pictures; it must shriek or it will not be seen. Such a situation obviously encourages such qualities as over-statement, paradox, violence, and the search for novelty at any price. Novelty is not revelation; not in the least. But sometimes people confound them.

I remember my predecessor at Oxford, Professor Bywater, telling me how, when he and his friends were students, they had two great prophets, 'John' and 'Thomas'. On every important question the thing was first to find out what John said and what Thomas said. (John's surname, as you may have guessed, was Ruskin, and Thomas's, Carlyle.) My own generation at College thought little of John and detested Thomas. But the demand for prophets has continued and increased.

The general movement of thought and society in Europe has been, of course, towards democracy and emancipation. And the most successful prophets have naturally been on the revolutionary side.

First came the great revolutionaries of 1848, Victor Hugo and Mazzini, and their disciples, such as Swinburne and Browning. Then came the less political revolutionaries, aiming at the dethronement not of kings, but of more internal and spiritual potentates. Ibsen and the dethronement of all convention; Dostoievsky and the dethronement of human reason; Strindberg and the dethronement of love; Tolstoy and the dethronement of all the glories of the world, all pleasure, all desire, save the search for truth and the love of Christ; Nietzsche and the dethronement of good and evil, and of all that was not mere vitality and force. I will not speak of my own English contemporaries; and among the European writers I mention only the best, or at least the most conspicuous; but behind these, in every country of the world, are scores of less influential prophets, journalists, accidental celebrities, deliberate boomsters and stray imposters; cliques with new theories of poetry, new theories of painting, new theories of morals, education, diet, cookery, clothing; theories how to live without hats, or without boots, or without washing, or without self-denial or without work.

I suppose we have at the present day an extraordinary harvest of false prophets. I doubt if the Court of Ahab in its flower could compete with us. There was a certain degree of truth in a queer reactionary book written by one Max Nordau in the early nineties, and dedicated to the German Emperor. It was called *Degeneration*; and it argued that, if ever a new book or new theory had a startling success, it meant that the author probably suffered from some very slight but widespread form of mental disease. He was slightly mad in a particular way; and all the people throughout the world who were mad in the same way were perfectly delighted with him. If he had real luck his fellow-sufferers might amount to millions.

There is a fragment of truth in that theory, no doubt. And no doubt at any moment most of our hot gospellers and speakers of revelation will, if severely tested, prove to be false. It is certainly true that, as the generations pass, the fashionable teachers are all or almost all rejected, one after another.

> They are thrust
> Like foolish prophets forth; their words to scorn
> Are scattered and their mouths are stopped with dust.

And others take their place to form new sects of followers and to share sooner or later in the same fall.

Ought that to discourage us? Why no; because we have all the time left out of account most of the silent factors in the situation. We have forgotten especially the enormous and almost incredible number of decent honest men and women who are on the whole working well and making for progress; we have forgotten the considerable number of fine workers or writers, men with intellectual or moral greatness in them, who do not advertise. When I am disposed, as I suppose all of us sometimes are, to despair of modern civilization and to think that the world has gone mad, I always counteract the impression in one way. I turn from contemplating vast masses of life, which one cannot fully survey and cannot possibly divide into elements and add up into totals, and take some one particular branch of human activity. Ask the various specialists and they will generally tell you that, though the world as a whole is very likely going to the dogs, the particular part they know about has improved. Ask the engineer; he will tell you of the enormous advance made in engineering; the schoolmaster, he may complain that education does not advance faster, but he has no doubt that it is advancing; the doctor, he thinks the world is in a very poor state because it does not attend sufficiently to medical men, but medicine itself is improving hand over hand; the sociologist or social reformer, he will denounce the present state of things as heartily as any one could wish, but he will generally admit that in detail everything that has been worked at has been made rather better.

And after all, if most of our pilots in these strange waters sooner or later turn out mistaken and have to be left behind or even thrown overboard, why should any reasonable person be surprised at that? It is all in the bargain. It is all in the ordinary bargain that man perforce makes with life. There is no finality. There is no full and exact statement, even about those parts of experience which are already reduced to order and marked down on the charts. And meantime Man is moving always, every hour, forth into the uncharted; into the region, not of knowledge and certainty, but of experiment, and guesswork, and daring and wisdom. I believe with all my heart in human progress. But progress is not an advance along a straight path; it is the groping of people with darkness ahead of them and light behind; the questing this way and that of men climbing an unknown precipice; the search for good paths through an unexplored bog, where the best way of advance is no doubt generally discovered by guides who have studied the ways and habits of bogs but may sometimes be hit upon by a child. And the popular prophets, the speakers of burning words, are generally those who at least believe that they have seen some path, and cry to us some advice that seems to them the one thing most needed at the moment.

At the moment their words seem to be of extreme importance; and when the moment has passed, as a rule, their advice has passed too. Only there still remain—and this is perhaps the greatest difference, next to differences in sincerity, between the various breeds of prophet—there still remain some whose words seem to apply not only to the moment for which they spoke them but to the permanent or constantly recurrent needs of humanity. These are the men for whom we scholars seek in the literature of diverse and widely removed ages. They are the people who have felt most profoundly and expressed most poignantly those facts about life which are always important and always easily overlooked, those visions and aspirations in which the human race is always afresh finding its calm in the midst of storm, its 'deliverance from the body of this death'; and their words stay with us as something more than literature, more than mere art of writing or pleasant help for the passing of leisure hours: 'the precious life-blood of a master-spirit, treasured up for a life beyond life'.

CHAPTER VI

Pagan Religion and Philosophy at the time of Christ[1]

---

1. RELIGION AND PHILOSOPHY

The life of man can be divided, like the old maps of the world, into the charted and uncharted. The charted is finite and the other infinite; yet for a well-situated member of a successful and peaceful civilization the part of life which is fairly subject to reason and control outweighs enormously the parts about which he cannot calculate. He can anticipate the result of most of his actions, can work at his profession, till his fields and plant fruit trees, nay, even educate his children, with some reasonable expectation of success. He is guided by experience and reason: he values competent work and exact thought. He realizes his dependence on society, and accepts his duties towards it: he obeys the laws and expects to be protected by them. And such a man, when trying to form a conception of the universe or of life as a whole, will tend to do so in the same sober spirit, and regard the vague terrors and longings that sometimes obsess him as likely to be sources of error. Such a society, at its best, will produce science and philosophy.

It is different with a man who, through his own character or through circumstances, finds life beyond him. If the society in which he lives is torn by war and anarchy, or if he himself is very poor and ignorant, he can neither control his fortune nor understand why things happen to him. He is now taxed, now beaten, now enriched, now stricken with famine or pestilence, and such results do not seem to depend much upon ascertainable causes. His confidence in the charted regions grows less and he throws himself on the unknown. He feels from the beginning that he is in the power of incalculable beings or forces, and makes passionate, though uncertain, efforts at placating them. These efforts will be guided little by observation of the external world, and much by the man's own

[1] From *The History of Christianity in the Light of Modern Knowledge*, Blackie & Sons, 1929.

instincts and subconscious desires. They may lead to good conduct or bad, to high forms of religion or to degraded superstition. The frightened man may determine to give alms to the poor, or to pay his debts, or even to live in mystic contemplation. He may be content to persecute heretics or to perform filthy and cruel rites.

There is nobody, of course, whose mind is devoted entirely to the charted region, nor yet to the uncharted. To the most rational and sober of men there must come from time to time a consciousness of the presence all round him of undiscovered and perhaps undiscoverable forces, a vast night surrounding the small illuminated patch in which he moves; while to the most blindly superstitious a very large part of his daily life must be conducted on principles of observation and reason. The deadest rationalist has some consciousness of mystery, the most helpless mystic some gleams of common sense. Still, on the whole, as society advances in security and human beings in intellectual culture, there is an increase in the range of knowledge and reason and the proportion which they occupy in life. As the social order decays and the level of culture falls, the irrational element in life grows and the little island of light amid the darkness grows smaller still.

When we speak of 'ancient philosophy' as contrasted with 'the Christian religion' we must realize that religion is something common to the highest and lowest of human societies, while philosophy has always been the attainment of a small class in a high state of culture. Philosophy implies a view of the world which uses the knowledge and thinking power of man to their utmost limit, though every good philosophy recognizes the limits of human intelligence and leaves room for the unknown beyond the border. When civilization decays philosophy must needs decay with it: a disintegrating society may produce an age of faith or one of brutal materialism, but it cannot well produce philosophy.

Among the various causes or symptoms of the decay of ancient civilization Professor Rostovtzeff has rightly emphasized the disappearance, through economic and political causes, of the cultured class. The governing class of the Roman Empire, originally drawn from senatorial families in Rome and Italy but afterwards from distant provinces as well, had not only a high tradition of public service, but also very considerable literary culture, while it commanded the services of highly skilled officials and technical assistants in every department of government. A dialogue of Plutarch, written in the early part of the second century AD, describes the meeting at Delphi of cultured Roman citizens from the most diverse parts of the world, a Greek country gentleman, an administrator, a poet, a grammarian, a professor from Britain, much as, at the present day, one might find together in Cairo an English M.P., an American professor, a Scotch engineer, an Indian civilian, and a professional archaeologist—all of them, whatever their diversities of training or interest, united in the service of modern civilization. The Imperial cultured class may have been limited, but it had wide experience; it knew its business and, at this time, it felt perfectly secure. It took little interest in the beliefs of the vast unlettered proletariat beneath it. Plutarch, with all his variety of interests, never notices Christianity. Three centuries later Christianity was dominant, and the cultured class was in the last stage of dissolution. Synesius, the Platonist bishop of the Libyan tetrapolis, complains that he can find in his diocese almost no person who knows Greek or philosophy, no body of men who can be trusted to collect money for public purposes, no one who knows how to make good roads or weapons of war, or how to collect or command a competent military force to protect the settlement against the negroes of the interior. The careful agriculture on which the prosperity of the place depended was now above people's heads. The bishop's friend, Hypatia the Neoplatonist, was brutally murdered by the Alexandrian mob. The mob was now Christian, and less under control; but it had behaved in much the same way when it was pagan, and was just as far removed from 'ancient philosophy'.

We must remember, therefore, in making any comparison between Christianity and ancient philosophy, that Christianity belongs to a time when ancient culture was on the down grade and to a class which had always been shut out from it. The greater part of ancient philosophy originated in the fourth century BC, before the free and highly cultivated city-states had been superseded by the large military empires, and their more or less manageable problems swamped in those of a limitless and undisciplined world. Philosophy weathered the storms of the Roman conquest and the civil wars, and became permanently the possession and guide of educated men without distinction of race or nation, but it hardly touched the uneducated. Thus, with some exceptions to be noticed hereafter, classical philosophy represents the view of society and of duty which is natural to men of position, with a sense of responsibility. Christianity, and the various passionate religions which competed with it in the great industrial towns, represented the aspirations of the poor and outcast.

These considerations explain the mutual indifference to one

another of Christianity and ancient philosophy. The professor or administrator did not inquire what his foreign slaves talked about in the kitchen, nor did the slaves try to understand the books and papers which they were told not to disturb in the study. But sometimes, instead of this indifference, there was, in many places if not throughout the empire, a passionate hostility. Liberal pagans, who would not have thought of persecuting ordinary free speech, drew the line at Christians and sometimes at Jews. Christians who preached, and no doubt in some respects practised, a religion of meekness exhausted their vocabulary of curses against Rome. This needs some explanation.

The restoration by Augustus of peace and order after the civil wars was felt, not merely by flatterers or adherents, but by the whole law-abiding population of the Roman world, as something like a miracle of beneficence. It was impossible to prevent the Eastern Provinces, accustomed to such ideas, from worshipping Augustus as a god; and even Italy and the West gradually lost their repugnance to that exotic conception. The peace had really brought something like a heaven upon earth. And though Augustus might die and Tiberius stubbornly refuse to be worshipped, there was something divine which remained. It was Rome herself, 'Rome the Goddess', 'Rome the Benefactress'. Together with the Emperors as her representatives, it was the spirit which made Caesar and Rome invincible, the *Genius*, the *Fortuna*. Rome meant peace, order, good government, and the welfare of man. Her old brutality had been greatly humanized by Greek philosophy. Rome was *caput orbis*, the 'head' of which the whole world was the 'body'. She drew little or no distinction of race or nationality among her subjects or citizens, and the well-to-do classes throughout the world were ready, as a rule, to give her more worship than she claimed. For all she demanded was, on certain specified occasions, a prayer for the Fortune of Rome and Caesar, and a gift of incense at their altars. The act required meant little more than singing 'God save the King', but it happened to be the very thing that most Christians and Jews could not give. For one thing, they could represent it to themselves as the worship of a false god. That scruple might perhaps have been met: but, more than that, it was the worship of something which they hated. For Rome had always had three types of enemy, the conquered nations, the predatory tribes and classes, and the oppressed proletariat within her own borders.

The Roman governing class, tamed and educated by Greece, had saved the ancient world, and their overthrow ruined it. Yet it must be remembered that, in spite of the humanity of their best men, their régime and the world order that it maintained involved not only slavery on a vast scale, but a system of much hardship to its poorer subjects and atrocious severity to those who rebelled. Where the interest of Rome or, as they called it, the peace of the world was endangered the Roman governing class stuck at nothing. It was always remembered how the mortally dangerous slave-revolt led by Spartacus was ended by the exhibition along the whole stretch of the Appian Way of six thousand crucified slaves. The free workman and peasant were also exposed to many of the abuses of capitalism and usury in their earliest and crudest forms. The sayings against the rich which abound in the Gospels, and the imprecations against the Roman Empire which fill the *Book of Revelation*, are echoes of many centuries of misery endured and resented by the proletariat of Italy and a large part of the whole populations of the conquered provinces. As Professor Arnold Toynbee has pointed out, when Jesus in the Gospel declares that 'The foxes have holes and the birds of the air have nests, but the son of man hath not where to lay his head,' he is only repeating the old aching cry of the dispossessed peasant in the very words uttered long before by Tiberius Gracchus (Plut., *Tib. Grac.* IX).

'Blessed are the poor, blessed are they that mourn, blessed are the meek, blessed they that hunger and thirst. . . . It is easier for a camel to go through the eye of a needle than for a rich man to enter into the kingdom of God.' Blessings of the same purport, and perhaps of equally mysterious beauty, had doubtless been spoken in many different ages by many thousands of men whose mission was to comfort the poor, both pagan and Christian.

And it was not blessings alone that thus arose from the *ergastula* and the wasted farms. 'Fallen, fallen is Babylon the Great, the harlot that sitteth upon seven hills, and is drunken with the blood of the saints . . . with her merchandise of gold and silver and precious stones and chariots and slaves and the souls of men. . . . In one day shall her plagues come, death and mourning and famine; and she shall utterly be burned with fire. She shall be trodden in the wine-press of the wrath of God and blood shall come out of the wine-press even unto the bridles of the horses, as far as a thousand and six hundred furlongs'—nearly as far, perhaps, as stretched the crosses of those slaves on the Appian Way. To any contented and loyal Roman citizen such imprecations must have seemed to be the ravings of a veritable 'odium generis humani'.

Almost as significant as the things said are those left unspoken.

There are no blessings on the strong and unselfish administrator, on the governor who braves unpopularity and prevents corruption, on the judge who does strict justice without fear or reproach. These suffering people do not understand justice. They can only say, 'Blessed are the merciful!' They would have little use for that inflexible 'severity' which the kindly Cicero so specially admires in a judge.

How could the poor fishermen of the Galilean Lake or their followers in the slums of Antioch, who thought of tax-gatherers merely as wicked people and had never held or expected to hold any post of public responsibility, have understood the Roman ideal of public duty? The Roman moralists were enthusiastic about their general, Regulus. He had been taken prisoner by the Carthaginians together with other soldiers of noble family. The Carthaginians hoped to exact a highly profitable peace by means of these prisoners, and Regulus was sent back to Rome to negotiate, promising to return if the negotiation failed. He considered that the lives of the prisoners were not worth such a concession. He went to Rome, stated the Carthaginian terms, and argued that it was more in the interest of Rome to let the prisoners die. He convinced the Senate and returned voluntarily to Carthage where he was duly tortured to death. His 'virtue', resolute self-sacrifice for a public object, would have seemed to the Galileans unintelligible and perhaps, since it involved the death of many people whom he might have saved, wicked. It is very interesting to compare Cicero's book, *De Officiis (On Duty)*, with the precepts of the Gospel. Infinitely less sublime and moving, it also differs from the Gospels in being concerned with a whole range of duties, administrative, judicial and military, which are outside the experience or imagination of the Asiatic villager or artisan. Cicero, for example, accepts as an axiom that Virtuous Conduct hinges on four cardinal virtues: Wisdom, or 'the pursuit and perception of truth'; Justice, i.e. 'the preservation of human society by giving to every man his due and by observing the faith of contracts'; Fortitude, i.e. 'the greatness and firmness of an elevated and unsubdued mind'; and lastly, 'Moderation or Temperance in all our words and actions'. One sees in every phrase the man of culture, the man with a stake in the country, the soldier, statesman and governor. Such men were not to be found in the class from which the Christian movement arose.

2. CULTURE AND IGNORANCE

Apart from this social difference between the early Christian literature and that of contemporary pagan philosophy, there is another marked difference between the habits of mind of the ignorant and of the cultured. When St Paul was preaching in Athens his audience listened with interest until he spoke of the 'resurrection of the dead', or more literally 'the uprising of the corpses'. Then they laughed. They were familiar with the doctrine of the immortality of the soul, but when this eloquent Asiatic tent-maker began to explain that the dead bodies would get up and walk, they could not take him seriously. And we can see that Paul himself felt troubled over the form of his doctrine, and had to explain it rather elaborately. It seems as if the physical Resurrection of the Body was the only form in which the doctrine of immortality could be grasped by the very ignorant populations of the villages and big manufacturing towns of Asia Minor. One may think of a cultivated theologian at the present day listening to a Salvation Army preacher or still more to a negro revivalist. The doctrine preached may be essentially what he believes himself, but the expression of it is suited to a cruder intelligence.

Ignorance, of course, was no more confined to the Christians than hatred of Rome was. The same lack of intellectual training can be seen in some pagan writings of late antiquity. Abstract terms, for example, become persons or concrete objects. It is said that, during the World War, a body of Russian peasants being told that the war was being continued for the sake of 'annexation', and that 'annexation' must be given up, took 'Annexation' (Annexia) to be a princess of the Imperial house and set off to hang her. The negroes in certain of the Southern States when told, after the civil war, that they were at last to receive the suffrage, came to fetch it with wheelbarrows. In the same way in some late pagan documents 'the providence (Pronoia) of God' becomes a separate power; 'the wisdom of God' (Sophia), becomes 'the divine Sophia' or 'Sophia, the daughter of God', and even in one case gets identified with Helen of Troy. The doctrinal history of the conception 'Logos', the 'word' or 'speech' of God, shows similar developments. The results of intense abstract thought can only be understood by following, in some degree, the same process: when handed over mechanically to a generation entirely unaccustomed to abstract thought they change their meaning. Here again the contrast is not so much between pagan and Christian, but between the society of Aristotle or of Cicero and that of the Gnostics or the slave congregations.

Of course the advantage is never altogether on one side. It is hardly necessary to remind ourselves that the Galilean fishermen, by the very simplicity of their lives, by the fact that they knew nothing of complicated social responsibilities or problems, retained a power of direct vision which is not only far more moving but may actually be more profound than the good judgement of those with more knowledge of life. The Sermon on the Mount, though not so useful as a handbook to a Proconsul, may clearly cut far deeper toward the roots of things than Cicero's *De Officiis*. Furthermore, the age of general decadence and shaken nerves which began just before the rise of Christianity and returned in the third century AD was remarkable for some extraordinary qualities. Conduct, as far as one can judge so difficult a matter, was not better than in fourth-century Athens or first-century Rome. It was probably worse. There was more brutality, weakness, cowardice and disorder. Yet there was at the same time a widespread thirst for some sort of spiritual salvation; a sense of the evil of the world and a desire, at any sacrifice, to rise above it and be saved. There was also, both in Christian and pagan, a conviction of the need of some gigantic effort to overcome the sins of the flesh. Ancient philosophy was always ascetic. But in this period there was a passionate asceticism which often took strange and unwholesome forms, and which it is the fashion nowadays to treat with ridicule; yet it was perhaps something like an instinctive biological necessity, if the European world was not to sink into a condition of helpless sensuality like that of some oriental and savage societies. If we judge the world of the Gnostics and early Christians by standards of good citizenship and intelligence, it is far below the Rome of the Antonines or the Athens of Plato; if we bring them all before a Last Judgement to which this whole world is as dross and passionate aspiration counts for more than steady good character, the decision will be more doubtful.

3. PREVIOUS PHILOSOPHY: PLATO AND ARISTOTLE

The early philosophers of the sixth and fifth centuries BC were more like men of science with a strong taste for generalization. Their problems were concerned with the physical world: they made researches in geometry, geography, medicine, astronomy, natural history, and were apt to sum up their conclusions in sweeping apophthegms. 'Moisture is the origin of all things' (Thales). 'All things were together till Mind came and arranged them' (Anaxagoras). 'All things move, nothing stays; all things flow' (Heraclitus). 'All things perish into that from which they sprang. They pay retribution for their injustice one to another according to the ordinance of Time' (Anaximander). Socrates, the father of the

Attic school of philosophy, turning away from natural science with its crude generalizations, concentrated his attention on man, and particularly on the analysis of ordinary speech and current ideas. People talked of 'justice' and 'courage'; of things being 'beautiful' or 'ugly'; but no one could tell him what these words meant. Socrates still remains a problematical figure. A humorist and a saint, a mocker and a martyr, he made different impressions on different people of his acquaintance, but evidently had extraordinary powers as a teacher. Certain doctrines, mostly paradoxical, can with some probability be attributed to him—e.g. that virtue is knowledge, but cannot be taught, and that no one does wrong willingly—but in the main he set himself not to inculcate his own doctrines but to elicit from his pupils the full consciousness of what they themselves really believed or knew. This explains how, in the next generation, many divergent schools of philosophic thought professed themselves followers of Socrates.

The most famous of his disciples, Plato, preserved to an extraordinary degree his master's aversion to dogmatism. A dialogue of Plato's hardly ever leads to a positive conclusion. It is always a discussion, not a pronouncement. It may reject many dogmas as demonstrably false; but it never claims to have reached the whole truth. It probes deeper than before, climbs higher, uses every means —similes, parables, jests and all the resources of a prose style which has never perhaps been equalled since for variety and eloquence— to suggest the sort of thing that the truth is likely to be, or the way in which we can get nearest to it, but it ends almost always on a note of question or wonder. The particular doctrine, however, which is especially associated with Plato, and has divided the world ever since, is a purely intellectual one.

The plain man feels quite certain of two classes of facts. He is sure that what philosophers call 'the external world' exists; that is, if he is sitting on a chair before a table, and looking out of the window at a river, he is confident that these things exist. If he can see, feel, lift, the chair and table; if he can go outside and see the river from a different point of view and put his hand into it, he has tested his belief and is more certain than before. Then again he is perfectly certain that twice two is four, and (if he has learnt a little mathematics) that the three internal angles of any triangle are equal to two right angles. But here comes a difficulty. The two systems of certainties do not confirm one another: rather the reverse. The rule 'twice two equals four' is seldom or never true of the external world. No actual set of four apples is exactly double a particular set of two apples: not only have all the apples different individual qualities, but, if you have very exact weighing machines, you will find that even in weight the real four is seldom or never double the real two. Also, such triangles as you meet in the real world never satisfy the rules of mathematics. Their sides are never straight, for example. They are only imitation triangles, useful as signs or symbols of the triangles that you really mean.

Then again, suppose you do find some statement which you can make with truth about an object in the external world—'this river is about six feet deep', 'this coat is blue', 'this is the man I met last year', when you come to observe the objects again you may find it no longer true: the river has dried up to five feet, the coat has lost colour in the sun, the man has certainly become different. The world is all flowing and changing: you can never be sure of it; whereas the mathematical or arithmetical rule stays unchanged. Twice two is still four, and the three internal angles are still equal to two right angles, though a deluge may in the meantime have swept over the world.

Two views of this difficulty are possible. One man may say: 'The real things are these chairs and tables; the mathematical rules are merely hypothetical or abstract statements about them': i.e. statements which would be true if the objects were different, or which are true if we disregard certain factors in the problem. Thus 'twice two equals four' is only true of the apples if we disregard the accidental differences between the apples, or would be true if the apples were all exactly alike. The mathematical rule is a convenient generalization, no more. This man would call himself a realist.

The Platonist, on the contrary, starts at the other end: for him the rule 'twice two equals four', or the rule about the internal angles, is exactly true and always true. It is the real truth, and the fluctuating, imperfect objects which we meet in the external world are only images or imitations of reality—like reflections in a bad mirror, distorted to start with and transitory as well. The only way to reach truth is to concentrate on the ideal world. Thus, in mathematics you can never get on by merely counting or weighing the existing triangles and tables and chairs. you start with your principles of arithmetic and then by reason deduce the whole world of number. And it must follow that the same method will lead to truth in all other regions too.

If you want to know what Justice is, you will not get very far by observing the behaviour of a number of honest men. Among other difficulties, no actual honest man is perfectly honest: he is only an imitation in flesh of true Justice as the wooden triangle is an imitation in wood of the ideal triangle. You must first get a clear conception of Justice—as clear as your conception of 'two' or of 'triangle'; then you will be able to deduce with mathematical exactitude the true properties of Justice. Truth is to be found, not in this fluctuating world of sense perception, but in the world which is reached by thought, i.e. by a clear and strictly rational introspection. For if the question is raised how we know that twice two is four, or that things which are equal to the same thing are equal to one another, it seems to be by some sort of intuition or introspection, or, as Plato half metaphorically puts it, by 'recollection' (*Anamnêsis*) from a previous life. As we look into our own minds and discover that 'twice two is four', so we can discover with equal certainty that Justice is beautiful or that a son should honour his father.

The obvious criticism here is that Plato is transferring the methods suitable to a system of exact knowledge, like arithmetic, to a chaotic world of words half understood and ideas incapable of definition. We do know what we mean by 'two', but we do not know what we mean by 'justice' or 'beautiful'. Plato himself criticizes his own suggestion more than once, and is never carried away into dogmatism. But this way of thinking formed a dangerous heritage for Greek and early Christian thought. The philosophers tended to conceive all knowledge as analogous to mathematical knowledge, either entirely right or entirely wrong. They failed to recognize or admit that most of what we call knowledge is only an approximation to the truth. A realization of this fact, which to us seems obvious, might have saved the world many desperate heresies and persecutions.

It is sometimes said that everyone is born either a Platonist or an Aristotelian, but the opposition between the two philosophers is not nearly so sharp as this would suggest. Though Aristotle rejected the doctrine of Ideas and was himself more concerned with biology and various forms of the 'humane' sciences than with pure mathematics, yet he started as a Platonist, and retained always a profound admiration for his master. One quality that strikes one in reading Aristotle is the desire of the great researcher and collector to have a philosophic framework into which all real facts will fit. He will not be inhospitable to the discoveries of physical science, as many idealist philosophers were; neither will he rest content with any contradiction of common sense; nor yet will he shut the door against any genuine spiritual experience. A system so all-embracing roused little of the fighting spirit which seems necessary to enthusiasm among the later pagan philosophers. Aristotle was respected but not adored. Consequently he was not hated. And he had his reward in having his system taken over by various Christian theologians, especially by Thomas Aquinas, as the almost complete basis of the philosophy of the new religion.

Aristotle denied the existence of Plato's world of Ideas—Justice and the number Two did not exist separately in 'some heavenly place', but were in the objects of the sensible world. One discovered them by a process of 'Induction' (*Epagôgê*). By experience of a number of particular cases, the mind grasps a universal truth about them, which then and afterwards is seen to be self-evident. It sees the 'Idea' or the 'Form' by means of a review of individuals, but the 'Idea' or 'Form' is not something separate. The object of science thus becomes classification and the discovery of the attributes of objects. A new animal, for example, has to be assigned to the right genus, and the right species, and then distinguished from others by the attributes that are essential to it. Through this system of thoroughgoing classification he seems to have arrived at his discovery of the syllogism, and thus laid the foundation of Logic. The syllogism is a form of reasoning consisting of two premisses and a conclusion, in which one term which is common to both premisses disappears. From the relation of A to B, and from B to C, you conclude the relation of A to C. This discovery has been extraordinarily fruitful, though perhaps Aristotle was too apt to regard it as the sole type of deductive reasoning. Again, in all existence he distinguished between 'form' and 'matter': a statue consists of so much wood or stone—matter—on which a particular form is impressed, a sword of so much iron worked into a particular form. Connected with this division was another, which not only answered certain ancient philosophic puzzles, but gave a characteristic quality to his whole system. Suppose you say, 'That man sitting in the chair is Phidippides, the swift runner,' how can you be speaking the truth? How can a man sitting down be a runner? Aristotle's answer is that the man is 'in act' (*energeia*) sitting, but 'in power' (*dunamis*) or 'potentially' a runner, and the idea thus suggested became fruitful in many ways. A man or city or any object not only is what it actually is at the moment; it is also, 'in power', all that it may become. That mass of stone in the quarry is potentially a temple; this child is potentially a sage or a patriot. Influenced by his studies in biology Aristotle is full of the idea of a perfect or characteristic form to which all life tends, each species working towards its own perfection. In theology, both pagan and Christian, this idea led to a conception of the universe as fulfilling the purpose of God, or, rather differently, striving towards God as 'the desire of the World'. In modern science it pays an important part in the theory of evolution.

This meagre sketch is intended merely to show the kind of problem with which ancient Greek philosophy was occupied, in the domain of logic and metaphysic. Natural science we have entirely omitted, but of ethics or moral theory we must treat more fully.

4. ETHICS IN PLATO

It may be that ethics form a derivative and secondary kind of philosophy, dependent at every turn on Logic and Metaphysic, since a man cannot know what is good without knowing what is true. Nevertheless the information that interests a historian most about any religion or philosophy is both how its professors behaved and how they thought they ought to behave. Now Greek ethics in the classical period stand apart from those of most ancient societies. Like those of Confucius, they are singularly untheological. The Hebrew in all his conduct considered whether he was obeying or disobeying the rules given to Moses by Jehovah, and knew that if he disobeyed them Jehovah would be 'angry' and punish him. The rules might or might not be consistent with the welfare of humanity; that question should not be raised, and in any case the welfare of the Gentiles did not much matter. The Greek philosophers, with few exceptions, considered conduct with an eye on the welfare of the community, and the way in which the citizen could best serve his State. True, if he committed some offence, such as betraying a trust, the indignation felt against it might depend on purely 'moral' considerations—e.g. the amount of treachery, impiety, cruelty, etc., involved—and not on the mere amount of harm done to the city; but the ultimate problem of human conduct was the problem of producing welfare or good life for the community.

Even in Plato, where idealism reigns and the spring of all good conduct seems to be Erôs, or passionate Love, for the Idea of the Good—that one ultimate aim of all right desire—morality is always an affair of the citizen, not of the isolated man. It is in practice a relation of man to his fellows, though no doubt it may ultimately rest on a relation of the soul to God. It still surprises a modern reader when the great problem of the *Republic*—what Righteousness is—is answered by the elaborate and to our minds obscure process of constructing an imaginary Republic. The answer also is a paradox. Plato sees in the man and the State alike three elements: one that craves, one that fights, and one that thinks, and finds righteousness in a harmony between them. There is the element of natural desire—for food, drink, sleep, bodily pleasure and all that is bought with money; the 'spirited element', which fights against that which seems evil or hostile to the man or the community; and the element of thought, which judges, reflects and knows. When all these three serve the common good in harmony the result is Righteousness both in man and city. We can make no attempt here to analyse the extremely subtle and not always consistent theory of morals which we find in Plato. Of all great philosophers he is the least dogmatic and the most suggestive. He also combines in a remarkable way the attitude of the statesman, adapting means to ends, and the saint, doing right in scorn of consequences. His two longest works, the *Republic* and the *Laws*, are both attempts at constructing an ideal constitution, and in real life he faced much hardship, danger and ridicule in trying to put his political projects into practice. Yet at the same time no one insists more eloquently on the principles that it is better to suffer wrong than to do wrong, better to be punished than not to be punished, and that it is better to be righteous than to seem righteous, even if the former leads to death on the cross, and the latter to every kind of human reward. In contrast to the common conceptions of the ancient Hebrews or the modern vulgar, the Greek thinkers are never content to say, 'Be righteous because you will be punished if you are not.' They almost always keep a firm hold on two principles: one, that good conduct is conduct that is good for the community as a whole; the other, that if righteousness or wisdom is good, then it is good in itself, and not because it leads to rewards in other coin.

5. ETHICS IN ARISTOTLE

But the most characteristic philosopher of the Hellenic period is Aristotle. He is Greek in his *sophrosynê* or moderation; in his complete remoteness from primitive superstition; in his combination of intense intellectuality with human sympathy and interest in practical life; and in his essentially civic point of view.

His theology and metaphysic were largely taken over by Thomas Aquinas and used as the basis of mediaeval and modern Christianity. His political philosophy is still a mine of thought and information. His researches in the physical sciences have of course been superseded in different degrees. It is in his ethics or theory of conduct that we find the characteristics of Greek thought at their clearest.

In the first place, conduct is an art, the art of living, and like all the arts it has an aim. In each department of conduct it aims at 'virtue' or 'goodness' (ἀρέτη), and this is always, as in the other arts, an exact point or degree, a mean between too much and too little. As a musician can go wrong by striking a note too high or too low, too loud or too soft, so a man may be too daring or not daring enough, not generous enough or too generous. This combination of common sense and exact thinking is highly characteristic. As to the aim of this art as a whole, as the aim of medicine is health, or of strategy victory, so the aim of ethics is the good life. The art of private ethics aims at the good life for the individual, but is subordinate to public ethics, or politics, which has for its aim the good life of the community. Aristotle decides after some discussion that this 'good' must be something aimed at in all kinds of action, it must be desirable for itself and not merely as a means to something else, it must be self-sufficing. It must be 'an unhindered activity of the soul', and a fulfilment of the true function of man as man, as good harping, for instance, is the function of a harp player. It must obviously be an activity 'in accordance with virtue' (i.e. as we should say, 'on the right lines'): and, characteristically, Aristotle adds that it must be 'in a complete life', for it cannot operate when a man is miserably poor or deprived of freedom. This unhindered activity of the soul he identifies with *Eudaimonia*—a word which is usually translated 'happiness'. It is worth remembering however, that etymologically the English word 'happy' means 'lucky', the Greek *eudaimon* means 'with a good Spirit or Daemon'.

We may observe that such happiness is social; 'man was born for citizenship'. It is not pleasure, though pleasure comes as a crown or completion to the activity when it goes right, just as—so Aristotle puts it—physical charm (ὥρα) comes as a completion to youth and health. The motive for good action, however, is not the pleasure that may accompany it; nor yet the happiness which normally does so. When a brave man faces danger or a martyr faces suffering he does so ἕνεκα τοῦ καλοῦ, i.e. literally 'for the sake of the beautiful'. This phrase gives us modern English a shock. We do not habitually think on these lines, and we have no native English word corresponding to the Greek *kalon*. It does not mean the 'showy', nor yet 'the artistic'. It denotes the sort of action which, as soon as we contemplate it, we admire and love, just as we admire and love a beautiful object, without any thought of personal interest or advantage. The brave man has the choice, let us suppose, of dying for his friends or betraying his friends: as he imagines the two actions he sees that one is 'ugly' (αἰσχρόν, the regular Greek word for 'base') and the other 'beautiful' (καλόν); so he chooses it though it involves pain and death.

He may of course be influenced by all sorts of other motives, love of his friends, patriotism, anger, the mere habit of courage, or the like: but the strictly moral motive is preference for the beautiful action over the ugly.

Such *Eudaimonia* implies freedom; a slave can have pleasure, but not *Eudaimonia*. If we consider what kind of 'activity of the soul according to virtue' is the highest, most perfect and most characteristic of man as a reasoning animal, it proves to be Contemplation. That is the only activity we can well attribute to God, who must be infinitely blessed and happy. It may be said that, since Reason is not the whole of man but only the highest part, to live entirely in the activity of Reason, i.e. in Contemplation, is a thing too high to aim at. Man is mortal, they tell us, and should have mortal thoughts; but Aristotle, on the contrary, urges that we should 'make ourselves as immortal as we can, and strain every nerve to live in accordance with the best thing in us'.

Even so we do not escape from material considerations, since even for contemplation, if it is to be good in quality, we need health and leisure. And, after all, in human life, when there are things to be done, the end must be not merely to contemplate but to do. In the practical world, we must try 'any way there may be of being good', especially in educating and legislating. And thus we are led straight, and without any change of aim, from the most lofty speculations of ethics to the science of practical politics. Political activity is the conduct of a society seeking *Eudaimonia*, and trying to live according to virtue.

This philosophy, it is easy to see, is civic through and through. It accepts the State as a good thing. It assumes that 'Man is born to be a citizen' and is 'by nature a social animal'. He finds his virtue in performing his civic duty, and only in the service of his community can he become fully 'Wise, Temperate, Courageous and Righteous'. It is rather a surprise to find that Aristotle was writing at a time when the Greek City State was everywhere failing, and the world being re-shaped on a totally different model by Aristotle's own pupil, Alexander, and his successors. Evidently Aristotle did not regard the system of large military monarchies, backed by a lower civilization, as an improvement on that of the old City States, small, weak and poor, but highly civilized. It is characteristic of Greek democratic feeling that in the whole of Aristotle's works there is no word of flattery to his royal pupil.

6. REVOLT OF THE SOUL AGAINST THE STATE

The School of Aristotle, the Peripatetics, clung firmly for many generations to their master's point of view. But a rebellion of the individual Soul against the State had already begun and was never again without a witness in the Greek world.

It is important, if we would understand the various phases of Greek religion and ethics, to realize it as a philosophy of service, of citizenship, a loyalty of the individual to the whole of which he is a part. There are conditions under which this conception is entirely satisfying. In a ship on a long and stormy voyage the mind of a member of the crew may well be entirely occupied in saving the ship, and the more so the more he loves the ship and admires the captain. This was roughly speaking the position of a good citizen of Athens or Sparta in the early fifth century BC. But suppose he realizes that his ship is only one of a large fleet; or suppose he thinks that the ship is badly managed or the captain trying to sink her or the object of the voyage slave-trading or piracy? His loyalty will be in different degrees modified or undermined and his duty may become entirely different.

The thought that loyalty must be due not to Athens alone but to all Hellas or all humanity, meets us with increasing frequency from Herodotus onward; the suspicion that the whole government of Athens is incompetent and unjust and, worse still, that her aim in the Great War was tyrannical, is prominent in Euripides, Thucydides and Xenophon. And Plato especially found himself confronted by the paradox of the condemnation of Socrates, in which the City and the Laws, to whom he owed allegiance, were murdering the Just Man because he told them the truth. Plato's answer to the problem is a still more passionate devotion to the State, provided only that the State will be righteous; and, as we have seen, he spent his life in the search for that Righteous City. Isocrates, Xenophon and Lysias in different ways preached a Pan-Hellenic patriotism, as we might today preach a Pan-European patriotism, contrasted with the narrow devotion to a man's own city. But in the main philosophy detached itself from earthly patriotisms and, while keeping the ideal of loyalty or social duty, directed it towards some goal at once less limited and less tarnished. Where Aristotle continued to urge the duty of practical 'politic', and the importance of studying 'what enactments suit what circumstances', most of the other philosophers, despising such worldliness, considered that the proper thing was to pursue 'righteousness' or 'virtue' as the crow flies, and to know that any City which objected was no true City.

7. ETHICS IN EPICURUS

Two main schools of philosophy arose towards the end of the

fourth century and have, in a sense, divided mankind ever since, the Epicurean on the one hand and the Cynic or Stoic on the other. Epicurus was an Athenian of good birth, son of an elementary schoolmaster, who had passed through poverty, defeat in war, exile, bad health and distress in a colony of refugees; had discovered that there is still 'sweetness' (ἡδονή) in life; that it can be produced by moderate and temperate living, and that the secret of it lies in not being afraid and in loving one's companions (τὸ θαρρεῖν, φιλία). This 'sweetness', sometimes translated 'Pleasure', is the Good, or the aim of life. Virtue is only good as a means towards it. Epicurus set to work to free mankind from all their false fears. Why fear death? The dead feel nothing. Why fear the Gods? The Gods cannot harm you. They are blessed beings, and nothing can be blessed which gives pain to another. Why fear pain in this world? Long continued pain is never intolerable; intense pain is generally brief; a brave man can endure either. He can live the life of the soul, in memory or contemplation, and ignore the petty pains of the present. Next, Epicurus sought to set men free from all the 'humbug' of the conventional world. Rank and power and ambition were delusions; better a picnic by a river than all 'the crowns of the Greeks'. Learning and culture were worthless and deceiving; 'From all higher education, my friend, spread sails and fly!' Remember above all that human bliss—'sweetness' or 'blessedness', as he sometimes calls it—is not a remote dream but a thing easily won. It is here in your hands, if you will only live temperately, love those about you and not be afraid.

This school was never very numerous. It seems to have owed much to the personality of the founder. Its great work was to liberate the educated Greek world from superstitious terrors. When that work was done its message was largely exhausted, and it was perhaps too modest in its promises and too difficult in its practice to attract multitudes of adherents. Also it suffered deservedly for its founder's contempt for the advance of knowledge. Its two main doctrines, the Atomic Theory in physics, and the Utilitarian Theory in ethics, have come to their kingdom in modern times, but in antiquity the advance of science fell mostly into the hands of the Aristotelians, and the religious struggle against Christianity into those of the Platonists and Stoics. Indeed the pious pagans of the fourth century AD were fond of denouncing the Christians and Epicureans together as 'atheists'.

8. ETHICS OF THE CYNIC AND STOIC SCHOOLS

Yet the Stoics, especially if we couple with them the Cynics from whom they were derived, were largely the source of the moral ideas of Christianity. The difference between Cynic and Stoic seems to have been essentially a difference of education and culture rather than one of doctrine. The Cynics were the Stoics of the slum and the street corner. They were like the Buddhist mendicant monks as compared to the Buddhist philosophers. The first Cynic, Antisthenes, set up his school in a gymnasium appropriated to the use of bastards without citizenship. The most famous, Diogenes, lived like St Francis in utter poverty, and without even a roof over his head. In later times the Cynic dressed as a beggar, refused all possessions beyond a beggar's staff and wallet, and preached in the streets. It is worth mentioning that women as well as men were found among their preachers, as well as in the quieter ranks of the Stoics and Epicureans; that under the Roman Empire some persons were at the same time Cynic philosophers and Christian monks; and that the abolition of the gladiatorial games was due to the self-sacrificing protest of three persons in succession, two Cynics and the Christian Telemachus. Thus in the Cynic school the transition from the old religion to the new took place almost without a conscious change.

The doctrine of the Cynics was that Virtue ('Ἀρετή, Goodness) was the Good, and nothing else of any worth at all. Virtue was a direct relation of the naked soul to God. Like the Dominicans (Dominicani—'*Domini canes*') after them, the Cynics (κυνικοί, 'canine') were the watchdogs of God on earth; like a dog they needed no possessions, no knowledge, no city, only Courage, Temperance, Justice and Wisdom, which consisted in absolute fidelity to the divine Master. The Cynic saint, like the Christian, had affinities not only with the respectable poor, but with sinners and outcasts. Diogenes came to Athens as an ill-mannered young foreigner, whose father, a fraudulent money-changer, had been convicted of 'defacing the coinage' and was now in prison. When asked what he wanted in a philosophical school, Diogenes answered: 'to deface the coinage'. He meant to strip from life all the false stamps and labels put on it by human conventions. He obeyed no human laws, for he recognized no City: he was 'citizen of the Cosmos', or universe, and obeyed the laws of God. Through that citizenship he was 'free' while all the world was in bondage, 'fearless' while others were afraid. He was brother not only to all men, but to the beasts also. When about to die he recommended that his body should be thrown out to the dogs and wolves, who were doubtless hungry. 'I should like to be some use to my brothers when I am dead.'

He differs from the Stoics and from many of his own followers in having no social message, except the call to repent. Similarly he differed from many leaders of the ancient proletariat, in that he never preached rebellion or attempted to reconstitute society. The most oppressed slave, he considered, had already full access to God and to Virtue, and the greatest king had no more. He did not even correct the possible excesses of his followers by saying, as St Paul did, 'Slaves, obey your masters.'

The modern use of the word 'cynic' is of course a complete travesty of its original meaning. To most of us the Cynic school seems to suffer not from any lack of idealism, but from an idealism that has run mad through its own narrowness and intensity and its neglect of the secondary values of life. The Stoic school, starting from the same premiss, that 'Nothing but Goodness is good', built out of it a system of ethics and—one may fairly say—of religion which, whether one accepts it or not, seems to have a permanent value for mankind. 'Nothing but Goodness is good': there is no importance whatever in such things as health or sickness, riches or poverty, pleasure or pain. Who would ever claim credit for such things when his soul stood naked before God? All that matters is the goodness of man's self, that is, of his free and living will. Goodness is to serve the purpose of God, to will what God wills, and thus co-operate with the purpose of the Cosmos. In that spirit Zeno wrote his *Republic*; he conceived a world-society in which there should be no separate States; one great 'City of gods and men', where all should be citizens and members one of another, bound together not by human laws but by Love.

In the world as a whole, then, there is a purpose, and Virtue, or Goodness, is co-operation with that purpose. It was easier then than it is now to see a purpose revealed in the discoveries of science. For science had in the fourth century just reached a conception of the world which was singularly satisfying to the human mind. Astronomy had shown that the heavenly bodies followed perfectly regular movements. The stars were no wandering fires, but parts of an immense and eternal order. And though this order in its fullness might remain inscrutable, its main essence at least could be divined from the fact—then accepted as certain—that the orbits of all the celestial bodies had for their centre our earth and its ephemeral master, Man. Whatever else the Purpose might be, it was the purpose of a God who loves Man and has placed him in the centre of the Universe.

Add to this the conception of Nature which the Stoics had learned from Aristotle and others, as a system of Phusis or 'growth' towards perfection—of the seed towards the oak, of the blind puppy towards the good hound, of the primeval savage towards the civilized man—and one can see how this *'Phusis'* becomes identical with the Forethought or *'providentia'* of God. The whole movement of the Cosmos is the fulfilment of God's will. Virtue is action harmonious with that will; wickedness, the attempt to assert one's own contemptible will against it, an attempt which besides being blasphemous must always be futile. This line of thought ends in a paradox or an apparent contradiction, sublime and perhaps insoluble, which is common to Stoicism and Christianity. We recognize that in this great Cosmos or Order each living creature has its part. It is the part of the deer to grow swifter and stronger; of the artist to produce beauty; of the governor to govern well, so as to produce a prosperous and well-ordered city. At the same time we must remember that none of these things at which we aim, speed, beauty, prosperity or the like, are of any real value in themselves; nothing matters at all except the Good Will, the willing fulfilment of the Purpose of God. It does not really matter if all our efforts in this world are defeated. It is His will that we should strive, it may not be His will that we should succeed. We must not be too bitterly disappointed. If our friends die and we suffer great sorrows we may groan; that is human and pardonable. But ἔσωθεν, in the centre of our being, we must not groan. We must accept the eternal purpose and be content, though we perish.

Most adherents of evolutionist or 'meliorist' systems fall into the speculatively unsound position of justifying the present by the future. Imperfect man is so constantly preoccupied with the morrow, and so well content if he can see the labour and discomfort of the present repaid by success hereafter, that he is apt to transfer the same conception to the divine and perfect scheme. The world may be a miserable place now; that does not matter, he argues, if it is going to be a happy place hereafter. He sees no difficulty in supposing that the purpose of God, like that of a man, may be thwarted for a long time as long as it is ultimately triumphant. The conception seems clearly to be unsound. Even in human action one would feel some compunction about a plan which condemned a number of individuals to misery in order that after their death some other people should be happy. The Stoics at any rate were firm against any such lines of thought. Virtue is the good now; the Purpose is being fulfilled now; the Cosmos is infinitely beautiful now—now and always. They entirely refuse to promise future rewards to Virtue or to justify the present injustices of the world by the prospect of a millennium. The sufferings are of no importance: the only thing that matters is the way in which we face them.

The special advantage of Stoicism over most other systems is that, like Christianity, it adapts itself equally to a world order which we accept as good or to one which we reject as evil. Though it originated in a rebellion of the soul against society, it can equally well become a religion of social service. Many of the Hellenistic kings and great Roman governors were Stoics. Some of the great revolutionary reformers were inspired by Stoic advisers. Stoicism taught them to fulfil the divine purpose by governing as well and justly as they could, while at the same time it afforded a theoretical comfort if their efforts failed. Consequently it held its own both in the good periods and the bad. It comforted Brutus and Cato in the death agonies of the Roman republic; it fortified the lame slave Epictetus; it inspired the good Emperor, Marcus Aurelius, in his care for a peaceful and well-administered world. Doubtless it tended at times to protest too much; to try to solve the riddles of life by sententious preaching and rhetorical paradoxes, as in Seneca; but it never compromised its lofty spirit and never sank into vulgar superstition or emotionalism.

9. THE 'FAILURE OF NERVE': MYSTICISM AND SUPERSTITION

But we must realize that there was plenty of superstition and emotionalism about. It hardly appears in the classical writers who have come down to us, and we are tempted to think it was not there. But the evidence is abundant. We do not need the testimony of Epicurus, Lucretius, the early Christian fathers, or Theophrastus in his account of 'The Superstitious Man', to show the prevalence and strength of superstition. It is shown by many incidents in history, and brought home by the religious inscriptions, the rites recorded by the antiquarian Pausanias, the fragments of mystical and magical literature. And there seems now to be evidence to show that the kind of conception which has hitherto been supposed to be characteristic of the decadence of the Hellenic world was really present in pre-Hellenic Crete. (See Evans in *J.H.S.*, vol. XLV, 'The Ring of Nestor'.) There is no cause for surprise in this. Many words which occur in Homer disappeared in classical Greek only to re-emerge in late Ptolemaic papyri or in modern speech. The common people, in Greece as elsewhere, went on comparatively unaffected by the great spiritual and intellectual movements of Hellenism. Socrates or the Stoics might preach, Epicurus might disprove, but the Boeotian peasant went on placating the same old bogies in the same old way as his remote ancestors. And it is notable how the various periods of economic distress or prolonged warfare which fell upon the Greek world brought about a decline of culture and a revival of primitive beliefs. Men are apt to regard their misfortunes as the punishment of unforgiven sins. The famous earthquake of Lisbon was expiated by the burning of a large number of Jews: the eruption of Mount Pélée in our own day was followed by great public ceremonies of repentance. Greece was the home, from pre-Hellenic times, of rites of initiation or mysteries, such as exist in many barbarous tribes at the present day. In their simplest form these rites formed the initiation of the boys of the tribe into manhood, and the exposition to them of certain secret truths or doctrines that only the grown men of the tribe might know. But in practice we find that, as tribes disappeared or turned into voluntary societies, the rites began to have a different meaning. They brought purification from sin or pollution; they brought the communicant into close relation with some mediating god and gave him some assurance of bliss in the next world. Those who were not initiated, and thus accepted into the community of the faithful, would remain outcast from bliss. Plato and other writers are scornful of these doctrines and the votaries who live by them, professing to 'forgive sins' and secure that an initiated thief would fare better in the next world than an uninitiated just man. But the doctrines lived and spread.

For similar reasons, perhaps, there had early been a religion of the 'Sôtêr', the Saviour or Deliverer. Sometimes it is a mere title, as in 'Zeus Sôtêr': sometimes it is 'the Saviour' alone, or more especially 'The Third, the Saviour', or 'the Saviour who is Third' (τρίτος Σωτήρ). The origin of this conception seems probably to lie in the old agricultural religion which created and worshipped so many beings to represent the Year, or the Season, or the Vegetation, gods whose coming was the coming of spring or else of harvest, and whose annual death was celebrated when the harvest was cut or the vegetation died. The God had been killed—most often torn in pieces and scattered over the fields—by a Second Being, his Enemy, through whose victory the life of the earth seemed dead, till there came a Third Being, a Saviour, who slew the Enemy and brought back the dead God, or was himself the dead God restored. Modern travellers have found remains of this worship in modern Greece, and something like it continues in many parts of Europe.

In Hellenistic times, and particularly in the terrible times of strain that came between the Punic Wars and the Battle of Actium, this Saviour religion took a more spiritual or mystical character. It was associated with many names from the old mythology or from new Oriental systems, from the old Heracles to the new Isis and Sarapis, or the compound Hermes-Thoth. Notably Asclepius, the divine physician, not previously a god of much importance outside his temple at Epidaurus, became for some generations the most passionately worshipped god in the eastern Mediterranean. The world was sick, and cried out for the Healer.

In some of the earliest and most primitive rituals the climax of ecstatic worship was to bring the worshipper into 'communion', to make him one with his God. The communion originally involved drinking the blood and eating the flesh of the god, though in some of the sects called 'Gnostic' it came through ecstasy and contemplation. For to 'know' God, in this context, meant to be made one with him. ($\Gamma\nu\hat{\omega}\sigma\iota\varsigma$=knowledge.) The Gnostic writings have come down to us mixed up with later additions from many sources, and it is hard to separate out the original pre-Christian doctrines. But the Saviour seems generally to be a 'Third', the other two being God the Father and some such being as the Divine 'Wisdom' (Sophia) or 'Spirit'. (In some sects the second person is still the Enemy, as in the old Year-Daemon rituals, and 'the god of the Jews' made into a kind of Satan.) The method of redemption is sometimes that of the dying or suffering God, as he appears in the oldest agricultural religions; sometimes that of the 'righteous man' in Plato, who is happy though he be condemned of men and in the end impaled or crucified. Meantime the old ideas of astrology newly imported from Babylon have run riot through Greek thought, and the Saviour descends, by his own will or that of the Father, through all the spheres of the sinister Seven Planets, who rule the earth, to save mankind, or it may be to re-awaken in man the Soul, or the divine Sophia or Wisdom, who has forgotten her true nature.

Many details might be added to illustrate the various forms taken by these Saviour Religions, and the curious and often beautiful speculations which they engendered. But the main root of them seems to be a feeling of disillusion or despair of the world; the feeling of men in the presence of forces which they can neither control nor understand. They cry to their new God because the old gods have failed and there is none other to hear or help them. They seek to be saved not by 'justice' or wise conduct, but by some act of sacrifice or purification, some intensity of adoration. The forms and theories are merely those which happen to be supplied by old tradition or by the customs of some foreign hierophant, coming perhaps from Egypt or Babylon.

10. MITHRAISM

Historically the most important of these religious communities, at once the nearest and the most hostile to Christianity, came not from the Levant but from higher and remoter regions of the East. There were worshippers of Mithras in extreme antiquity, before the ancestors of the Persians separated from those of the Hindus. Even under the Roman Empire they liked to worship in caves, as they had before temples existed, and drew their myths and parables from pastoral life, as it had been before the building of cities. Of old Mithras had been a high God; but now he had lost in rank and gained in vitality. He was a hero, a redeemer, a mediator between man and god, a champion ever armed and vigilant in the eternal war of Ormuzd against Ahriman, of light against evil and darkness.

This religion hardly touched Greece at all. The severe Iranian dualism held out almost as rigorously as did the monotheism of the Jews against the general Hellenization which followed the conquests of Alexander. There are no Greek names derived from Mithras, as there are none from Jehovah, though 'Isidotus', 'Serapion', etc., are fairly common. Mithraism is said to have come to Rome from Cilicia and Pontus, after the campaign of Pompeius against the pirates and the rebel King Mithridates (65–61 BC). From thence onward it was carried by a stream of slaves and captives to Rome and the Mediterranean ports, and still more by a stream of soldiers out to the legions. Mithraism stretched at this time from Persia to the Euxine Sea, and covered some of the best recruiting-grounds. It spread along all the frontiers of the Empire, especially on the east and north, where life was most dangerous.

It was the religion of an unconquered people, the religion for a man and a soldier, not like Christianity, a doctrine for the conquered and subject. It had no place for the emotional women who swarmed in the Oriental cults and had a considerable influence in Christianity. We hear of no priestesses or female initiates: only of virgins, to share the worship of a virgin soldiery. It was in many ways more like an order of chivalry than a religious sect. There were ascetic vows, and an organized self-denial. The Mithraic might accept no earthly crown: 'His crown was Mithras.' There were rites of baptism and confirmation; but the confirmation was preceded by stern ordeals, and the baptism was not a dipping in water, but a branding with hot iron. The adherent of Mithras was throughout life a warrior, fighting for Ormuzd, for the Light, for the Sun, as against all that was dark and unclean. Since Mithras was 'The Sun, the Unconquered', and the Sun was 'the royal Star', the religion looked for a King whom it could serve as the representative of Mithras upon earth: and since the proof that the 'Grace' of Ormuzd rested upon a king was, of course, in addition to his virtue and piety, his invincibility, the Roman Emperor seemed to be clearly indicated as the true King. In sharp contrast to Christianity, Mithraism recognized Caesar as the bearer of the divine Grace, and its votaries filled the legions and the civil service.

Yet the similarities between Mithraism and Christianity are striking, and may be taken as signs of the spiritual and psychological needs of the time. Mithraism arose in the East, among the poor, among captives and slaves. It put its hopes in a Redeemer, a Mediator, who performed some mystical sacrifice. It held a Communion Service of bread and wine. It rested on the personal *Pistis* (Faith, or faithfulness) of the convert to his Redeemer. It had so much acceptance that it was able to impose on the Christian world its own Sun-Day in place of the Sabbath; its Sun's birthday, December 25, as the birthday of Jesus; its Magi and its Shepherds hailing the divine Star; and various of its Easter Celebrations.

On the other hand, its Redeemer, Mithras, makes hardly any pretence to have had an earthly history. His saga is all myth and allegory, elaborate ritual, sacraments and mystic names, and the varied paraphrasing that is necessary for bringing primitive superstitions up to the level which civilized man will tolerate. Above all, it differed from Christianity in that, having made its peace with Rome, it accepted not only the Empire but the other religions of the Empire. Rome saw in the second century the usefulness of Mithraism, and the Emperor Commodus was initiated: Mithraism became inextricibly involved in the other Sun worships as well as those of Isis and the Great Mother, and thus sank into the slough of turbid syncretism in which the Empire of Septimius Severus and Elagabalus tried to find a universal religion.

Mithraism must have lost much of its purity and vigour before it met its great military disaster. In the Dacian Revolt of AD 257, following on the Gothic invasions, Mithras proved too weak to withstand the barbarians. He was no longer 'The Unconquered'. His cave-chapels, or Mithraea, were destroyed all along the frontier where they had been at their strongest. The sect never recovered. Doubtless they had encouraged persecution of the Christians in previous times, and now the Christians had their chance. The little chapels, never with a congregation of more than a hundred, were a fairly easy prey to large mobs. A candidate for Christian baptism in St Jerome's letters offers as a proof of his piety his exploits in wrecking them. Excavations of the Mithraea, which are exceedingly numerous all over the imperial frontiers, show sometimes how the priests had walled them up, with the holy objects inside, in the hope of reopening the worship in better days; sometimes how the Christian mobs had polluted them for ever with the rotting corpses of the faithful. A bloody and cruel story, like so much of the history of religion; but it is clear that Christianity gained in strength by defying the Roman world longer than Mithras did, and by denying instead of accepting its numerous gods.

11. WHAT THE AGE NEEDED

A study of the Gnostic and Hermetic collections, and such evidence as exists about the worships of Isis, Serapis, Mithras and various Saviours, together with the magical remains and the accounts of early heresies, leaves on the mind the impression of a mass of emotional and spiritual aspiration, marred by nervous and intellectual wreckage. The world passed through a bad period after the Second Punic War, and another in the troubles of the third century AD and then in the final fall, but it is difficult to assign dates to movements of which one does not know the local or social origin. The mystic literature as a whole bears a message of despair and consolation—despair of living a good life by one's own efforts in so unrighteous a world, and consolation by promises of ultimate reward whose extreme splendour makes up for their regrettable uncertainty. Here and there the future bliss for ourselves is crossed by a vision of the well-deserved torments that await our enemies and persecutors. It is the cry of the failure of the old Graeco-Roman civilization, though of course that failure may have been felt in different degrees at very different places and dates.

It seems clear that any new religion which was to have a chance of success at this time must be one that appealed to the ignorant masses—though no doubt it would be a great advantage if it were capable also, like Stoicism, of being adapted to the needs of the philosophers. It must promise a personal salvation by the active help of a personal god, who must also be as solid and human as possible. A god who was pure thought 'without body, parts or passions' would be of no avail. It must be a religion of the poor, though whether the rich should be given their deserts now or left to receive them in hell was a point which depended upon circumstances. (In 130 BC, when suffering was intense, the madder alternative had been tried with disastrous results; in the first century of the Empire there was peace and good government, and consequently far less suffering and more meekness.) It must in the main satisfy man's moral nature, for the present discontent was not merely due to personal suffering but also to a rage against the injustice of the world and a feeling that such misery must somehow be the result of sin. Lastly, it must clearly profess doctrines which were natural and acceptable to the masses of the Mediterranean world; that is, it must be based on the old religions. At the same time it could not belong to one nation only, but must have some wider appeal, the old familiar emotion being stimulated by the new revelation. Thus the Hermetic system is derived from Greece and Egypt, Mithraism from Iran and Babylon with a touch of Hellenism, Christianity from Greece and Judaism.

Whether Christianity is to be explained as a natural development from the existing factors, or whether it is a miraculous revelation vouchsafed after long delay to a world that had been allowed to grow exactly ripe for it, is a problem which cannot be settled by historical research and must be answered by each man according to his own bent. But it is curious how all the main articles of Christian faith and practice were already latent in the ancient religion. The parts of Christian doctrine which a Levantine pagan of the first century would deny are chiefly the historical statements. Like Paul before his conversion, he would be ready enough to discuss the doctrine of a Hebrew Messiah or a Hellenistic 'Saviour', but would refuse to believe that this supernatural being had just arrived on earth in the person of a certain Jew or Nazarene. He would feel no surprise at the moral teaching; he would have met parts of it in the Jewish tradition and parts in Stoicism. At worst he might be alarmed at the revolutionary tone of certain parts and the exaltation of one who was, after all, a condemned criminal, as the ideal good man and Son of God. The rejection of bloody sacrifice he had learnt from the Peripatetics and the Jews; conceptions like the Good Shepherd, the Mother and Child, the worship of a divine Baby, the halo round the heads of saints, and innumerable other incidents of Christian tradition, were of course not new inventions but things ancient and familiar. The transition consisted largely in giving a new name and history to some object of worship which already had had many names and varying legends attached to it. Nay, more, in the metaphysical and theological doctrines formulated in the Creeds, except where they were specially meant to controvert the old system, he would at least recognize for the most part ideas which he had heard discussed.

12. THE CREEDS, CHRISTIAN AND PAGAN: THE AREA OF AGREEMENT

He believed in God as a 'Father' and would have no quarrel with a Christian as to the exact meaning of that metaphorical term; the attribute 'Almighty' he accepted, though both Christian and pagan theologians had the same difficulty in dealing with the implications of that term and explaining how the All-good and Almighty permitted evil. The average Greek did not think of God as the 'maker of heaven and earth'; the thought was Hebrew or Babylonian, but was not strange to the Hellenistic world. The idea of an 'only-begotten Son' of God was regular in the Orphic systems, and that of a Son of God by a mortal woman, conceived in some spiritual way, and born for the saving of mankind, was at least as old as the fifth century BC. In a simpler and more natural form it was much earlier. That this Saviour 'suffered and was buried' is common to the Vegetation or Year religions, with their dying and suffering gods; and the idea had been sharpened and made more living both by the thought of Plato's 'righteous man' and by the various 'kings of the Poor' who had risen and suffered in the slave revolts. That after the descent to Hades he should arise to judge both the quick and the dead is a slight modification of the ordinary Greek notion, according to which the Judges were already seated at their work, but it may have come from the Saviour religions.

The belief in God as a Trinity, or as One substance with three *'personae'*—the word simply means 'masks' or 'dramatic roles'—is directly inherited from Greek speculation. The third person was more usually feminine, the divine Wisdom, or Providence, or the Mother of the Son: the 'Spirit' or 'Breath of God' comes from the Hebrew. Belief in the Holy Catholic Church was again not the pagan's own belief, but it was the sort of belief with which he was quite familiar. He accepted belief in some church or community, be it that of Mithras or Hermes-Thoth or some similar Healer. If the 'communion of the Saints' originally meant the sharing of all property among the faithful, that practice was familiar in certain congregations; if it meant, as is now generally understood, the existence of a certain fellowship or community between those who are 'pure', whether dead, living, or divine, it was an idea prevalent in Stoicism. The 'forgiveness of sins' was a subject much debated in antiquity as at the time of the Reformation. The traditional religion dealt largely in 'purification', which involved forgiveness of sins and slipped from time to time into a mechanical or mercenary treatment of the matter, which roused the usual protest of indignation and denial. It is interesting also to note that a closely cognate idea, the 'forgiveness of debts', was one of the regular cries of the proletarian movements. A connection was probably felt between a generous Leader—like Cleomenes III or C. Gracchus—who annulled poor men's debts on earth and a God who forgave them their offences in heaven. Of the Resurrection of the body we have already spoken; it was a concession to the uneducated, who would not be content with a 'life everlasting' of the soul alone, freed from bodily substance and form, and perhaps even from personality.

The greatest blot upon Christianity was the savage emphasis which it laid upon the doctrine of Hell—and that a Hell specially reserved, not so much for the wicked, but for all those who did not belong to the Christian community. Yet here also there is nothing absolutely new. Mithras and Isis and even the God of Neoplatonism tolerated some tormenting demons. And after all Hell for the persecutor in the next life is the natural retort of the victim who cannot hit back in this life. One may well imagine that the followers of Spartacus, Aristonicus or Mithridates believed in a Hell for Romans. And the peculiar notion of treating false belief as a form of sin, and a particularly dangerous form, goes back to the wise and gentle Plato himself.[1]

In the same way, if we compare briefly with the Christian Creeds the document drawn up by Sallustius for the education of the young pagans in religion, we shall not find much that a modern Christian would care to deny, though we shall notice how much more intellectual, abstract, and in a sense aristocratic, is the doctrine of the Neoplatonist.

The young are to be thoroughly trained in the knowledge that God is free from passion and change, eternal, unbegotten, incorporeal, not in time or space. He is good and the cause of good; He is never angry nor appeased. (Much of this would clash vividly with parts of the Hebrew and Christian story but not much with modern theology.) They are to know that the ancient myths are all allegories; they mean not what they say, but reveal hidden wisdom. (This is the usual refuge of a society which has outgrown its sacred book.) The Cosmos is eternal and can never come to an end. (The Christians, of course, were eagerly expecting the end of it.) The

[1] *Laws*, p. 908.

first Cause is the Good; i.e. all things throughout the Cosmos move from love of the Good, though as a rule they do not know it: there is no positive evil, and of course no evil caused by God. The soul is immortal; human freedom, Divine Providence, Fate and Fortune have all their place and can be reconciled. Virtue consists in four parts, Wisdom, Courage, Temperance, Righteousness. Men worship God, not to benefit Him or show honour to Him; for of course we cannot affect Him in any way. We merely rejoice in Him as we rejoice in the beauty of the Sun. Similarly those who deny or reject God (i.e. the Christians and Epicureans) do Him no injury; they are like men in the sunlight who cannot see the Sun, either because they are blind or because they insist on looking away from it. Goodness is not a painful thing to be rewarded by future bliss; it is blessedness both now and hereafter.

13. CHRISTIANITY ON THE SIDE OF PROGRESS

It is difficult at this distance of time to form any judgement about the comparative morals of the early Christian communities and the pagan societies in which they lived. We may indeed be fairly sure that the average mass of sensual men, with their commonplace vices and dishonesties, did not trouble to become Christian before Constantine made it the easier course, nor dare to stay pagan afterwards. The polemical writings of the Christians are preserved, those of the pagans have mostly perished; but we can see that the lurid accusations hurled by each against their opponents are nearly all based on what is called constructive evidence. The pagans argue that people who deny the gods, who worship a condemned criminal, and who pray that the whole world may soon be destroyed, must be inconceivably wicked and malignant; the Christians, that people whose mythical gods committed adultery and cannibalism, must themselves be ready for any enormity. Such accusations are like the stories circulated about Jews and Anabaptists in the Middle Ages. They are only symptoms of the accusers' state of mind, not evidence against the accused.

In general we must remember that the Christians belonged mostly to the seething town proletariat of the eastern Mediterranean; the pagans, as that name implies, seem to have been the unprogressive peasants of the country villages (*pagi*), though the word has a secondary meaning, 'civilian', and may have been intended to denote the common herd as distinct from the soldiers of Mithras or Christ. One can easily understand how the excesses of the town mobs would be attributed by the timid respectable classes to the terrible inroads

Christianity. But the mob was really neither pagan nor Christian. The idealists, rebels, reformers, among the working class, would be mostly either Christians or followers of some other mystic sect, though the more intellectual might become philosophers. The Jewish element in Christianity, also, was a separating influence and made for a higher morality. The Jews uncompromisingly denounced certain practices, notably homosexuality and abortion, which the world as a whole tolerated and only philosophers and certain special communities condemned. The crusade against the lusts of the flesh which marked the centuries just before and after the Christian era was by no means specially Christian, though doubtless here as elsewhere Christianity was against the dead mass and for the reforming few.

But there is certainly one point in which Christianity, at any rate in its earlier forms, did a unique service to the world. In its rejection of superstition it stands far higher than the rival religions, higher even than the Neoplatonism of Proclus and Julian, infinitely higher than the paganism of the vulgar. When Julian condemns the Christians as 'atheists' or 'rejectors of God' he is giving them the highest praise. The beautiful dialogue *Octavius*, attributed to Minucius Felix, shows how, to an educated man, Christianity came as a liberation from the perpetual presence of objects of superstitious worship. It performed the same cleansing task as Judaic monotheism among the worshippers of the Baalim, as Islam among the Arabian pagans, and as one side at least of the Reformation. The ancient world, as civilization declined, was overburdened by the ever-increasing mass of its superstitions, and its thought devitalized by a blind reverence for the past. Philosophy as well as religion could hardly find life except through a process of which the first step was a vigorous denial of false gods. That step once taken, it is curious to observe how little of ancient philosophy has perished, how much has merely been taken over by Christianity, and how few new ideas in the realms of metaphysics or morals have occurred to the human mind since the fourth century before Christ.

CHAPTER VII

The Stoic Philosophy[1]

I PROPOSE to give here in rough outline some account of the greatest system of organized thought which the mind of man had built up for itself in the Graeco-Roman world before the coming of Christianity with its inspired book and its authoritative revelation. Stoicism may be called either a philosophy or a religion. It was a religion in its exalted passion; it was a philosophy inasmuch as it made no pretence to magical powers or supernatural knowledge. I do not suggest that it is a perfect system, with no errors of fact and no inconsistencies of theory. It is certainly not that; and I do not know of any system that is. But I believe that it represents a way of looking at the world and the practical problems of life which possesses still a permanent interest for the human race, and a permanent power of inspiration. I shall approach it, therefore, rather as a psychologist than as a philosopher or historian. I shall not attempt to trace the growth or variation of Stoic doctrine under its various professors, nor yet to scrutinize the logical validity of its arguments. I shall merely try as best I can to make intelligible its great central principles and the almost irresistible appeal which they made to so many of the best minds of antiquity.

From this point of view I will begin by a very rough general suggestion, viz. that the religions known to history fall into two broad classes, religions which are suited for times of good government and religions which are suited for times of bad government; religions for prosperity or for adversity, religions which accept the world or which defy the world, which place their hopes in the betterment of human life on this earth or which look away from it as from a vale of tears. By 'the world' in this connection I mean the ordinary concrete world, the well-known companion of the flesh and the Devil; not the universe. For some of the religions which think most meanly of the world they know have a profound admiration for all, or nearly all, those parts of the universe where they have not been.

[1] The Moncure Conway Memorial Lecture, 1915.

Now, to be really successful in the struggle for existence, a religion must suit both sets of circumstances. A religion which fails in adversity, which deserts you just when the world deserts you, would be a very poor affair; on the other hand, it is almost equally fatal for a religion to collapse as soon as it is successful. Stoicism, like Christianity, was primarily a religion for the oppressed, a religion of defence and defiance; but, like Christianity, it had the requisite power of adaptation. Consistently or inconsistently, it opened its wings to embrace the needs both of success and of failure. To illustrate what I mean, contrast for the moment the life of an active, practical, philanthropic, modern bishop with that of an anchorite like St Simeon Stylites, living in idleness and filth on the top of a large column; or, again, contrast the bishop's ideals with those of the author of the Apocalypse, abandoning himself to visions of a gorgeous reversal of the order of this evil world and the bloody revenges of the blessed. All three are devout Christians; but the bishop is working with the world of men, seeking its welfare and helping its practical needs; the other two are rejecting or cursing it. In somewhat the same way we shall find that our two chief preachers of Stoicism are, the one a lame and penniless slave to whom worldly success is as nothing, the other an Emperor of Rome, keenly interested in good administration.

The founder of the Stoic school, Zeno, came from Cilicia to Athens about the year 320 BC. His place of birth is, perhaps, significant. He was a Semite, and came from the East. The Semite was apt in his religion to be fierier and more uncompromising than the Greek. The time of his coming is certainly significant. It was a time when landmarks had collapsed, and human life was left, as it seemed, without a guide. The average man in Greece of the fifth century BC had two main guides and sanctions for his conduct of life: the welfare of his City and the laws and traditions of his ancestors. First the City, and next the traditional religion; and in the fourth century both of these had fallen. Let us see how.

Devotion to the City or Community produced a religion of public service. The City represented a high ideal, and it represented supreme power. By 320 BC the supreme power had been overthrown. Athens, and all independent Greek cities, had fallen before the overwhelming force of the great military monarchies of Alexander and his generals. The high ideal at the same time was seen to be narrow. The community to which a man should devote himself, if he should devote himself at all, must surely be something larger than one of these walled cities set upon their separate hills. Thus the City, as a guide of life, had proved wanting. Now when the Jews lost their Holy City they had still, or believed that they had still, a guide left. 'Zion is taken from us,' says the Book of Esdras; 'nothing is left save the Holy One and his Law.' But Greece had no such Law. The Greek religious tradition had long since been riddled with criticism. It would not bear thinking out, and the Greeks like to think things out. The traditional religion fell not because the people were degenerate. Quite the contrary; it fell, as it has sometimes fallen elsewhere, because the people were progressive. The people had advanced, and the traditional religion had not kept pace with them. And we may add another consideration. If the Gods of tradition had proved themselves capable of protecting their worshippers, doubtless their many moral and intellectual deficiencies might have been overlooked. But they had not. They had proved no match for Alexander and the Macedonian phalanx.

Thus the work that lay before the generation of 320 BC was twofold. They had to rebuild a new public spirit, devoted not to the City, but to something greater; and they had to rebuild a religion or philosophy which should be a safe guide in the threatening chaos. We will see how Zeno girded himself to this task.

Two questions lay before him—how to live and what to believe. His real interest was in the first, but it could not be answered without first facing the second. For if we do not in the least know what is true or untrue, real or unreal, we cannot form any reliable rules about conduct or anything else. And, as it happened, the Sceptical school of philosophy, largely helped by Plato, had lately been active in denying the possibility of human knowledge and throwing doubts on the very existence of reality. Their arguments were extraordinarily good, and many of them have not been answered yet; they affect both the credibility of the senses and the supposed laws of reasoning. The Sceptics showed how the senses are notoriously fallible and contradictory, and how the laws of reasoning lead by equally correct processes to opposite conclusions. Many modern philosophers, from Kant to Dr Schiller and Mr Bertrand Russell, have followed respectfully in their footsteps. But Zeno had no patience with this sort of thing. He wanted to get to business.

Also he was a born fighter. His dealings with opponents who argued against him always remind me of a story told of the Duke of Wellington when his word was doubted by a subaltern. The Duke, when he was very old and incredibly distinguished, was telling how once, at mess in the Peninsula, his servant had opened a bottle of port, and inside found a rat. 'It must have been a very large bottle', remarked the subaltern. The Duke fixed him with his eye. 'It was a damned small bottle.' 'Oh', said the subaltern, abashed; 'then no doubt it was a very small rat'. 'It was a damned large rat', said the Duke. And there the matter has rested ever since.

Zeno began by asserting the existence of the real world. 'What do you mean by real?' asked the Sceptic. 'I mean solid and material. I mean that this table is solid matter.' 'And God', said the Sceptic, 'and the soul? Are they solid matter?' 'Perfectly solid,' says Zeno; 'more solid, if anything, than the table.' 'And virtue or justice or the Rule of Three; also solid matter?' 'Of course,' said Zeno; 'quite solid.' This is what may be called 'high doctrine', and Zeno's successors eventually explained that their master did not really mean that justice was solid matter, but that it was a sort of 'tension', or mutual relation, among material objects. This amendment saves the whole situation. But it is well to remember the uncompromising materialism from which the Stoic system started.

Now we can get a step further. If the world is real, how do we know about it? By the evidence of our senses; for the sense-impression (here Stoics and Epicureans both followed the fifth-century physicists) is simply the imprint of the real thing upon our mindstuff. As such it must be true. In the few exceptional cases where we say that 'our senses deceive us' we speak incorrectly. The sense-impression was all right; it is we who have interpreted it wrongly, or received it in some incomplete way. What we need in each case is a 'comprehensive sense-impression'. The meaning of this phrase is not quite clear. I think it means a sense-impression which 'grasps' its object; but it may be one which 'grasps' us, or which we 'grasp', so that we cannot doubt it. In any case, when we get the real imprint of the object upon our senses, then this imprint is of necessity true. When the Sceptics talk about a conjuror making 'our senses deceive us', or when they object that a straight stick put half under water looks as if it were bent in the middle, they are talking inexactly. In such cases the impression is perfectly true; it is the interpretation that may go wrong. Similarly, when they argue that reasoning is fallacious because men habitually make mistakes in it, they are confusing the laws of reasoning with the inexact use which people make of them. You might just as well say that twice two is not four, or that 7×7 is not 49, because people often make mistakes in doing arithmetic.

Thus we obtain a world which is in the first place real and in the second knowable. Now we can get to work on our real philosophy, our doctrine of ethics and conduct. And we build it upon a very simple principle, laid down first by Zeno's master, Crates, the founder of the Cynic School: the principle that Nothing but Goodness is Good. That seems plain enough, and harmless enough; and so does its corollary: 'Nothing but badness is bad.' In the case of any concrete object which you call 'good', it seems quite clear that it is only good because of some goodness in it. We, perhaps, should not express the matter in quite this way, but we should scarcely think it worth while to object if Zeno chooses to phrase it so, especially as the statement itself seems little better than a truism.

Now, to an ancient Greek the form of the phrase was quite familiar. He was accustomed to asking 'What is the good?' It was to him the central problem of conduct. It meant: 'What is the object of life, or the element in things which makes them worth having?' Thus the principle will mean: 'Nothing is worth living for except goodness.' The only good for man is to *be* good. And, as we might expect, when Zeno says 'good' he means good in an ultimate Day-of-Judgement sense, and will take no half-measures. The principle turns out to be not nearly so harmless as it looked. It begins by making a clean sweep of the ordinary conventions. You remember the eighteenth-century lady's epitaph which ends: 'Bland, passionate, and deeply religious, she was second cousin to the Earl of Leitrim, and of such are the kingdom of heaven.' One doubts whether, when the critical moment came, her relationships would really prove as important as her executors hoped; and it is the same with all the conventional goods of the world when brought before the bar of Zeno. Rank, riches, social distinction, health, pleasure, barriers of race or nation—what will those things matter before the tribunal of ultimate truth? Not a jot. Nothing but goodness is good. It is what you are that matters—what you yourself are; and all these things are not you. They are external; they depend not on you alone, but on other people. The thing that really matters depends on you, and on none but you. From this there flows a very important and surprising conclusion. You possess already, if you only knew it, all that is worth desiring. The good is yours if you but will it. You need fear nothing. You are safe, inviolable, utterly free. A wicked man or an accident can cause you pain, break your leg, make you ill; but no earthly power can make you good or bad except yourself, and to be good or bad is the only thing that matters.

At this point common sense rebels. The plain man says to Zeno: 'This is all very well; but we know as a matter of fact that such things as health, pleasure, long life, fame, etc., are good; we all like them.

The reverse are bad; we hate and avoid them. All sane, healthy people agree in judging so.' Zeno's answer is interesting. In the first place, he says: 'Yes; that is what most people say. But the judges who give that judgement are bribed. Pleasure, though not really good, has just that particular power of bribing the judges, and making them on each occasion say or believe that she is good. The Assyrian king Sardanapalus thinks it good to stay in his harem, feasting and merry-making, rather than suffer hardship in governing his kingdom. He swears his pleasure is good; but what will any unbribed third person say? Consider the judgements of history. Do you ever find that history praises a man because he was healthy, or long-lived, or because he enjoyed himself a great deal? History never thinks of such things; they are valueless and disappear from the world's memory. The thing that lives is a man's goodness, his great deeds, his virtue, or his heroism.'

If the questioner was not quite satisfied, Zeno used another argument. He would bid him answer honestly for himself: 'Would you yourself really like to be rich and corrupted? To have abundance of pleasure and be a worse man?' And, apparently, when Zeno's eyes were upon you, it was difficult to say you would. Some Stoics took a particular instance. When Harmodius and Aristogeiton, the liberators of Athens, slew the tyrant Hipparchus (which is always taken as a praiseworthy act), the tyrant's friends seized a certain young girl, named Leaina, who was the mistress of Aristogeiton, and tortured her to make her divulge the names of the conspirators. And under the torture the girl bit out her tongue and died without speaking a word. Now, in her previous life we may assume that Leaina had had a good deal of gaiety. Which would you sooner have as your own—the early life of Leaina, which was full of pleasures, or the last hours of Leaina, which were full of agony? and with a Stoic's eyes upon them, as before, people found it hard to say the first. They yielded their arms and confessed that goodness, and not any kind of pleasure, is the good.

But now comes an important question, and the answer to it, I will venture to suggest, just redeems Stoicism from the danger of becoming one of those inhuman cast-iron systems by which mankind may be browbeaten, but against which it secretly rebels. What *is* Goodness? What is this thing which is the only object worth living for?

Zeno seems to have been a little impatient of the question. We know quite well; everybody knows who is not blinded by passion or desire. Still, the school consented to analyse it. And the profound common sense and reasonableness of average Greek thought expressed the answer in its own characteristic way. Let us see in practice what we mean by 'good'. Take a good bootmaker, a good father, a good musician, a good horse, a good chisel; you will find that each one of them has some function to perform, some special work to do; and a good one does the work well. Goodness is performing your function well. But when we say 'well' we are still using the idea of goodness. What do we mean by doing it 'well'? Here the Greek falls back on a scientific conception which had great influence in the fifth century BC, and, somewhat transformed and differently named, has regained it in our own days. We call it 'Evolution'. The Greeks called it *Phusis*, a word which we translate by 'Nature', but which seems to mean more exactly 'growth,' or 'the process of growth'.[1] It is Phusis which gradually shapes or tries to shape every living thing into a more perfect form. It shapes the seed, by infinite and exact gradations, into the oak; the blind puppy into the good hunting dog; the savage tribe into the civilized city. If you analyse this process, you find that Phusis is shaping each thing towards the fulfilment of its own function—that is, towards the good. Of course Phusis sometimes fails; some of the blind puppies die; some of the seeds never take root. Again, when the proper development has been reached, it is generally followed by decay; that, too, seems like a failure in the work of Phusis. I will not consider these objections now; they would take us too far afield, and we shall need a word about them later. Let us in the meantime accept this conception of a force very like that which most of us assume when we speak of evolution; especially, perhaps, it is like what Bergson calls *La Vie* or *L'Élan Vital* at the back of *L'Évolution Creatrice*, though to the Greeks it seemed still more personal and vivid; a force which is present in all the live world, and is always making things grow towards the fulfilment of their utmost capacity. We see now what goodness is; it is living or acting according to Phusis, working with Phusis in her eternal effort towards perfection. You will notice, of course, that the phrase means a good deal more than we usually mean by living 'according to nature'. It does not mean 'living simply', or 'living like the natural man'. It means living according to the spirit which makes the world grow and progress.

This Phusis becomes in Stoicism the centre of much speculation

[1] See a paper by Professor J. L. Myres, 'The Background of Greek Science', *University of California Chronicle*, xvi, 4.

and much effort at imaginative understanding. It is at work everywhere. It is like a soul, or a life-force, running through all matter as the 'soul' or life of a man runs through all his limbs. It is the soul of the world. Now, it so happened that in Zeno's time the natural sciences had made a great advance, especially astronomy, botany, and natural history. This fact had made people familiar with the notion of natural law. Law was a principle which ran through all the movements of what they called the *cosmos*, or 'ordered world'. Thus Phusis, the life of the world, is, from another point of view, the Law of Nature; it is the great chain of causation by which all events occur; for the Phusis which shapes things towards their end acts always by the laws of causation. Phusis is not a sort of arbitrary personal goddess, upsetting the natural order; Phusis is the natural order, and nothing happens without a cause.

A natural law, yet a natural law which is alive, which is itself life. It becomes indistinguishable from a purpose, the purpose of the great world-process. It is like a fore-seeing, fore-thinking power—*Pronoia*; our common word 'Providence' is the Latin translation of this *Pronoia*, though of course its meaning has been rubbed down and cheapened in the process of the ages. As a principle of providence or forethought it comes to be regarded as God, the nearest approach to a definite personal God which is admitted by the austere logic of Stoicism. And, since it must be in some sense material, it is made of the finest material there is; it is made of fire, not ordinary fire, but what they called intellectual fire. A fire which is present in a warm, live man, and not in a cold, dead man; a fire which has consciousness and life, and is not subject to decay. This fire, Phusis, God, is in all creation.

We are led to a very definite and complete Pantheism. The Sceptic begins to make his usual objections. 'God in worms?' he asks. 'God in fleas and dung beetles?' And, as usual, the objector is made to feel sorry that he spoke. 'Why not?' the Stoic answers; 'cannot an earthworm serve God? Do you suppose that it is only a general who is a good soldier? Cannot the lowest private or camp attendant fight his best and give his life for his cause? Happy are you if you are serving God, and carrying out the great purpose as truly as such-and-such an earthworm.' That is the conception. All the world is working together. It is all one living whole, with one soul through it. And, as a matter of fact, no single part of it can either rejoice or suffer without all the rest being affected. The man who does not see that the good of every living creature is his good, the hurt of every living creature his hurt, is one who wilfully makes himself a kind of outlaw or exile: he is blind, or a fool. So we are led up to the great doctrine of the later Stoics, the Συμπάθεια τῶν ὅλων, or Sympathy of the Whole; a grand conception, the truth of which is illustrated in the ethical world by the feelings of good men, and in the world of natural science.... We moderns may be excused for feeling a little surprise... by the fact that the stars twinkle. It is because they are so sorry for us: as well they may be!

Thus Goodness is acting according to Phusis, in harmony with the will of God. But here comes an obvious objection. If God is all, how can anyone do otherwise? God is the omnipresent Law; God is all Nature; no one can help being in harmony with Him. The answer is that God is in all except in the doings of bad men. For man is free.... How do we know that? Why, by a *kataleptikē phantasia*, a comprehensive sense impression which it is impossible to resist. Why it should be so we cannot tell. 'God might have preferred chained slaves for His fellow-workers; but, as a matter of fact, he preferred free men.' Man's soul, being actually a portion of the divine fire, has the same freedom that God Himself has. He can act either with God or against Him, though, of course, when he acts against Him he will ultimately be overwhelmed. Thus Stoicism grapples with a difficulty which no religion has satisfactorily solved.

It will be observed that by now we have worked out two quite different types of Stoic—one who defies the world and one who works with the world; and, as in Christianity, both types are equally orthodox. We have first the scorner of all earthly things. Nothing but goodness is good; nothing but badness bad. Pain, pleasure, health, sickness, human friendship and affection, are all indifferent. The truly wise man possesses his soul in peace; he communes with God. He always, with all his force, wills the will of God; thus everything that befalls him is a fulfilment of his own will and good. A type closely akin to the early Christian ascetic or the Indian saint.

And in the second place we have the man who, while accepting the doctrine that only goodness is good, lays stress upon the definition of goodness. It is acting according to Phusis, in the spirit of that purpose or forethought which, though sometimes failing, is working always unrestingly for the good of the world, and which needs its fellow-workers. God is helping the whole world; you can only help a limited fraction of the world. But you can try to work in the same spirit. There were certain old Greek myths which told how Heracles and other heroes had passed laborious lives serving and helping humanity, and in the end became gods. The Stoics used such myths as allegories. That was the way to heaven; that was how a man may at the end of his life 'become not a dead body, but a star'. In the magnificent phrase which Pliny translates from a Greek Stoic, God is that, and nothing but that; man's true God is the helping of man: *Deus est mortali iuvare mortalem*.

No wonder such a religion appealed to kings and statesmen and Roman governors. Nearly all the successors of Alexander—we may say all the principal kings in existence in the generations following Zeno—professed themselves Stoics. And the most famous of all Stoics, Marcus Aurelius, found his religion not only in meditation and religious exercises, but in working some sixteen hours a day for the good practical government of the Roman Empire.

Is there any real contradiction or inconsistency between the two types of Stoic virtue? On the surface certainly there seems to be; and the school felt it, and tried in a very interesting way to meet it. The difficulty is this: what is the good of working for the welfare of humanity if such welfare is really worthless? Suppose, by great labour and skill, you succeed in reducing the death-rate of a plague-stricken area; suppose you make a starving countryside prosperous; what is the good of it all if health and riches are in themselves worthless, and not a whit better than disease and poverty?

The answer is clear and uncompromising. A good bootmaker is one who makes good boots; a good shepherd is one who keeps his sheep well; and even though good boots are, in the Day-of-Judgement sense, entirely worthless, and fat sheep no whit better than starved sheep, yet the good bootmaker or good shepherd must do his work well or he will cease to be good. To be good he must perform his function; and in performing that function there are certain things that he must 'prefer' to others, even though they are not really 'good'. He must prefer a healthy sheep or a well-made boot to their opposites. It is thus that Nature, or Phusis, herself works when she shapes the seed into the tree, or the blind puppy into the good hound. The perfection of the tree or hound is in itself indifferent, a thing of no ultimate value. Yet the goodness of Nature lies in working for that perfection.

Life becomes, as the Stoics more than once tell us, like a play which is acted or a game played with counters. Viewed from outside, the counters are valueless; but to those engaged in the game their importance is paramount. What really and ultimately matters is that the game shall be played as it should be played. God, the eternal dramatist, has cast you for some part in His drama, and hands you the role. It may turn out that you are cast for a triumphant king; it may be for a slave who dies in torture. What does that matter to the good actor? He can play either part; his only business is to accept the role given him, and to perform it well. Similarly, life is a game of counters. Your business is to play it in the right way. He who set the board may have given you many counters; He may have given you few. He may have arranged that, at a particular point in the game, most of your men shall be swept accidentally off the board. You will lose the game; but why should you mind that? It is your play that matters, not the score that you happen to make. He is not a fool to judge you by your mere success or failure. Success or failure is a thing He can determine without stirring a hand. It hardly interests Him. What interests Him is the one thing which he cannot determine—the action of your free and conscious will.

This view is so sublime and so stirring that at times it almost deadens one's power of criticism. Let us see how it works in a particular case. Suppose your friend is in sorrow or pain, what are you to do? In the first place, you may sympathize—since sympathy runs all through the universe, and if the stars sympathize surely you yourself may. And of course you must help. That is part of your function. Yet, all the time, while you are helping and sympathizing, are you not bound to remember that your friend's pain or sorrow does not really matter at all? He is quite mistaken in imagining that it does. Similarly, if a village in your district is threatened by a band of robbers, you will rush off with soldiers to save it; you will make every effort, you will give your life if necessary. But suppose, after all, you arrive too late, and find the inhabitants with their throats cut and the village in ruins—why should you mind? You know it does not matter a straw whether the villagers' throats are cut or not cut; all that matters is how they behaved in the hour of death. Mr Bevan, whose studies of the *Stoics and Sceptics* form a rare compound of delicate learning and historical imagination, says that the attitude of the Stoic in such a case is like that of a messenger boy sent to deliver a parcel to someone, with instructions to try various addresses in order to find him. The good messenger boy will go duly to all the addresses, but if the addressee is not to be found at any of them what does that matter to the messenger boy? He has done his duty, and the parcel itself has no interest for him. He may return and say he is sorry that the man cannot be found; but his sorrow is not heartfelt. It is only a polite pretence.

The comparison is a little hard on the Stoics. No doubt they are embarrassed at this point between the claims of high logic and of human feeling. But they meet the embarrassment bravely. 'You will suffer in your friend's suffering,' says Epictetus. 'Of course you will suffer. I do not say that you must not even groan aloud. Yet in the centre of your being do not groan! "Ἔσωθεν μέντοι μὴ στενάξῃς.' It is very like the Christian doctrine of resignation. Man cannot but suffer for his fellow-man; yet a Christian is told to accept the will of God and believe that ultimately, in some way which he does not see, the Judge of the World has done right.

Finally, what is to be the end after this life of Stoic virtue? Many religions, after basing their whole theory of conduct on stern duty and self-sacrifice and contempt for pleasure, lapse into confessing the unreality of their professions by promising the faithful as a reward that they shall be uncommonly happy in the next world. It was not that they really disdained pleasure; it was only that they speculated for a higher rate of interest at a later date. Notably, Islam is open to that criticism, and so is a great deal of popular Christianity. Stoicism is not. It maintains its ideal unchanged.

You remember that we touched, in passing, the problem of decay. Nature shapes things towards their perfection, but she also lets them fall away after reaching a certain altitude. She fails constantly, though she reaches higher and higher success. In the end, said the Stoic—and he said it not very confidently, as a suggestion rather than a dogma—in the very end, perfection should be reached, and then there will be no falling back. All the world will have been wrought up to the level of the divine soul. That soul is Fire; and into that Fire we shall all be drawn, our separate existence and the dross of our earthly nature burnt utterly away. Then there will be no more decay or growth; no pleasure, no disturbance. It may be a moment of agony, but what does agony matter? It will be ecstasy and triumph, the soul reaching its fiery union with God.

The doctrine, fine as it is, seems always to have been regarded as partly fanciful, and not accepted as an integral part of the Stoic creed. Indeed, many Stoics considered that if this Absorption in Fire should occur, it could not be final. For the essence of Goodness is to do something, to labour, to achieve some end; and if Goodness is to exist the world process must begin again. God, so to speak, cannot be good unless he is striving and helping. Phusis must be moving upward, or else it is not Phusis.

Thus Stoicism, whatever its weaknesses, fulfilled the two main demands that man makes upon his religion: it gave him armour when the world was predominantly evil, and it encouraged him forward when the world was predominantly good. It afforded guidance both for the saint and the public servant. And in developing this twofold character I think it was not influenced by mere inconstancy. It was trying to meet the actual truth of the situation. For in most systems it seems to be recognized that in the Good Life there is both an element of outward striving and an element of inward peace. There are things which we must try to attain, yet it is not really the attainment that matters; it is the seeking. And, consequently, in some sense, the real victory is with him who fought best, not with the man who happened to win. For beyond all the accidents of war, beyond the noise of armies and groans of the dying, there is the presence of some eternal Friend. It is our relation to Him that matters.

A Friend behind phenomena: I owe the phrase to Mr Bevan. It is the assumption which all religions make, and sooner or later all philosophies. The main criticism which I should be inclined to pass on Stoicism would lie here. Starting out with every intention of facing the problem of the world by hard thought and observation, resolutely excluding all appeal to tradition and mere mythology, it ends by making this tremendous assumption, that there is a beneficent purpose in the world and that the force which moves nature is akin to ourselves. If we once grant that postulate, the details of the system fall easily into place. There may be some overstatement about the worthlessness of pleasure and worldly goods; though, after all, if there is a single great purpose in the universe, and that purpose good, I think we must admit that, in comparison with it, the happiness of any individual at this moment dwindles into utter insignificance. The good, and not any pleasure or happiness, is what matters. If there is no such purpose, well, then the problem must all be stated afresh from the beginning.

A second criticism, which is passed by modern psychologists on the Stoic system, is more searching but not so dangerous. The language of Stoicism, as of all ancient philosophy, was based on a rather crude psychology. It was over-intellectualized. It paid too much attention to fully conscious and rational processes, and too little attention to the enormously larger part of human conduct which is below the level of consciousness. It saw life too much as a series of separate mental acts, and not sufficiently as a continuous ever-changing system. Yet a very little correction of statement is all that it needs. Stoicism does not really make reason into a motive force. It explains that an 'impulse', or $\dot{o}\rho\mu\dot{\eta}$, of physical or biological origin rises in the mind prompting to some action, and then Reason gives or withholds its assent (συγκατάθεσις). There is nothing seriously wrong here.

Other criticisms, based on the unreality of the ideal Wise Man, who acts without desire and makes no errors, seem to me of smaller importance. They depend chiefly on certain idioms or habits of language, which, though not really exact, convey a fairly correct meaning to those accustomed to them.

But the assumption of the Eternal Purpose stands in a different category. However much refined away, it remains a vast assumption. We may discard what Professor William James used to call 'Monarchical Deism' or our own claim to personal immortality. We may base ourselves on Evolution, whether of the Darwinian or the Bergsonian sort. But we do seem to find, not only in all religions, but in practically all philosophies, some belief that man is not quite alone in the universe, but is met in his endeavours towards the good by some external help or sympathy. We find it everywhere in the unsophisticated man. We find it in the unguarded self-revelations of the most severe and conscientious atheists. Now, the Stoics, like many other schools of thought, drew an argument from this concensus of all mankind. It was not an absolute proof of the existence of the Gods or Providence, but it was a strong indication. The existence of a common instinctive belief in the mind of man gives at least a presumption that there must be a good cause for that belief.

This is a reasonable position. There must be some such cause. But it does not follow that the only valid cause is the truth of the content of the belief. I cannot help suspecting that this is precisely one of those points on which Stoicism, in company with almost all philosophy up to the present time, has gone astray through not sufficiently realizing its dependence on the human mind as a natural biological product. For it is very important in this matter to realize that the so-called belief is not really an intellectual judgement so much as a craving of the whole nature.

It is only of very late years that psychologists have begun to realize the enormous dominion of those forces in man of which he is normally unconscious. We cannot escape as easily as these brave men dreamed from the grip of the blind powers beneath the threshold. Indeed, as I see philosophy after philosophy falling into this unproven belief in the Friend behind phenomena, as I find that I myself cannot, except for a moment and by an effort, refrain from making the same assumption, it seems to me that perhaps here too we are under the spell of a very old ineradicable instinct. We are gregarious animals; our ancestors have been such for countless ages. We cannot help looking out on the world as gregarious animals do; we see it in terms of humanity and of fellowship. Students of animals under domestication have shown us how the habits of a gregarious creature, taken away from his kind, are shaped in a thousand details by reference to the lost pack which is no longer there—the pack which a dog tries to smell his way back to all the time he is out walking, the pack he barks to for help when danger threatens. It is a strange and touching thing, this eternal hunger of the gregarious animal for the herd of friends who are not there. And it may be, it may very possibly be, that, in the matter of this Friend behind phenomena, our own yearning and our own almost ineradicable instinctive conviction, since they are certainly not founded on either reason or observation, are in origin the groping of a lonely-souled gregarious animal to find its herd or its herd-leader in the great spaces between the stars.

At any rate, it is a belief very difficult to get rid of.

CHAPTER VIII

The Conception of Another Life[1]

ALL we gregarious beings are swept along in the great stream of obvious social life. We are caught in the wheels of an enormous engine, pushed and carried by the half-conscious drift of the herd. And no doubt, as a rule, while things go entirely well with us, this is all the life we need. Yet constantly, in a man's ordinary experience, there is an undercurrent of discontent or home-sickness; a feeling that this is not our complete or ultimate life; that there is somewhere another life which is more our own and which matters more. The commonest view places it after death, but mystics and contemplatives have believed it to exist now in our own souls. In any case it is described as something peculiarly real and transcendantly important. Indeed the language used about it, and about the rewards and punishments which it carries with it, is usually so strong as to excite suspicion in the plain man. The offer of such enormous interest seems calculated to compensate for some exceptionally large element of uncertainty.

The object of the present paper is to suggest some thoughts about the history of this wide-spread conception of Another Life, and then to make some comments on its validity.

This conception, it will be seen at once, is not the same as the immortality of the soul. Either might exist without the other. Suppose, in the words of the Fourth Book of Esdras, '*The Most High hath created not one world but two*', it does not necessarily follow that one of them lasts for ever. Man might be mortal and yet have an inner life more important than his outward life. And again one might have an immortality which was shadowy and unimportant.

For example, in what we may call the classic tradition of Greek poetry there are conceptions of immortality which for our present purpose can be disregarded. In Homer as a rule there is some life beyond the grave, but it is a feebler life. The psychology is of course

[1] From the *Edinburgh Review*, 1914.

confused. At one time the man's soul still lives in his other home, but the man himself is dead on the earth, torn by dogs and birds. At another time the man himself is in Hades, but he is only part of himself. There is breath; there is a phantom shape; but something is lacking which the primitive psychologist finds it hard to describe. There are no φρένες in him—literally no midriff; or again there is no life-blood. And the dead without life-blood are flitting shadows.

Even in a document like Aeschylus's *Chöephoroe*, where the whole plot turns on the awakening of the dead, it is a very dim awakening. Agamemnon lies motionless in his grave; he can just, after due ritual, be stirred to hear the cry of his children and to drink their drink-offerings. He is stung to life for a moment by the memory of a great anger, and then sinks back into the old sleep.

These Homeric conceptions, when analysed, have been shown to correspond to two separate strata of funeral customs, burning and burial. The shadowy ghost, the thing of air, is that θυμός or *Animus* which has passed away in the smoke of the funeral pyre; the more solid earthfolk, χθόνιοι, or ἔνεροι, to whom libations are poured through holes in the ground, are the dead lying in their graves. Both worlds, of course, are influenced by dreams and memories. The dead man is conceived as still performing his characteristic actions or bearing the deathwounds which we cannot forget. Hector appears *raptatus bigis ut quondam*.

Of course, this kind of life beyond the grave can be idealized. We find it set in an ancient garden beyond all seas, at the 'springs of night and openings of Heaven'; in some region not shaken by wind or storm, far away, to be reached only by making the great leap over the Rock of Leucas and passing the ocean river to the Δῆμον Ὀνείρων, the old Land of Dreams.[1] But it is only a land of dreams; it is not a reality that reduces this present world to a dream. And it is that that we are looking for.

To find that kind of Other Life in Greek literature we must go to a different stream of tradition, a stream interrupted by gaps, known to us chiefly by allusions and not by positive statements, hard to trace to a definite authentic source, yet all the same clear and constant. In the Homeric Hymn to Demeter (l. 480) we hear of certain people who are for ever blessed, and others who are for ever deprived of their portion. If we ask who they are respectively, the answer is simple: the Initiated of Eleusis and the Uninitiated. The same conception occurs frequently in Pindar. In the Second Olympian, in practically all the θρῆνοι or Dirges—a natural place—

[1] *Odyssey* vi. 43; iv. 563; Sophocles fr. 870; *Odyssey* xxiv. 11 ff.

we hear of the infinite consequences which a man's 'holiness' or 'unholiness' brings him in the Other Life. Indeed the body, in which our present life centres, is nothing permanent; it must die. There is something else which is greater, which lives on, which is indeed the only part of man that comes really from God. It is by our ordinary standards a thing infinitely frail, αἰῶνος εἴδωλον, 'the reflection of a breath'; it sleeps while the limbs are in action, but when the noisy, restless body is once hushed it sees, or perhaps reveals, things beyond mortal sight. And hereafter, in the world beyond death, there is long peace and joy for the Blessed Heroes, for the Innocent, for those who 'have endured even thrice'—let us observe the phrase—and kept their hands free from sin. And there are others suffering . . . what? Ah, Pindar is a writer of the high classic style; he will not soil his page with the description of torments. It is only 'toil that eyes dare not look upon'.

Again and again in Plato we find this same thought; in the *Phaedo*, in the *Phaedrus*, several times in the *Republic*. It is expounded at some length in Book X. It is parodied in Aristophanes's *Frogs*, parodied in detail after detail, with a freedom of allusion which indicates it as a doctrine widely familiar. It must clearly have been so, apart from the literary evidence, because it was exhibited to all Greece at Delphi, in the famous painting of Polygnotus, which portrayed the joys of Heaven and the pains of Hell almost in the style of the Campo Santo at Pisa. References to the same conception are scattered about freely in classical literature, in Euripides, in the Speech against Aristogeiton, in the fragments of Empedocles, in the gold tablets discovered in graves at Petelia and elsewhere,[1] in quite a number of funeral inscriptions. Most of the passages are collected in Professor Dieterich's book, *Nekyia*. It is needless to examine the evidence in detail, but there is a highly significant point to be observed: wherever we meet this particular conception of an immensely important future life, involving rewards and punishments, which in modern language we could describe as Heaven and Hell, it is in every case connected with Mysteries and Initiations. Sometimes it is the Eleusinian Mysteries; often the Orphic or Pythagorean; sometimes again the allusions are simply to Dionysus or Osiris or the Satyrs, or to other initiations such as were abundant in the Greek world.

He who believes and is initiated shall be saved; he who is not

[1] These tablets are accessible in the Appendix to Miss Harrison's *Prolegomena to Greek Religion*, or in Guthrie's *Orpheus* (Cambridge 1935).

initiated shall be cast out. That is the normal rule of all exclusive religions, a rule which tends to seem natural and right to those inside and obviously preposterous to those outside. We hear of a famous jibe of Diogenes the Cynic at the idea that one Pataikion, an initiated burglar, should go to everlasting bliss while the great Epaminondas is cast into torment.[1] Of course Diogenes is right; we all agree with him. But we should realize that to the pious Orphic it probably did not seem conceivable that a man could really be initiated, and receive his initiation properly, and hold firmly all the true doctrine and perform the blessed rites, and still be a bad man. He might perhaps err or slip, fall into sin, in extreme cases even into a burglary... but his heart must after all be in the right place. Orpheus or Osiris or the Mother can purify him of his accidental errors. In any case he is far preferable to those whited sepulchres who pass as good citizens, who commit no positive crimes perhaps, but have never had the inner filth cleansed from their souls, and never given their hearts to the true God. For all practical purposes the *Amuêtos* is *Anosios*, the Uninitiated is Unholy.

And what were the Mysteries? Thirty years ago, or even less, the question would have raised a sigh of weariness. It had too often been asked fruitlessly, and sensible men had simply set it aside. Any scholar who wrote about the Mysteries was supposed to need a truss of hay on his horns. And now the question is solved and the answer known. It came partly through Mannhardt and Frazer and Spencer and Gillen. It is specially made clear by the writings of Webster and Schurtz, whose results again are well criticized in Van Gennep's *Rites de Passage*. The Mysteries are simply Initiation Ceremonies, and initiation ceremonies are a normal feature of primitive society over the greater part of the globe. The age appointed for a boy's initiation varies, and sometimes there are many successive initiations; but as a normal type we may say that initiation is a ceremony emphasizing the vital moment when a boy, παῖς, becomes a man, ἀνήρ. The novice puts away childish things and takes upon him manly things. His ἀνδρεία—his manhood—is put to the ordeal; he is instructed in the full knowledge of his elders and ancestors; he is admitted to the three great duties of a full man of the tribe—to slay the tribe's enemies, to beget the tribe's children, and last but not least to speak with full knowledge in the tribal council.

In studying these tribal initiations in detail any imaginative

[1] Plutarch, 'de audiendis poetis', p. 21 E.

student will be struck by two sides of them. There is a grotesque and ugly side, proper to the low level of culture from which they spring; and a sublime side, proper to the permanent spirit of man struggling to find its way. The initiations are in essence an emphasis, an over-emphasis, of something that in itself is true and fine. To the boy it is the dedication of himself to his life's work. He wants to be a man, a warrior, a counsellor. For that he is ready to bear ordeals of privation, pain, and terror, to face the most terrific arcana of his religion, ready even to die. For in the more complete initiations the novices are regularly supposed to be killed, to move for a time among the dead, to see gods and daemons and their own great ancestors, and afterwards, completely changed, with a new name, and a new personality, to be born again to this world.

We have seen that these conceptions of Another Life consisting of bliss and torments are, in ancient literature, always connected with the Mysteries. The writer wishes now to point out, or at least to suggest, that the mental pictures of Heaven and Hell which were current in ancient times and are still to a certain extent traditional among us, are based upon the actual ritual of the Mysteries. The scenery and arrangements, so to speak, of the other world are, in the first instance, projections of the initiation ceremonies.

The full mustering of the historical evidence on this point would need a large volume. But the point at issue can be illustrated by taking one good typical description of Heaven and Hell and showing how many of its details correspond with what we know of modern and ancient initiation rites. For instance, there is an early Christian document, which is also, as Dieterich has proved, quite in the pagan tradition, the so-called *Apocalypse of Peter*. It was found on a papyrus at Achmin and belongs to the second century. The following passages may be quoted:

The Lord said: Let us go away to the Mountain.

This is normal in initiations. The initiands are taken away from human society, often to a mountain, sometimes to a forest. Compare the Cretan and Dionysiac Oreibasiai or Mountain-Rites:

We begged him to show us one of our brethren, the righteous who have departed out of the world, that we might see what they are like in form and so bring comfort to men who hear us.

This is the normal aim or end of initiation ceremonies; cf. the accounts given in Schurtz, the hermetic documents, and especially the account given by Appuleius, Book XI, of his own initiation:

> Two men appeared to whom we were not able to raise our eyes. Radiance came from their faces like the light of the sun, and their raiment was shining, such as the eye of man has never seen.

In the Eleusinia we have definite statements that the initiands were kept in darkness, and then dazzled and half-blinded by the appearance of divine beings in a blaze of light. A similar use of darkness followed by light is attested for savage mysteries. But let us note the next point:

> The bodies of these two beings were whiter than any snow and redder than any rose. I simply cannot express their beauty. Their hair was curly and bright coloured. It glowed over their faces and shoulders, like one crown woven of spikenard and flowers of all hues, or like a rainbow in the air.

Let us realize this description. Bodies snow-white and brilliant red, and hair all the colours of the rainbow standing out like a halo. A curiously exact counterpart to these blessed beings is to be found in the divine ministers, or πρόπολοι, who accompanied the God in initiations and represented the blessed ancestors. They were painted all over with white chalk and vermilion, while their hair was made to stick out in a halo, and was interwoven with ribbons and dyed grasses and brilliant objects of every colour. The evidence for the white and red is clear both for ancient and modern times. The hair is to be seen in any good collection of Papuan, Australian, or Polynesian photographs.

It is explained to Peter that these are the Righteous Departed; he asks where they live, and is shown

> a great place outside this world, shining with light, the soil of it blooming with immortal blossoms, and full of perfumes and sweet-smelling flowers. ... The fragrance was so great that it was borne across even to this world.

This heaven seems like the region of light in which the divine beings appeared at the Eleusinia and in Appuleius's initiation. We may notice also the emphasis laid upon the sweet smells. Novices in initiations regularly pass through evil regions of darkness and foul smells and emerge into a heaven of light and fragrance. For the hierophant or stage-manager, if we may use such a word, the perfumes formed a comparatively easy and safe side of the revelation; easier certainly than the light and darkness.

And how were these blessed beings employed? The pseudo-Peter does not dwell on the point so long as some other Apocalyptists, but he speaks no less clearly. Just like the ministers of Dionysus or Isis or Mithras, or the Australian Durramulun, they were with one voice singing hymns to the glory of their god. The point, though so familiar, is instructive. This eternal hymn-singing has often been the subject of jokes: it strikes the outsider as odd and monotonous, but if we refer it to the ceremony from which it arose it is natural enough. Our savage stage-manager, who has to produce a brief and dazzling vision of the Blessed surrounding the Mystery of God, naturally accompanies his blaze of light and perfume with a blaze of song. The awkwardness, if it is one, arises only when the song is made everlasting, when the outburst of one dazzling moment is transformed into a normal employment for the whole of life.

After this the pseudo-Peter passes to the description of hell. The first note struck is that of filth, the second darkness; then came tormenting angels in dark raiment. Especially prominent is the lake of mud, of mud and fire, of indescribable filth and blood and putrefaction, which recurs in slightly different forms again and again. The wicked are plunged in it, to varying depths, head first or otherwise.

The mire and filth of Hades are emphasized by Plato and Aristophanes and others, and the source of the conception is clear. Mud and filth were used in ancient initiation ordeals and purifications; and 'immersion in dust and filth' is given by Webster as one of the commonest ordeals in savage initiation ceremonies. There is no need to prove this point in detail. But it is worth remembering that a pious savage's feeling about dirt is probably very different from ours. To us dirt is no doubt a highly disagreeable thing, but it is purely temporary and superficial, to be removed by a wash or a rinse. To the savage any dirt really worthy of the name is a thing of religious horror, polluting to the soul and unpurgeable. Mr Edwyn Bevan has published an interesting story of the unspeakable horror produced in the mind of a pious Brahman by the English habit of using a toothbrush; to put every day into one's mouth—actually one's mouth!—the bone of a dog covered with the bristles of a pig . . . his imagination reeled at the wanton loathsomeness.

So much for the mire. It is naturally in a pit or depression of some kind. In many initiations the novices have to go down into a pit or chasm. In Crete and elsewhere they descended into a cave; in the rites of Trophonius into an artificial chasm, where they presently lost consciousness.

Some of Peter's sufferers were in a pit full of snakes. There were snakes in the pit of Trophonius, and snakes were largely used in the Bacchic rites. They naturally bit the wicked and caressed the initiated. The evidence on this point is abundant for ancient times, and we may compare the well-known snake dances of the Hopi and other Indians.

Other sufferers are scourged by daemons. Scourging is normal in ancient hells and ancient initiation ceremonies; we think of the celebrated ordeal at the altar of Artemis Orthia. The scourging of Australian and African rites is apt to be performed by disguised daemons or spirits of the dead.

Others of Peter's victims scourge one another. One remembers the battles of youths which form a well-known ritual in ancient times, but it is not easy to find this particular variety of ordeal in an actual initiation ceremony. The present writer, however, has heard of a case where two Navajos, who wished to expiate their sins by scourging, found it more satisfactory to hit one another than for each to hit himself.

Others are tormented in various ways with fire and fire-brands. Ordeals of fire are, of course, common. In Australasian initiations great use is made of burning sticks to terrify or torment the novices. The Erinyes habitually carried firebrands. Dionysus in one of his mystic epiphanies came as fire, and so did divers other gods. This fire, as we might expect, followed the example of the snakes: it burnt the wicked and spared the initiated, as Euripides has described in the *Bacchae*.

Other offenders are thrown over precipices, picked up at the bottom and thrown over again, and so on for ever. This form of torment is a little puzzling. To make a guilty man leap over a rock into the sea was a fairly common ritual in Greece for expiating a crime or purifying a community. Normally the leaper had his chance of swimming, and one does not hear of his being thrown over again. Precipitation was also a regular form of ritual execution; we think at once of the Barathron and the Tarpeian Rock, and especially of the Rock of Leucas, which became a mystical synonym for death. It is beyond that rock that Homer's world of the dead begins. And it may be that this form of torment was taken not from an initiation rite, but simply from a form of legal punishment. In initiations you could not, unless in very exceptional circumstances, afford to throw your novices over a real precipice. Yet a question arises in one's mind whether the tragic hoax played on Gloucester in *King Lear* has perhaps some ritual tradition behind it. Was it possibly an ordeal in some initiations to set the novice, blindfold or in the dark, on the top of some harmless little bank, tell him that he was on the edge of an awful precipice and order him to throw himself over? From all one reads of the dazed and half-insane condition in which the novices emerge from their ordeals, it would probably be easier to play this trick on them than it was on Gloucester.

The Apocalypse of Peter is fragmentary, and perhaps that is the reason why it lacks many of the regular characteristics of apocalyptic hells and heavens. There is no tremendous Voice such as we find in other apocalypses, in Bacchic initiations and all the mysteries, ancient and modern, in which a part is played by the bull-roarer.[1] There is no mention of that Cup of Cold Water which alleviates the anguish of parching souls in many Orphic and Osirian prayers, or that 'light place with a fountain of water in the midst of it' which figures, for instance, in the book of Enoch (cap. xxii). Neither is there any torment by poison. Generally there are furies or similar beings holding cups of torment or of maddening philtres, or at least of Lethe. Such drugs are a regular feature of savage initiations. 'They give them pellitory bark and several intoxicating plants,' says Lawson of the Tuscarora Indians,[2] 'which make them go raving mad as ever were any people in the world; and you may hear them make the most dismal and hellish cries and howlings that ever human creature expressed.'

It is hardly necessary to press the detailed evidence further. A student who compares the ancient conceptions of Hell and Heaven, at any rate as expressed in all the Graeco-Christian tradition—the Jewish apocalypses are greatly influenced by other historical considerations—can hardly fail to see that they are intimately modelled on the Initiation Ritual—the Ordeal, the Vision, and the Re-birth. That is to say, Heaven is not primarily modelled on the palace, nor Hell on the torture chamber. In later times this statement would need qualifications. As the early Christians were persecuted they naturally began to hate their persecutors, and sometimes reshaped their conceptions of the future so as to satisfy that hatred. Some hells did become, in all probability, mainly projections of the torture chamber, mere orgies of unsatisfied passion. There is much of this

[1] See *Themis*, by J. E. Harrison, pp. 61–66.
[2] *History of Carolina*, pp. 380-382, quoted by Webster, *Primitive Secret Societies* (New York, 1908), p. 33, cf. ibid., p. 57, on the drinking of *wysoccan* = λήθη.

in the pseudo-Peter. There grew to be more passion in both the hells and the heavens, a passion of frantic hatred against the persecutor, a passion of pity and revenge for the oppressed innocent. But, apart from such disturbing elements, the normal conception of Another Life after death has in pagan and Christian tradition been modelled on the experience of the novice or devotee in the initiation ceremony.

Let us now think again of these initiations as they presented themselves to the mind of a believer. Let us forget the chalk and vermilion the bull-roarers and the patent frauds, the cruelties and absurdities. Let us take for guidance the dozen or so expressions of enthusiastic faith and gratitude towards the Mysteries that have come down to us from Greek times, and the fairly abundant evidence from Australia and North America which shows that the same enthusiasm and devotion are still evoked in our own day. What does the novice feel? He is faced with the great moment of his life, the ordeal which is to decide whether or no he is to become that greatest of things, a Man. (We omit for simplicity's sake all reference to female initiations, which were on the whole less prominent.) There is almost no bait of pleasure held out to the boy. Nothing but service and duty and self-respect. Everything that he has learned to admire is summed up in the achievement of manhood. A man must have perfect courage, true knowledge, and—in the sense in which he understands it—complete purity. All our modern witnesses express amazement at the endurance with which the Red Indian boys, without uttering a cry or moving a muscle, submit to be flogged almost to death, burned, mutilated, swung on hooks till the flesh breaks, and the like. And not only Red Indians, who are always brave, but Polynesians and Negroes and Australians. These physical ordeals are enough to stagger us; but one must suspect that ordeals of hunger and thirst, of the madness produced by strange drugs, of the ineffable terrors of the supernatural which they are compelled to face, are probably even a greater strain on the young men's constancy.

And we can see the meaning of it. It too is over-emphasis. The important thing in life for each of these boys is to become a man and all that a man should be. Now, as a matter of fact, becoming a man is a gradual process; in the full sense of the words it is a process which is being achieved, or not achieved, during the whole of life. This length, slowness, uncertainty, is just what puzzles and exasperates the natural human being in us. We want to get it over. 'Give it us now,' we cry: 'pile on all the ordeals, all the terrors and temptations, in one mass and let us face them now, now: let us either be men once for all, or else be consumed with fire or left rotting in the pit.' The experience of initiation thus acquires an enormous, a practically eternal significance.

In another way also this significance is deepened. All initiation ceremonies seem, if they last on, to pass through two stages. First, they are universally practised through the whole of a homogeneous tribe; next, after migrations, invasions, mixtures of races, and the like, they become the mark and property of a special society, a Church, as it were—usually more or less secret.

Initiations are only for the faithful; the higher initiation is only for those who have passed through the lower. We hear of three grades: we hear of seven. Now, let us think of an early Christian, or, better perhaps, of a faithful adherent of any of the ancient Mystery Religions. They all lived in a wrecked or hostile world. 'Zion hath been taken from us: we have nothing now save the Mighty One and His Law.' The Jews themselves were rather averse from mysteries; but these words of Baruch express the feeling of many ruined and bewildered nations.[1] Greek or Egyptian or Syrian or Anatolian, the mystery devotee was living in a great callous world of foreign soldiers and traders and governors and *publicani*, a world in which he seemed to be born an exile and hardly understood the language in which he was plundered or governed. Would he not feel that his true life, the life that mattered and enabled him to feel that he truly lived, was that which he passed among his fellow-believers? Out in the market-place he could not speak of the things for which he cared most. Neighbours might be civil or uncivil, magistrates and soldiers honest or dishonest; they could only touch the outside of him. At night, in his own θίασος, he could meet those who felt with him and had the same needs as he. He spoke their language. He was rapt with them into the same ecstasies. He could read in their eyes a history like his own. They had laboured under the same burden of sin, had conceived the same hope, and attained the same deliverance. Here and there, doubtless, would be one who had achieved the human soul's ultimate adventure and been for some single infinite instant united to the living God. This, it is easy to see, would be to such a man the true life; and this is the life that would be projected by his imagination into eternity: an eternity in which every experience would be intensified; an eternity in which these tyrannous outsiders, these Roman magistrates and hard men of the world and committers of impurity, would be put to the ordeals and

---

[1] Apocalypse of Baruch 85, 3: quoted by Burkitt, *Jewish and Christian Apocalypses* (1914).

fail. How they would fail! Miserably, inevitably; from their bestial ignorance, their manifold defilements, their lack of any true Helper and Saviour, as well as their obvious deficiency in all finer qualities. Doubtless they would get through in time: after a thousand years, perhaps, or ten thousand or thirty thousand . . . at least all except the really bad ones. Hell proper is generally reserved, as Peter's Apocalypse vividly shows us, for those who have committed sins against the Church itself—apostates, betrayers, persecutors, and hostile witnesses.

Thus the initiated have a true life of their own in this world, which is further strengthened by being projected into an imagined eternity.

Suppose now a man of more critical temper, a Jew, for instance, who is content to wrap himself in the Law, or—more instructive for our purpose—a Greek philosopher: one who does not believe the fables of the underworld nor yet the half-mad doctrines of the mystery-mongers. He does not yield himself up to 'projections'. He is severely anxious to keep to the seen and proven fact. Yet he will not go without his Other Life. Where is he to find it?

Stoic and Epicurean, the two poles of Greek philosophy, agree. The true life of man, the life that matters, is within. It is the life of the soul. The outer worldly life is real enough—the philosopher does not pretend that it is a mere dream or Maya—but it is of no consequence. The Stoic doctrine, as explained elsewhere in this book, is quite clear on this point. Life is like a play acted or a game played with counters. The play is only make-believe. The counters have no value: it matters not who wins or loses. All that matters is that the play should be acted well, the game played as it should be played. God is the judge and does not go by outward results. What interests Him is the one thing which He cannot determine, the action of your free will.

It is quite simple. Act one way and you are a good thing; another, and you are a bad thing; and to be good or bad is heaven or hell. In this region of the free will lies the life that is your own, your true heaven, quite other than the obvious life, independent of it, untouched by it. For even Epicurus himself has confessed that the Good Man will be happy on the rack. Even the average unregenerate man confesses it in his heart. Give him the choice in his calm moments, while his nerves are still firm, to be either the martyr or the tyrant who tortures him; he will choose the martyr.

Fascinating, triumphant, almost irresistible, this great Stoic gospel seems at first sight to have rejected all mythology, all bribes and threats and dreams, and to have opened up a vision of the meaning of life as true as it is noble. But it is not so. This imaginary blessedness of the Wise Man, blessedness impervious to the shocks of fortune, to the pain of oneself or others, to the praise or blame, the love or hate, of all one's associates and fellow-creatures, is almost as deep a dream, almost as violent an over-emphasis, as the Elysium or Tartarus of the vulgar. The Stoics could see that the furies with their burning torches were only metaphors to denote a tormented mind. They tried hard to face the facts of life, to invent no fancied eternal recompense for the good or punishment for the evil, but to leave virtue strictly its own reward. They made the attempt with wonderful self-restraint, but the effort was too great for them. They cared so intensely about the matters at issue that they could not help over-emphasizing what they considered most important. And the passion of their over-emphasis almost created for itself a new mythology.

But apart from that, apart from the mere element of exaggeration in the Stoic conception of this inward untroubled life which belongs for ever to the righteous and the innocent, we may raise the question whether it was in its main direction a good ideal. It is a good thing that we should accustom ourselves to feel, when we are cast down or disgusted by ordinary realities, that there is in our possession Another Life, more or less independent of the great stream, which matters infinitely more?

A strong case can be made against it, especially in these days when social duties are so much more valued then private virtues. Man is born a member of some society; his whole being is a network of intimate relations, of attractions and repulsions, helpings and hinderings, from which it is neither possible nor desirable that he should cut himself free. His relations to his fellow-men form, in normal circumstances, far the greater part of his happiness or unhappiness, even of his self-respect or his despair. For the most personal of all things, a man's own conscience, is mostly formed for him by other people. Anyone who tries first fully to realize the biological fact that man is a gregarious animal, and then, by an effort of introspection, to realize the infinitely complex stream of aims and impulses and affections on which he moves, must, it would seem, answer the Stoic claim with a definite rejection: Here or nowhere is man's true life; not in any imagined heaven, not in the rituals or dreams of any exclusive society; not even in the supposed calm of that treacherous fortress, a man's own soul.

And yet, on the other side, the voices of nearly all the saints and sages call to us in warning that this present obvious life cannot be all in all. For one thing the judgements of the herd are almost always wrong in value. If they do not often call bad things directly good and good bad, they constantly think cheap things precious and fine things unimportant. Everyone who cares at all for truth needs some court of appeal from the mere judgement of the world. The appeal will take various shapes and directions; but in the last analysis, when stripped of all its disguises, it will generally be an appeal exactly like that of the Stoics or of the seventeenth-century Quakers, from the world to oneself, from the now and here outwardly prevailing judgement to the judgement of one's inmost mind. One need not say that it is only that, much less that it is consciously that. In practice, for one thing, a man is hardly ever quite alone. He has his friends, his fellow-workers, his Church. They, in so far as they really support him, help to build up that Other Life whose canons are greater than the canons of the world. And, even when a man is quite alone, he generally feels himself to be appealing to some unknown friend, to the judgement of posterity, or to a righteous God. He projects another society to counterbalance the society which he has rejected; for a gregarious animal cannot be alone in heaven. But always he himself is the centre and pivot of this higher society of his own creating. It never really gives its verdict against him. If it did, it would have gone over to the enemy and would cease to be heaven. Its function is to fortify the man's own soul and enable him to defy his environment. The Stoic was so far right. There is another tribunal; and it is, ultimately, the tribunal of a man's own soul.

And not only a tribunal but also a refuge. The Stoic saw that too. Man must retire to that same inner region when he is strained and buffeted by the outer life, and needs peace or strengthening. For experience seems to show that those who have loved their kind most effectively have needed some refuge in which to be free from them. In order to help men you must be able to defy them. In order to give them the best you can, you must needs have within you something better, or at least more intimate, which you cannot give them. For how can you help and understand a man unless you are a separate and different person from him, standing on your own feet? And this is true not only of the selected Wise Man, described by Plato in words which at every turn are borrowed from the Mysteries, who deliberately descends into the cave to help his weaker brethren. It is true, in some degree, of every human being. We are, after all, individuals as well as members of a community. We are all, when a certain limit is passed, strangers one to another. There is a region in each of us where no other can penetrate; and every man is alone in his highest thoughts as every man is alone when he dies.

We are accustomed to treat this fact as something hard or piteous, a kind of horror in the background of life. Yet perhaps such a judgement is wrong. It is not a horror. It is only a necessary condition of social living, that we are individuals as well as members of a social whole. And it seems to be this nucleus of fact which lies at the root of most of the wide-spreading dreams that we have been dealing with. It is this truth, that the whole of our life cannot be contained by any human society but some part of the soul must be always alone—this truth so austere, so frail, a thing which we can so easily forget and which must never be forgotten—that has caused so much passionate dreaming and equally passionate denial. It has been overemphasized in divers ways in different ages of history; set up as an ideal in contemplative societies; more enthusiastically glorified and concentrated in world-wide mysteries and initiations; projected beyond the bounds of the physical world in dreams of some ultimate perfect acceptance or utter rejection, some everlasting home or eternal exile. The truth itself, if properly understood, ought of course to be sufficient motive for good action; but man is slow, and likes his motives for good over-emphasized and made tremendous before he will stir.

There is, then, another tribunal to which we can appeal from the world's judgement; there is another life in which we can find some refuge. And doubtless, if we must have one of the tribunals against us, it is better that it should be the loud and violent outside tribunal with all its harsh sanctions, not the intimate and silent one which exercises no sanctions but permits of no escape. But the advocates of this Other Life must not promise too much. They must not speak to us of regions of light and truth made perfect, nor of fields unshaken by snow and tempest where joy grows like a tree. Our tribunal is not perfect; it only tries to see and to do right. Our refuge promises no eternal bliss. It gives only a rallying-point, a spell of peace in which to breathe and to think, a sense not exactly of happiness, but of that patience and courage which form at least a good working substitute for happiness. For real full-blooded happiness, as for any satisfaction of our complete natures, we are thrown for good and evil on the realities of the outer social life and the turbid mercies of our fellow-men.

CHAPTER IX

What is Permanent in Positivism[1]

AUGUSTE COMTE was actually born in the eighteenth century, and there is a touch of the eighteenth century in his thinking. By the time of his death in 1857 his influence was immense upon all progressive European thought. Nowadays he is awarded a very small place in most histories of philosophy, and the Church or organized body of teachers which he founded, once so brilliant and influential, may almost be described as moribund. Such neglect seems a sign of complete failure; but in reality it is due almost as much to the general acceptance of his main doctrines as to their rejection. No doubt he was overbold. He attempted to build a complete and final system of philosophy based upon all the sciences. Necessarily any such system was conditioned by the state of science at the time, by the social environment of post-Revolutionary France in which he lived, by the traditions of Catholicism by which he was surrounded. As the conditions have changed the system has ceased to fit. Also, the era of hope and confidence into which he was born, and which made the creation of his system possible, was succeeded by an age of mistrust in which scientists were shy of all wide principles and generalizations, and took refuge in their separate specialisms. The specialists had been his chief enemies in his lifetime and they triumphed over him after his death. Again, the two opposing armies of Faith and Science, whom he sought to reconcile, and who seemed in many ways to be approaching one another in the nineteenth century, seem now to have lost any particular desire to be reconciled. The Catholic Church holds as firmly as ever that it possesses the monopoly of truth, subject to no progressive reinterpretation. 'That meaning of the sacred dogmas is to be perpetually retained which our Holy Mother, the Church, has once declared.'[2] And the post-war sceptic on his side has no particular desire to reinterpret dogmas which have ceased to interest him.

[1] Annual Comte Lecture, 1939.
[2] Judgement on Dr Mivart: Bridges, *Illustrations of Positivism*, 1907, p. 126.

Yet Comte was a very great figure in the history of thought, and Positivism remains a great coherent statement, imperfect indeed and showing signs of its period, of certain permanent and all-important truths.

One reason why Comte seems so often to have been superseded is that he often anticipated later thought or knowledge. Pioneers are always superseded. Otherwise they would not be pioneers. His three stages—Theological, Metaphysical, Positive—differently phrased and subdivided, have become a commonplace of history and anthropology. His *nisus conativus*, taken presumably from Leibniz, has become Bergson's *élan vital*. The word and the idea of 'sociology' as a science, a conception destined to bear such abundant and ever-increasing fruit, were his invention.[1] He proved from the biological researches of Gall and others that unselfishness was not a miracle produced by divine grace in the selfish animal man; on the contrary, there were in man's nature not merely egoistic instincts concerned with self-preservation or the good of the *Ego*, but also social instincts concerned with the good or preservation of others, of '*autrui*'; and to describe them he invented the important word 'altruism'. It was he, following no doubt in the tracks of Montesquieu and others, who emphasized the growth of one civilization out of another, using the word 'filiation', which in the form 'affiliation' plays so large a part in, for instance, Mr Toynbee's *Study of History*. It was perhaps a touch of prophetic foresight that made him long for that Society of Civilized Nations which he called 'The Republic of the West', and expect a great renaissance in China with effects reverberating through the world. Among other views of his which roused the opposition of J. S. Mill and other generally sympathetic contemporaries, but would find more support now among thinkers who are called progressive, were his insistence on the difference rather than the equality of Man and Woman; on the abundant faults and weaknesses of Democracy; and on Man's need for a Church and a system of prayer and worship, though not for a personal God.

This after all was his main problem. I will try to formulate it in the way that seems to me most intelligible.

Man is surrounded by unknown forces of infinite extent and almost infinite power. It is man's consciousness of these forces, or, shall we say, of the infinite extent of the Unknown compared with the small sphere of Knowledge in which we live, that constitutes the attitude towards life which we call a religious attitude. A man who

[1] In 1837. The word was adopted by J. S. Mill and Spencer, who had both been groping towards the idea.

never thinks at all about the Unknown but is confident that outside his approved range of knowledge there is nothing, or at least nothing that matters, is clearly without Religion; I conclude therefore that he is equally without religion whether his approved range is the *Encyclopaedia Britannica* or the dogmas of some infallible Church. To be cock-sure is to be without religion. The essence of religion is the consciousness of a vast unknown. Call it Faith or call it Doubt: they are two sides of the same medal.

The most obvious reaction towards this vast unknown is Fear. *Primus in orbe deos fecit timor.* The more man is exposed to the action of the unknown the greater is his fear of it. Primitive man is helpless and therefore superstitious. Society, as it becomes civilized, is always protecting itself. Civilization consists largely in a process of building or extending the walls round that little island of space, that City or Fatherland, in which life is known and friendly, in order to keep off the infinite unfriendly and unknown that is outside. Hence the rigidity of custom, the fixed pattern of life, usual in primitive societies, and due to the omnipresent fear of that which is unknown, unaccustomed, unintelligible. Hence the superstition that grows in times of danger and dies down when life seems safe and the world kind.

How does man represent these forces to himself? Naturally, inevitably, his thinking is conditioned by his human nature. It is anthropomorphic in the fullest sense, including that for which Mill coined the awkward word 'anthropophuism'. It sees everything in human terms. The old saying of Xenophanes, that if cattle or lions could picture the gods they would make them like cattle or lions, is more than superficially true. If man sometimes makes his gods in non-human form, in animal form like the Egyptians, in pillar or tree form like the Minoans, that does not alter the main fact of anthropomorphism; for the worshipper thinks of the animal or the pillar as having the same feelings as himself. He fears its anger; he appeases it with gifts, he cajoles it with compliments, avoids stirring its jealousy, and the like.

There is no essential difference here between what Comte calls 'fetichism' and Dr Marett 'animatism' on the one hand, and ordinary polytheism on the other. Either the non-human object feared behaves like a man, or, if for some reason that conception strikes the worshippers as improbable, there is a more definitely anthropoid being connected with the object. If the torrent or the thunderbolt is not actually alive and angry, then an angry being in the background has swollen the torrent or thrown the thunderbolt. Man thinks in this way because he cannot help it. His gods see, hear, smell, touch, with human senses; are pleased and displeased, kind and hostile, just as men are. They are, though superhuman, human in nature. Mostly they are thought of as Fathers or members of the tribe and therefore on the whole as friends, but subject unfortunately to the most unpredictable impulses.

Man thinks anthropomorphically because he cannot help it. For the rest, most of his thinking is determined, in the general absence of other evidence, by his wishes and fears. The proportion between them depends, it would seem, mainly on the degree of security a particular society has attained. When insecure, a man is haunted by fears, and thinks of his gods as constantly needing propitiation. Sailors are traditionally superstitious, but have become much less so since the invention of large steamers has made them less dependent on the unknown. So are soldiers in wartime; so are refugees and the like. As life becomes safe, fears dwindle and wishes predominate. We wish never to die; we wish to have for ourselves and our own community, who are of course our friends and good, a life of eternal happiness; so we create Heaven. The bad, the uninitiated especially, those who have persecuted and wronged our friends and us, must be repaid in their own coin. For them there is Hell—a conception dependent originally on membership or non-membership of a sacred society, but kept alive by the wish for vengeance. A persecuted generation revels in the thought of the torments in store for its persecutors, as one sees from the various Apocalypses.[1]

That is the crude raw material of most religious belief. It soon passes into something more disinterested, more in accord with the higher development of human society. Man longs for something like Heaven and Hell to correct the intolerable injustices of this mortal world. Dante must have meant something when he spoke of Hell as created by

La somma sapienza e il primo amore.

Horrid as the paradox is, one can understand that man's natural sense of justice, maddened by the oppressions of the innocent, craves not merely that the innocent should be comforted but also that the oppressor should suffer. If we set aside the traditional though immoral claim of various organized Churches that Hell is the correct punishment for non-membership of their body, one can see that, apart from the direct desire for revenge on the persecutor, that

[1] See p. 158, ff.

passionate and disinterested sense of justice which lies near the foundation of society tends to create some 'bright reversion in the sky' for the wrongs of mankind. I suspect it is this craving, carried to higher and subtler forms, which finds vent in books like the *Imitatio Christi* and the mystic dogmas or speculations of various creeds.

Here again, as in all the realm of wish-thinking, the lower and more selfish forms of wish tend to creep in, like weeds, into the garden of the ideal. We long for some higher law to set right the wrongs of the world. Yet, after all, do we really want all our own offences to be punished as they deserve? As Dr Freud has pointed out, our attitude towards the Law, civil or moral, is always 'ambivalent'. We love it and uphold it as maintaining the wish or conscience of Society against wicked law-breakers who may do wrong to us and our community; but we feel, in our own exceptional case, a conscious or subconscious desire sometimes to escape from it. The gods, being human, can be got at, propitiated, persuaded. From the earliest times to the latest, special societies like the Orphics, the Brahmins, the Catholic Church, provide guaranteed processes of initiation, baptism, purification, absolution, by which to evade the due penalty for our offences.

A third characteristic of religious thought is its emotional quality, due, apparently, to a subconscious recognition that its most cherished doctrines are really mere wish-beliefs, not facts proved or provable, but hopes without which we cannot be happy. The craving for certainty where all is uncertain betrays itself by passionate and continual over-emphasis. Genuine intellectual certainty is generally serene; it does not seek to kill or burn those who differ from it in opinion.

It is not necessary to follow in any detail the course of criticism to which these anthropomorphic conceptions have been continually subjected from the time of Xenophanes onward. His splendid rejection of anthropomorphism as regards the outward form of the gods, or, as he preferred to say, of God, affected most Greek philosophic thought afterwards; but it is worth noting that, in spite of all his efforts, his dehumanized spherical God, though it has no eyes or ears or brain, but 'sees, hears, and thinks with its whole being', nevertheless does 'see, hear, and think'—which are, after all, human activities. So difficult is it to dehumanize our thought. Cicero ridicules the belief in *barbatum Iovem, galeatam Minervam* (*Nat. De.* 36). He recognizes that the visions in which various people have seen Jupiter with a beard or Minerva with a helmet are purely subjective, and have shown the divine being in the shape laid down by the social tradition. It was only a step further to see that the same social tradition was responsible not merely for the beard and the helmet, but for Jupiter and Minerva themselves. Being surrounded by unknown forces and seeking somehow to be on terms with them, Man made God in his own image. Throughout the whole process two influences are co-operating, which we may call man-thinking and wish-thinking. Man cannot help—at least not without extraordinary mental effort—thinking in human terms. The unknown forces which help and hinder him can only be thought of as moved by the motives and using the methods and instruments that he knows. And secondly, the thing that in his loneliness he wishes most is that some great Man, like himself but infinitely stronger, speaking his language and sharing his feelings of right and wrong, his friendships and his hatreds, should guide and protect his enterprises. The fishermen of the Greek islands liked to think of a Great Fisherman armed like themselves with a trident or fish-spear, presiding over their boats: so they created Poseidon. But, even if they could get free from their wishes, they could scarcely have conceived of their God in any other form. The form was dictated by the social tradition.

A very simple but attractive application of this principle was made by Freud in his book, *The Future of an Illusion*. The chief god of polytheists, the sole god of monotheists, is habitually called 'Father', a plain projection of the human father or patriarch. The father in a simple patriarchal society has two main functions; abroad he is the protector of his family against enemies, at home he is the judge and punisher of the disobedient. He is thus both loved and feared. This relation is not merely primitive, it is pre-human. When a herd of gregarious animals, such as deer or cattle, is threatened by danger, they form up to meet it, the leader or patriarch in the front centre, the young bulls beside him, the cows behind, and the young calves well covered in the middle of the ring. There the patriarch is the protector; a very present help in trouble. But he is also a terror to the rebellious or disobedient if any younger bull disputes his rule.

The chief God is a Father, but he is also a King. And in Europe, since our religious literature comes almost entirely from Oriental sources, he is a King of the despotic Oriental type. The conception of God in the Old Testament shows several strands of influence. Like an earthly pastoral king he has tribute paid to him which is a pastoral tribute, the 'first-born of every flock'; and, as on earth, the first-born can be redeemed. Like the Assyrian and Babylonian Kings in the British Museum he requires praise, continual praise, praise in all its forms; and, if the praise ever strikes him as insufficient, there is trouble for those responsible. He is jealous in the extreme, and likes constantly to dwell upon the fact: 'I the Lord, thy God, am a jealous God' grows into 'Jehovah whose name is Jealous' (Exod. xxxiv. 14), the 'name' standing for the essential nature. His jealousy is directed against other similar potentates, the gods of other nations in the neighbourhood. They are all his enemies, and woe betide anyone who speaks well of them. His people are to 'destroy their altars, break their images, cut down their groves' (ibid., 13). Any respect paid to them will be punished by utter destruction (Deut. iv. 26); Jehovah's jealousy will not be appeased until the third and fourth generation (Deut. v. 9). The land of such an offender will be sown with salt and brimstone (Deut. xxix. 23), so that it shall never bear fruit again—just as enemy land was treated by the Mesopotamian tyrants in their worst anger. And observe, though certain moral and legal offences are properly condemned in the Laws, the sin which above all others rouses Jehovah is Disobedience to him, or attention to other gods. For that, and for almost nothing else, he 'smites': indeed, the variety and ferocity of his smiting as detailed in Cruden's *Concordance*, would do credit to the most ferocious of Oriental despots.[1] On the other hand, his mercy or bounty is on the same great scale as that of Haroun al-Raschid or Suleiman the Magnificent; though apparently any absence of punishment counts as mercy because, being above the Law and having every right to smite his subjects as he pleases, he may well claim that it is kind of him not to smite them. I take these passages not for the purpose of ridiculing the magnificent records of ancient Israel, but to show how the Hebrews conceived of the unknown forces of the world as controlled by an anthropomorphic being, and how, further, they pictured that being partly in the guise of a pastoral patriarch and partly as a king of Babylon—only more formidable. The late Professor Kennett, one might add, has shown in a most interesting way how Jehovah has been affected by the sojourn of Israel in the desert. He has no consort; he is not concerned with fertility or interested in agriculture, but makes up for the vices which he is thereby spared by his arid and torrid severity. His extreme jealousy of the Baalim is

[1] He smites the knees, the legs, the loins; he smites the 'land of Egypt', smites 'all the first-born', smites 'every living thing'; he smites with frogs, pestilence, consumption, fever, botch, scab, blindness, madness, great plague, and a general curse.

explained by the fact that his chosen people when they came out of the desert and settled down to agricultural life were inevitably much tempted to practise the normal agricultural ceremonies. It would be curious to study the influence which this idea of the pastoral patriarch *plus* the Oriental despot still exercises over the imagination of Protestant Christendom.

It is perhaps this conception of God as an Oriental tyrant which gives rise in so many religions to the need of some kinder and more human being to mediate and intercede. In earthly despotisms it is usual, it is almost a necessity, that those who wish to make a request of the King should first make favour with some powerful subordinate who has access to him. It was a risky business to do so in person. When Pythios the Lydian, relying on promises of royal favour, asked Xerxes that his eldest son, instead of marching on Greece, might be left behind in Asia to comfort him, Xerxes granted the request by cutting the said son into two halves and leaving them. The mediator required is sometimes a woman, like Esther with Darius or Mme de Maintenon with Louis XIV; sometimes a being like the Faithful Son of Babylonian religious art. Christianity in its Catholic form looks chiefly to the Virgin, in its Evangelical form to Jesus, as the eternal mediator between us common men and the 'just wrath' of this formidable potentate.

One of the most striking differences between mediaeval and modern Christianity can be explained in the same way. God is the eternal judge. A mediaeval law court relied greatly on torture. Apart from man's natural enjoyment of cruelty, mediaeval society tried to make up for the inefficiency of its police system by extreme ferocity against those offenders whom it was able to catch. To strike terror was the duty and privilege of the earthly judge. The eternal judge must do the same and do it even better. He must apply eternal tortures, and of a kind far surpassing the puny efforts of earthly racks or flames. The modern world, on the other hand, has abolished torture, and regards the infliction of it by law as an abomination. Consequently, in spite of very explicit tests and an immense weight of uncontested tradition, modern civilized societies have either abolished Hell altogether or reformed it into something so metaphorical that it does not horrify the average conscience. I am disposed to think that one important element in this change of social psychology was the discovery of anaesthetics. Violent pain used, till lately, to be a normal element in human life: a thing to be shrieked over by the victim, commiserated or laughed at according to circumstances by the spectators, but never a strange unnecessary horror which ought to be entirely removed. Certainly some vast social change seems necessary to explain the distance we have moved from the state of mind indicated by certain well known and hideous phrases in Dante, Thomas Aquinas, and even Augustine.

It will be observed that in all this list, which could be extended indefinitely, of changes in the conceptions man has formed of the God or gods of his worship, he never really gets away from either his man-thinking or his wish-thinking. In our own day it seems to me that both are being re-emphasized. The ordinary Christian apologist has almost forgotten to argue that his creed is true; he concentrates so exclusively on arguing that it is a comfort, a source of good life, a psychological necessity: in fact that the only way to be happy is to believe it, or perhaps not so much to believe it, but to accept and act upon it. That is confessedly wish-thinking. And at the same time there is a revival of extreme man-thinking in reaction against the impersonal theisms of philosophers like Green and Bradley, Kant and Spinoza. Emphasis is laid, not merely in evangelical circles but much more widely, on the worship of the man-god Jesus and the intimate personal relation which his worshippers claim to have established with him as with a human friend.

Is it possible to rid ourselves of these two weaknesses, man-thinking and wish-thinking, and yet retain any effective conception of God? I doubt it. A certain Arab mystic has made the trenchant criticism that to call God 'righteous' implies just as profound anthropomorphism as to say that he has a beard. 'He is just', 'He is merciful', 'He is long-suffering', 'He loves mankind' ... all such phrases apply to God human qualities and human ways of behaviour. Take them away, and you are left with some purely abstract residuum, indescribable and inconceivable: not even a Reason or an Intelligence or a Purpose, for each of these is essentially a human thing, an attribute of a limited being who has to think, plan and take pains. I see no escape from the conclusion that if you take away the humanity of God, you take away the traditional conception of God altogether. Theism in its essence, if it means anything, means that behind the dead inhuman world which cares nothing for us, there exists something human which does care; there is Fatherly Love, Providence, Foresight, or some other emphatically human quality: there is, in the phrase used in a previous essay, 'A Friend behind phenomena.'

Of course that is not all that is demanded by theism, at any rate in its higher forms. The friend must be something far better than any human friend, more loving, more powerful. I am not sure that the normal man, if left to himself, would insist that his god should be by human standards a thing of absolute perfection, either in goodness or in power. The Greek and Indian and Nordic gods were neither. Furthermore, a perfect being could hardly, I think, be, strictly speaking, the object of love. We love the suffering God, the human God. We love the Being who strives, who shows courage, who endures, hopes, and makes sacrifices; but a Being perfect in power can do none of these things. He can never make that appeal for sympathy which seems essential to the power of arousing love.[1] But two influences at least seem to have been at work demanding infinite perfection of God. Many philosophers, from Plato onwards, have insisted that any imperfection whatsoever is inconsistent with the divine nature; and those nations whose religious ideas were largely formed by the Old Testament, with its sublimated despot insisting on unlimited glorification, were forced to regard their own hymns of praise as true, and to believe that the Ruler of the world was endowed with all the virtues they ascribed to him, perfect justice, perfect wisdom, and perfect love for his creature, mankind. They clung to this belief throughout the Middle Ages in spite of their equally firm belief in Hell. They cling to it still in spite of the obvious cruelty and imperfection of the world by which alone that ruler and creator makes himself known. They must insist on believing in the teeth of all the material evidence that 'God is Love'.

True, there is in all or almost all religions a violent difficulty when we insist that the God of love must also have perfect power. Nothing else will satisfy man's natural desire. The thing we cannot endure to think of is the omnipotence against us of the material or non-human world, with its utter disregard of what we call moral or spiritual values. God must deliver us from the body of that death, or else he fails us altogether. The simplest solution is a primitive dualism; if there is a friend, a good man, behind the phenomena, is there not equal plausibility, and better evidence, for supposing there is also

---

[1] It is interesting to note that Aristotle in seeking τὸ πρῶτον κινουν, the First Cause which moves the rest of the universe but is not moved itself, decides that it does so as 'an object of desire, or an object of thought', which equally is unmoved but causes movement (action) in others, and finally says κινεῖ ὡς ἐρώμενον, 'It moves as being loved.' This is obviously not love in the human sense, but more like magnetic attraction. (*Metaphysics*, p. 1072.) On the other hand ἄτοπον ἂν εἴη εἴ τις φαίη φιλεῖν τὸν Δία, 'It would be absurd for anyone to say he felt an affection for Zeus' (*Magna Moralia*, 1208 b 30).

an enemy, a bad man? God and Devil, Ormuzd and Ahriman, Jehovah and Satan the Adversary, always at strife, seem to afford a fair explanation of the world as we actually see it; our wish-thinking only insists that the end of the strife shall be an unconditional victory for the good. All the subtle explanations of modern theology really fail to provide us with a solution of the fundamental and glaring contradiction involved in all religions which maintain that a world, admitted to be full of evil, is created and ordered by the will of a being who is perfectly good and also omnipotent. The hypothesis of an 'intractable material' which the good God cannot control is inconsistent with his omnipotence. The hypothesis that he left man's will free to do good or evil as it chose is inconsistent with his perfect goodness, and fails entirely to meet the difficulties presented by a 'Nature red in tooth and claw with ravin', in which every creature normally lives by inflicting pain and death on others, and cannot live otherwise. Another hypothesis is that we are mistaken in supposing that there is any evil in the world: all is really just as it ought to be. Either no Jews are persecuted, no Chinese massacred, no men or animals perishing in torture, or, if there are, it is good for them, and if they had sense they would like it. This doctrine is, in its ordinary forms, heartless as well as senseless. It is not only obviously untrue, but like the doctrine of eternal damnation it is an untruth which, in the natural meaning of the words, no feeling man could believe. But there is another sense in which it can be understood and may, as far as logic goes, be true; only in that case it utterly wrecks the current conceptions of theism. It may be that what man calls 'good' is not at all the same as what the Power behind the world calls 'good'. That Power may well be no more 'good' or 'just' or 'merciful' than it is 'polite' or 'clever' or 'agreeable' or a 'good linguist'. All our moral ideas may be as inapplicable to it as our social phrases and conventional prejudices. Such a Power is neither good nor evil, neither friend nor enemy. It cannot be loved or hated. It is not anthropomorphic, not human, not describable in human language—not what we mean by God.

Along another line of thought a particular form of man-thinking and wish-thinking has been progressively undermined and made, not exactly impossible, but at least destitute of its chief claim to probability. The greatest shock sustained by theistic religion in historical times was perhaps that which came with the astronomical discoveries of Copernicus. The thought of post-Aristotelian Greece, of Rome, of the Middle Ages, was permeated by the researches and doctrines of the great Hellenistic astronomers. 'The stars, which had always moved men's wonder and even worship, were now seen and proved to be no wandering fires, but parts of an immense and apparently eternal Order or Cosmos. One star might differ from another star in glory, but they were all alike in their obedience to law. Their courses were laid down for them by a Being greater than they. The Order or Cosmos was a proven fact; therefore the purpose implied in it was a proven fact; and, though in its completeness inscrutable, it could in part be divined from the observation that all these varied and eternal splendours had for their centre our Earth and its ephemeral master. The Purpose, though it is not our purpose, is especially concerned with us and circles round us. It is the purpose of a God who loves Man.'[1]

On that conception the Stoic and Christian theologies were based. And now we know that it is not true. Our earth is not the centre of the cosmos; it is not even the centre of the solar system; and the solar system itself is only one out of very many systems, incalculably vast, incalculably numerous, to which the welfare or misery of us human beings is, as far as we can make out, of no consequence whatever. We are not the central care of the universe. The sun was not created to give us light by day, nor the moon by night. The animals were not, after all, made for man's sake, so as to provide him with food by eating them, with clothes by skinning them or with healthy amusement by trapping, hunting, shooting, and tormenting them. All such anthropocentric thinking proves to have been just a part of our inordinate human conceit.[2] It is wish-thinking or fear-thinking. It is the same sort of thinking which, with no evidence whatever except wishes and fears, created an infinite reward for the good and the wicked, those who have pleased or displeased the gods of our imagination, those who are with us or against us.

[1] *Five Stages of Greek Religion*, p. 125.
[2] Cf. Euripides, *Electra*, v. 726 ff. Old shepherds tell how the first sin committed on earth, Thyestes's theft of the Golden Lamb, convulsed all nature:

> Then, then the world was changed,
> And the Father, where they ranged,
> Shook the golden stars and glowing,
> And the great Sun stood deranged
> In the glory of his going.

We and our contemporaries, he says, merely smile at such simplicity.

What then? Must we say that all theism is a form of mere wish-thinking, the projection of man's own desires and fears, conditioned at every turn by the limitations of the human brain? The result is frightening. 'If there are no gods', says Cicero, 'or if such gods as there may be have no care for us, and pay no regard to our actions, what becomes of piety and religion?' And later: 'I do not feel sure, if we cast away piety towards the gods, that Good Faith (*fides*) and all the associations of human life, and the best of virtues, Justice, may not perish with it' (*Nat. De.* i. 2). For one thing, Heaven and Hell go. Is that a serious loss? It is hard to know how far considerations so remote and speculative have affected man's conduct. Legislators have generally found that men are not much influenced by promises of rewards or punishments to be realized even as far off as ten or twenty years hence. But, for what they may be worth, they go. More serious than that, the whole belief in a moral universe goes. We are left face to face with that 'Nature red in tooth and claw' which cares neither for the type nor for the individual; with those aeonian processes which make not merely the life of the individual man but the whole existence of human beings on the earth little flashes of movement in the history of a small planet which itself must in due course pass away to nothingness. One may recall a classical Japanese Haikai describing the value of man in eternity:

> In a still pool
> A frog jumped:
> A noise of splashing water!

We see good men living strenuous lives for their fellows. We see St Francis devoting all his powers to love and piety. We see man's conscience protesting against wrong, and resisting to the point of martyrdom. Is all that based on a mere delusion: is it mere wish-thinking to suppose that conscience really matters? In revulsion against such a thought comes a passionate rush of religious reaction, based usually not on reason but on emotional appeal. 'See what a loathsome creature man is', says Pascal, 'when once his divine guidance is taken away. See how divine he can be if he is safe in the fold of the Catholic Church.' The appeal is unconvincing to most of us. Not only would it be difficult to prove that those who have firmly rejected the wiles of Protestants and Freemasons are more virtuous than those who have embraced them; but, as soon as the claim is made that orthodoxy is necessary to moral salvation, there are too many conflicting revelations in the field, each with its own authoritative orthodoxy. Granted that the true faith will save us, which of the fifty-odd Christian sects is the true faith, to say nothing of the religions of Judaism, Islam, Hinduism, Buddhism, or the various systems of China and Japan? Far more plausible, as well as more civilized, is the claim that all these warring sects may be trying, imperfectly and confusedly, to say the same thing: that there is a God of Love and Justice, that there is a personal being who, in spite of our crabbed logic, is in some sense higher than we can comprehend both All-good and All-powerful, if only we will lay down our mortal judgement and stake all on faith? Immensely attractive to almost everyone; and yet that is just the theism which we have been examining and have found to be anthropomorphic in its essence and based on a wish, not on evidence. Modern Indian philosophers, like Radhakrishnan, have expounded eloquently the theme that religion is not a set of doctrines; it is an experience. And religious experience is based on the realization of the 'presence of the divine in man'. 'Dogma divides and sows enmity. Experience unites and makes concord. Dogma needs to be proven; experience needs no proof. It is a fact.'

Alas! The experience may be a fact, but the interpretation of experience is something different. What we mean by 'the divine in man' is, I fear, merely the same thing as the human in God; some sublimation of the highest human qualities which we have projected from ourselves on to the image of this intractably anthropomorphic god created by our own man-thinking and wish-thinking. It is our own dream returning to us in the guise of an external being.

Men accepting these somewhat mystical forms of belief are apt to find themselves professing or preaching some traditional theistic faith not quite because they believe it to be true, but because they are strongly convinced that it is good for other people to believe it; that in fact average human nature cannot get on without it.

The adherents of this line of thought inevitably find themselves confronted by a well-known problem: their creed, however it is expressed, means something quite different to the educated thinker and to the unthinking multitude. Cicero himself held the office of Augur: he considered it of the utmost importance that the Roman people should continue to observe the traditional pieties and sanctities of the Roman religion; he duly performed the rites and took the auspices. Yet, as we all remember, he quotes with approval Cato's expression of wonder that two *haruspices* can look each other in the face without laughing.[1] The priests of the modern Roman

[1] *De Div.* ii, 51; cf. *Nat. De.* i, 71.

Church when presiding over certain miracles in the South of Italy may well feel the same difficulty as the *haruspices* did, and no doubt surmount it as successfully. So much most people will admit. But the position of that eminent and high-minded body of men, the Broad Church leaders of the nineteenth century, is open to a very similar criticism. Dr Bridges in one of his essays[1] quotes certain passages from Dr Jowett's thoughts on religion; for example: '*Limits of change within the Christian religion. The conception of miracles may become impossible and absurd. Immortality may pass into present consciousness of goodness and of God. The personality of God may pass into an idea. Doctrines may become unmeaning words.*' And a little later: '*Christianity has become one religion among many. . . . We pray to God as a person; but there must always be a* subintelligitur *that He is not a person. Our forms of worship, public and private, imply some interference with the course of Nature, (yet) we know that the empire of law permeates all things.*' Dr Jowett's High Church critics found it easy to argue that such doctrines, or rather such radical scepticisms, were inconsistent not merely with the Articles of Faith which Dr Jowett had signed, but with the obvious implications of his position as a clergyman of the Established Church. His defence, that he was assisting in a vital movement for the liberalizing and enlightening of the Church, is a strong one, but not for the moment relevant to our discussion. It is clear that in these creeds with a *subintelligitur* attached, we are not far from the position attributed by Gibbon to the cultivated circles in Ancient Rome, that all religions were to the uneducated equally true, to the philosopher equally false, and to the statesman equally useful. A position which has a great deal to be said for it, but which cannot satisfy a speculative mind determined to preserve its honesty as well as its religious emotion.

Is it possible for us to do both? One of the Stoic arguments for the existence of the gods was the observation that, as a matter of fact, god-fearing or religious people live better and more successful lives than godless people, which would hardly be the case if they were wrong and the godless right in their main doctrine. A quaint piece of reasoning, but with some force in it. Man must at times be conscious of the vast mystery which surrounds his little island of knowledge; the inconceivable measures of astronomical distance, of the movement of light, of the extent of the wave-lengths which are neither visible to our eyes nor audible to our ears; the mere length of time involved in the history of man, of the earth, of the solar system. These things produce on any sensitive mind an

[1] Loc. cit., pp. 64 ff.

impression of awe and a feeling not so much of the insignificance of all our human interests, but perhaps rather a doubt whether we can know what is significant or not. An individual's mental attitude towards this mystery is one of the most revealing things about him, revealing just because he has no certain information to go upon and therfore acts and feels according to the general bias of his character. Utterly to ignore the mystery is what the Stoics called 'godless' or impious; yet, if we attempt to conceive it or speak of it, two results seem inescapable. In the first place, all our language will be metaphorical. To describe something utterly beyond our experience and power of conception we possess only words created by our experience to describe objects that we know. Secondly, though the material out of which we build our metaphorical Cosmos is no doubt our experience, the form we give it is determined, not by known facts, but entirely by our wishes or ideals. We build our conception of the divine out of what we take to be the best that we know or can imagine from our experience. What theists call 'the goodness of God' and mystics 'the divine in man' is precisely man's *humanitas*, the quality which specially exalts him above the beasts and progressively raises him higher and higher above himself.

This is essentially Comte's answer. He denies entirely that morality depends on any system of false beliefs, though of course it may often be accompanied by them. Morality is based on the results of many centuries and millennia of social experience and has its roots in human character. As for the belief in Hell and Heaven, it is not only not necessary as a basis for morality; it absolutely undermines morality. A good act done for the sake of a personal reward or under the terror of personal chastisement loses much of its value as a good act. The whole supposition that a system of violent and intense rewards and punishments is necessary to induce human beings to perform acts for the good of others is based on a false psychology which starts from the individual isolated man instead of man the social animal. Man is an integral member of his group. Among his natural instincts there are those which aim at group-preservation as well as self-preservation; at the good of *autrui* as well as of *moi*. Even among the animals, a cow, a tigress, a hen pheasant, does not need a promise of future rewards to induce her to risk her life to save her young from harm. The male bison or gorilla needs no reward before fighting devotedly for his females and children. They all instinctively care for *autrui*. And it would be a mistake to imagine that this devotion only shows itself in the form of fighting, or only in dangerous crises. It is part of the daily life of any natural group or herd: the strong members help the weak, the weak run for protection to the strong. In man even in his primitive state these instincts are much more highly developed than in the gregarious animals; with the process of civilization they increase in range, in reasonableness, in sublimity. In the late war, how many thousands of men—not particularly selected or high-minded men—risked their lives eagerly to save a companion wounded in No Man's Land? They did not ask or know why they did it. Some may have alleged motives of religion, or motives of ambition in the form of medals or promotions. But the basic motive was probably more or less the same all through; that instinctively they could not see a mate lying there wounded and not try to help him. Why did St Francis love his fellow-men, his birds, his enemies? He no doubt explained that it was all a part of his love of God. True, but his love of God was really his humanity, his *humanitas*, his ἀνθρωπότης, which made him love his group, and take into his group all life that met him, especially those parts that needed love most, the helpless, the despised, the angry and hostile. The humanity of man is an immense spirit, seen in the saints and heroes, seen in religious bodies; seen in dull prosaic societies of philanthropists, trying, skilfully or blunderingly, to help the unfortunate; seen in the ordinary social life of families and peoples. *Deus est mortali iuvare mortalem*: 'God is the helping of man by man'; or should we rather translate it: 'The spirit of mutual help among all mortal beings is the true object of worship?'[1] That, says Comte, is what God is. Not an external all-powerful Person, who will show favour to those who obey Him and terrible wrath to those who offend Him; not even an imaginary Infinitely Good Man whom we must serve out of love for His goodness; but a perfectly real spirit of goodness, which runs in some degree through all life, but finds its highest expression in the best men, the spirit that we can only call *Humanitas*, Humanity.[2]

[1] Pliny, *Nat. Hist.* ii. 7, 18.
[2] An objection may be raised that, morally speaking, Man is in many ways not better but far worse than the beasts, certainly more licentious, treacherous, and cruel. If we worship 'Humanity' must we not include these special human vices? The objection, so far as it is not merely verbal, is frivolous. What the Positivist proposes to worship is not everything that is characteristic of Man, but that quality, or that effort, by which Man is morally and intellectually higher than the beasts; exactly what Dr Radhakrishnan means by 'the divine in man'.

Where does the main difference lie between this faith and faith in a personal God? Only, I think, here: that in theism St Francis or any martyr is held to be always on the winning side; sure of his victory, sure of his reward. I do not, of course, say that he practises virtue merely for the sake of his reward: but at least he is sure that he will have it. In Positivism he takes his risk. He performs his act of love or sacrifice for the sake of others and their good, whether in the end it be fruitful of good to himself or utterly wasted. He does not wait to risk his safety until he is assured of success.

Comte always insists on seeing man as a member of Society. In society he realized his three-fold slogan: *Love the principle*: without love, no society can exist. *Order the basis*: without order no society can continue. *Progress the end*: for every human society by its own nature is imperfect and aims at removing its imperfections, looking higher as each flaw is cleared away. Comte is an evolutionist not in the purely biological sense but in the sociological; seeing the continuous development of man's *Humanitas* to higher achievement.

He calls this system a religion, not merely a philosophy. Is this justified? For example, is there a place in it for faith, for that 'substance of things hoped for, that evidence of things unseen', which has been one of the most moving forces of human history? History itself gives abundant answers. Men have had faith in the future of their country, faith in the cause for which they worked, when those with less vision could see no ground for faith. There is place for faith, place for hope; most royal and abundant place for charity. Is there a place for prayer? Not if prayer is merely a petition for personal favours, but ample place if prayer is, as it is in most of the higher religions, a concentration of thought and love upon our ideal of life. A place for worship? The whole system is a religion of worship, as can be seen, for example, in the Calendar of great men, where we not merely study and contemplate with reverence the actual life and work of those who have been Servants of Humanity, but above all, since each one of them has his faults, dedicate ourselves to the spirit which they imperfectly illustrate. He laid stress—most of us will say, too much stress—on the need of an organized liturgy and regular meetings of worship. He even kept the idea of sacraments, for entry to the Church, for marriage, and other occasions, using the word not in the ecclesiastical sense but in that of the Roman soldier's oath or *Sacramentum*: a solemn devotion of life to a great purpose.

It is not my business in this paper to try to point out particular weaknesses in Comte's vast system, or unattractive egotisms in his character. It may be that his literary style and the mind which it expressed were more conspicuous for rigid logic and strength than for sympathy and imagination. It may be that he was consciously or unconsciously inspired by Robespierre's curious project for leaving the Catholic Church fully established while removing the creeds. Certainly the system appeals more to those accustomed to the Catholic tradition than it does to Protestants. On the other hand he did try conscientiously to get free from the unconscious historic trammels in which the Christian tradition necessarily confines our Western civilization, and to speak intelligibly to Confucian, Muslim, or Buddhist. For my own part I cannot but think he attempted too much; he tried to build a great structure almost complete in detail when he had materials only for a foundation and some outside walls, and even those subject to reformation. But whatever the failures and imperfections of his actual statement, whatever the elements in it that will be superseded by future advances of thought, I cannot but feel, as did Mill, Morley, George Eliot, Spencer, as well as Bridges, Beesly, and Harrison, first, that his system forms a wonderful achievement of sincere and constructive thinking, and, secondly, that the thing he is trying to say, if only he could succeed in saying it is not only sublime but true.

CHAPTER X

Satanism and the World Order[1]

IN an old novel, still famous and once widely popular, the writer, oppressed with the burden of evil in the world, gives to her heroine the name Consuelo, 'Consolation', and makes her half-mad hero a a descendant of a strange sect. He is one of those Bohemian Lollards who, despairing of any sympathy from God, threw themselves into the protecting arms of their fellow-outcast, fellow-sufferer, fellow-victim of persecution and slander, the Devil. Their word of salutation was: 'The Injured One give you greeting,' or 'The Injured One give you blessing'. And they made of the Injured One a figure rather resembling the suffering Christ, a champion of the poor and lowly, a Being more than persecuted, more than crucified, but differing from Christ inasmuch as he was no friend of Pope, priest or Emperor, and therefore, presumably no friend of God; he was still unconquered and unreconciled. If the belief seems to us bizarre or even depraved, it can only be for a moment. The clue to it is that it is a belief of the persecuted and helpless, who know their own innocence and deduce the wickedness of their rulers. To these pious and simple mountain peasants, followers first of John Huss and Zyska, and then of leaders more ignorant and fiery, the world became gradually a place dominated by enemies. Every person in authority met them with rack and sword, cursed their religious leaders as emissaries of the Devil, and punished them for all the things which they considered holy. The earth was the Lord's, and the Pope and Emperor were the vicegerents of God upon the earth. So they were told; and in time they accepted the statement. That was the division of the world. On one side God, Pope and Emperor and the army of persecutors; on the other themselves, downtrodden and poor, their saintly leaders hunted like beasts, and, above all, their eternal comforter and fellow-rebel, that exiled Star of the Morning, cast into darkness and torment like his innocent children. Let them be true to him, and surely his day must come!

[1] The Adamson Lecture, Manchester University, October 1919.

Satanism in this sense is perfectly intelligible, and may be strongly sympathetic. We need pay no attention to the mere name of Satan or Lucifer; the name is a mythological accident. The essence of the belief is that the World Order is evil and a lie; goodness and truth are persecuted rebels. In other forms the belief has been held by many Christian saints and martyrs, and notably by the author of the Apocalypse. But we should notice that it is diametrically opposed to the teaching of almost all the great moral philosophers. Plato, Aristotle and the Stoics, St Augustine and Thomas Aquinas, Kant and J. S. Mill, and Comte and T. H. Green, all argue or assume that there exists in some sense a Cosmos or Divine Order; that what is good is in harmony with this Order, and what is bad is in discord against it. I notice that one of the Gnostic schools in Hippolytus the Church Father (vii. 28) actually defines Satan as 'the spirit who works against the Cosmic Powers'; the rebel or protestant who counteracts the will of the whole, and tries to thwart the community of which he is a member. Ancient philosophers are particularly strong on this conception of evil, and on the corresponding conception of human goodness as being the quality of a good citizen. The world or the universe is one community, or, as they call it, one city; all men, or perhaps all living things, are citizens of that city, and human goodness consists in living for its good. God's providence or foresight consists in providing the future Good of the Universe; and it is our business to be to the best of our powers ὑπουργοὶ τῆς θείας προνοίας, servants or ministers of the divine foresight (Diodorus I). Thus goodness becomes identical with loyalty, or with what some of the persecuted Christians called πίστις, faithfulness. There is an army of God, and there is an enemy. And the essential sin is rebellion or treason.

Loyalty is thus the central and typical virtue; but loyalty to what? So far we can only say it is loyalty to the Cosmic Process, or the Purpose of God, or the good of the whole, as representing that purpose. But in practice, for the ordinary human being who has no oddities or idiosyncrasies of belief, this central virtue takes the form of loyalty towards the most important active whole of which he is a member.

In practice, the good of any large society is accepted as sufficiently near to the Good of the Universe to justify a man's devotion to it. A man whose life was really devoted to the welfare of New York, assuming, of course, that his idea of the welfare of New York was reasonably adequate and sensible, would certainly count as a good man. It is speculatively possible that the good of the universe may demand the misery and degradation of the inhabitants of New York, but it is one of those possibilities which need not, in ordinary opinion, be taken seriously. *A fortiori*, a man who really devoted his life to the welfare of all the inhabitants of America or of the British Empire, or all the inhabitants of the German Empire, or, still more, the inhabitants of the ancient Roman Empire, would be accepted as a good man leading a good life by all but the eccentric or prejudiced. If a person of this type is blamed—such as Cecil Rhodes or Bismarck, or William II or Augustus—there is always an implication that his conception of what constituted the welfare of his whole was wrong. He professed, and perhaps thought, that he was promoting the welfare of his great society, whereas he was really doing something quite different: inflaming its ambitions, or flattering its vices, or the like.

The point of interest comes when one of these vast wholes begins to identify its own good with something which incidentally involves the evil of another whole, whether small or great. We most of us, for instance, look upon the late German Empire as an organization so hostile to humanity as a whole that it had to be destroyed. But it is worth noting that in any of these great organizations far the greater expenditure of time and energy is devoted to the good of its members, to such ends as education, transport, industry, agriculture, government and the administration of justice; and the evil it does, even when it is enormous, is mostly either unconscious or else accidental. The clearest, and perhaps the most tragic, case is that of the Roman Empire.

If we try to enter into the mind of a good Roman official, like Pliny, for instance, as shown in his letters to Trajan, he seems to feel that the service of Rome was for him the nearest approach possible to the service of God, or the helping of the human race as a whole. Rome, he would say, had doubtless her imperfections; and not all Roman proconsuls were worthy of their high calling. But, when all deductions were made, the Roman Empire meant peace throughout the known world; it meant decent and fairly disinterested government; it protected honest men from thieves and robbers; it punished wrongdoers; it gave effective help to towns wrecked by blizzards or earthquakes, or to provinces where the crops had failed. It spread education and civilized habits; it put down the worst practices of savage superstition. And, if any improvement in the practice of governing human beings could be pointed out, on the whole a good Roman governor was willing to consider it. If Pliny had been asked what was the greatest calamity that could befall the human race, he would probably have answered, 'The overthrow of the Roman Empire'; and it would have been hard to contradict him. One might have argued that, in nation after nation, Rome had crushed a native art and culture, and put in its place a very dull and mechanical civilization, with little life, or beauty, or power of growth; that it took the heart out of the local religions, and put in their place a dead official ceremonial. But such arguments would have been met with an incredulous smile, as similar arguments are met nowadays. Pliny would answer, very justly, that if the various subject nations all preferred Roman culture to their own, surely that must be because Roman culture was obviously superior. If they accepted the Roman official religion, it must be for the same reason. As a matter of fact, he would add, the religion of *Roma Dea*, the acceptance of the spirit of the Roman Empire as something to be regarded with awe and love and worship, was the nearest approach to a truly philosophical religion that uncultured men could assimilate; and, after all, Rome never suppressed or injured any local religion that was not criminal in its practices. All that Rome asked was the recognition of a common brotherhood, a common loyalty, expressed in the simplest and most human way, by an offering of incense and prayer at the altar of *Roma Dea*, Rome the Divine Mother, or sometimes at that of the existing head of the State.

And then, as we know, certain odd people would not do it. It seems curious that so simple a point of difference could not be got over. I do not see why Jews or Christians need have refused to pray for the welfare of Rome, provided they did so at their own altars, nor why the magistrates should have made a difficulty about the particular altar used. But evidently the affair was badly managed at the beginning. And by the time we have any detailed evidence we find the Christians uttering curses and incantations against the Empire in place of prayers, and the Roman working classes trying by pogroms to stamp out such incredible wickedness. When people met secretly and prayed to an alien and hostile God to do ill to the whole Empire; when they called our holy Mother Rome a harlot riding on a wild beast and drunken with the blood of the saints; when they saw visions and uttered incantations fraught with the most appalling afflictions upon mankind that any mind can conceive, seals and bowls of poisoned blood, and Riders upon strange horses, who should eventually trample the whole Roman world beneath their feet until the blood of that wine-pressing should wash the horses' bridles, while the Christians receive rich rewards and sing for joy—by that time the average working man or peasant began to look about him for clubs and stones, and the worried magistrate to decide that this new Jewish sect must be registered as an illegal society.

The mental attitude of the Book of Revelation is almost exactly like that of the persecuted Bohemian sectaries in *Consuelo*. The world and the rulers of the world are absolutely evil—not faulty men who make mistakes, but evil powers, hating all that is good and acting on earth as the representatives of evil gods: the earthly Cosmos is evil, and all that the righteous can desire is its utter destruction. This conception that the World Order may be definitely evil was, of course, not a new one. Four hundred years earlier, Athens had thrilled at Plato's conception of the ideal Righteous Man, who, coming to an unrighteous world, suffers every affliction, is bound and scourged and has his eyes burnt out, and at last is impaled or crucified, and yet is, on the whole, happy—i.e. he is a man you would like to be—because of his righteousness. Greek mythology itself possessed the traditional character of a divine rebel, Prometheus, who, for love of man, had defied the cruel Power which rules the world. The late and mystical Greek philosophers who were the founders of Gnosticism are eloquent on the badness of this world, and the malignity of the Powers who created it or who rule it. Such a view of the world as evil is, I think, seldom of any value as philosophy, but always of interest to the psychologist and the historian. When widespread, it is the result of some special and widespread unhappiness, either defeat and persecution or else of extraordinarily bad government. In isolated cases it may come merely from some sensitive idealism which pitches its hopes too high for human life to satisfy. It is the belief sometimes of the anchorite or the mystic; but normally it is the cry of the persecuted, the refugee, the sufferer of things past endurance, the victim of those Governments which are the enemies of their own people. It is never, I think, the belief of the good governor, the efficient public servant, or even the successful mechanic or man of business. But of that later: the point which I wish to lay stress on at this moment is a different one. It is that, unless I am mistaken, in every single case the man who believes that the order in which he lives is evil provides himself, either in this life or the next, with another order in which all is redeemed.

The writer of the Apocalypse looks forward, after the utter destruction of the hostile order of Rome, to a millennium upon earth, in which all the posts of authority are occupied by the faithful. Plato's righteous man, though in discord with the society which tortures him, is in harmony all the time with the true nature of things. Prometheus himself ultimately gains his point, and is reconciled to Zeus. The overpowering strength of this impulse in the persecuted, or unhappy, to project out of their own desires an imaginary order in which the injustices of the present order are corrected, a special Heaven in which the righteous are consoled, together with a special Hell in which the enemies of the righteous meet their deserts, is illustrated vividly in the apocalyptic literature of all persecuted faiths, both Christian and pagan. Persecution always generates vivid descriptions of Hell, the projection of righteous revenge unsatisfied. One of the most pathetic and amiable of these attempts to justify by imagination that which cannot be justified by the evidence is the theoretic optimism of the Neo-Platonic and Neo-Pythagorean communities. They had not suffered much. They did not revel in visions of revenge or recompense: they merely argued *in vacuo*. Their fundamental doctrine was that the Cosmos, the Universe, was good. If it was not good all their system reeled into ruins. But the world, as they actually saw it and lived in it, seemed to them a mere mass of gross matter, rolling in error and delusion, and wisdom could only be attained by abstention from it. How can these positions be reconciled? By a method so simple that it leaves one almost awed at the childlike power of living in dreams by which the human mind protects itself against the thorns of life. 'True,' said these philosophers, 'all of the world that we see is bad, all steeped in matter and in error. But what about the parts we do not see? If you could once get above the moon you would find it absolutely different. All those parts of the Universe about which we have no information are so extraordinarily and infinitely good, that the badness of the parts we do happen to know sink into insignificance. It is as though a judge had to try a number of accused people, of whom some could not be caught; all those who were brought into court were found guilty of various crimes, but the judge has such a strong inward conviction of the saintliness of those whom the police could not lay hands upon that he acquits the whole gang, and they leave the court without a stain on their character.

Quite absurd, I venture to say. And yet I think it is in essentials what I believe myself, and what we all believe. And I very much doubt whether human beings can go on living without some such belief. It is a matter of human psychology. But perhaps we do wrong in using the words 'good' and 'bad'; we really mean 'friend or enemy', on our side or against us. The division between 'friend' and 'enemy' goes far deeper down into human nature than that between good and bad. If you read the sort of literature that I have been treating, the ancient apocryphal or pagan apocalypses and descriptions of Hell, you will not find on the whole that Hell is primarily the place for people who do not come up to the received moral standard; it is the place for the enemy. It is the place for him who now persecutes us, robs us, hangs us, burns us, makes us fight with wild beasts, and laughs the while. Let him wait and he will be made to laugh on the other side of his mouth! And if a third person explains that a particular enemy is a decent and sober person, a good husband and father, the statement is almost irrelevant, as well as almost unbelievable. You may hate a man because he is wicked; or you may think him wicked because you hate him. You may love a man because you think him good, or you may feel him to be, with all his faults, a splendid fellow because he likes you. But in either case the psychological ground fact is not a moral judgement, good or bad, but an instinctive gesture, Friend or Enemy.

And as soon as we see this, we see also how it is almost impossible not to believe that ultimately in the real battle of life the Cosmos is with us. You cannot belong wholeheartedly to the Labour Party, or the Jesuits, as the case may be, without believing that God is on the side of the Labour Party or the Jesuits. You cannot belong to Islam without believing that God is on the side of Islam. In the main, whatever majority may be against you now, and however hostile you may find the present World Order, you cannot help believing in your heart that there is a better order which is on your side, and perhaps even that, as they say in melodrama, 'a time will come. . . .'

We all know, on Dr Johnson's authority, that the Devil was the first Whig. But the above argument enables us to see the difference between him and, let us say, the Whigs of later history. The Whig, while condemning and working against the existing order in some particular, is always consciously trying to institute another order which he regards as better. And through all the series, Whig, Liberal, Radical, Revolutionary, the same remains true; the only difference is that at each stage the ideal new order is increasingly remote from the existing order. But the Devil, unless I do him a wrong, is not trying to substitute another order which he prefers; he is merely injuring, marring, acting as an enemy—$\dot{a}\nu\tau\iota\pi\rho\acute{a}\tau\tau\omega\nu$ $\tau o\hat{\iota}s$ $\kappa o\sigma\mu\iota\kappa o\hat{\iota}s$. And here, perhaps, we get to the first result of this long argument: That goodness *is* the same thing as harmony with or loyalty to the World Order; but that, since the true World Order does not yet exist, Opposition to the present order is at times right, provided that the opposition really aims at the attainment of a fuller or better order.

Theoretically this seems sound. And I think, even in practice, the rule has a certain value, though of course it does not, any more than any other political rule, provide us with an infallible test of the good or evil, the sane or insane. It is rare to find any political lunatic so extreme as specifically to admit that he wishes to destroy and never rebuild, to make the present world worse than it is, with no intention even at the back of his mind, ever to 'remould it nearer to the heart's desire'. Yet a certain type of revolutionary does for all practical purposes take a position that is almost equivalent to this.

I once in my youth met the celebrated Nihilist, Bakunin, the unsuccessful Lenin of his day, who was credited with the doctrine that every act of destruction or violence is good; because either it does good directly, by destroying a person or thing which is objectionable, or else it does good indirectly by making an already intolerable world worse than before, and so bringing the Social Revolution nearer. Since he and his followers had no constructive scheme for this so-called Social Revolution, the theory is for practical purposes indistinguishable from true Satanism or hatred of the world. One of the deductions made from it was that, in the ordinary workaday business of political assassinations, it was far more desirable to murder innocent and even good persons than guilty or wicked ones. For two reasons; the wicked were some use, if left alive, in furthering the Revolution, and, also, to kill the wicked implied no really valuable criticism of the existing social order. If you kill an unjust judge, you may be understood to mean merely that you think judges ought to be just. But if you go out of your way to kill a just judge, it is clear that you object to judges altogether. If a son kills a bad father, the act, though meritorious in its humble way, does not take us much further. But if he kills a good father, it cuts at the root of all that pestilent system of family affection and loving kindness and gratitude on which the present world is largely based.

Let us become sane again and see where we are. What do we most of us, as a matter of fact, think about the existing World Order? I am thinking of all ordinary sensible people, whatever their politics, excluding only those who are prejudiced against the world by some intolerable private wrong, or in its favour by some sudden and delightful success. Strictly speaking, the world as a whole cannot be called good or bad, any more than the spectrum as a whole can be called light or dark. The world contains all the things we call good and all that we call bad: and since by the laws of language you call things bad if they are worse than you expect, and good if they are better than you expect, and your expectation itself is formed by your experience, you cannot apply any word of blame or praise to the whole. But when people speak of the world or the existing order, they are of course thinking of the part in which they are most interested: and that, for various reasons, is usually the part that depends on human society and human effort. And I shall feel a little disappointed if every one of my readers does not agree with me in thinking that on the whole, and allowing for exceptions, when people try to do something, and pay attention, they come nearer to doing it than if they did not try at all. Normally, therefore, that systematic organization of human effort which we call a civilized society, does on the whole succeed in being a good thing, just as the Roman Empire did. Doctors, on the whole, prolong human life rather than shorten it. Lawyers and judges, on the whole, bring about more justice than injustice. Even in a department of life so very imperfectly civilized as economics, on the whole, if you know of a young man who is hard-working, intelligent and honest, you do expect him to get on better than one who is lazy, stupid and a thief. This lands us in the belief, which any minute study of social history corroborates in letters of blood, that almost any Government is better than no government, and almost any law better than no law. And I think we may safely go further. If we take any of those cases where a civilized society obviously shows itself evil, where it rewards vice and punishes virtue, produces misery and slays happiness; when it appoints unjust tribunals, when it bribes witnesses to tell lies, when it treats its own members or subjects as enemies and tries to injure them instead of serving them; when it does these things it is not really carrying out its principles, but failing. It is not a machine meant for doing these bad things; it is a very imperfectly designed machine for doing just the opposite, at any rate inside its own boundaries.

If we accept this position, we see that the organized life of mankind is on the whole organized for good, and that the great pilgrimage of the spirit of man from the beginnings of history onward has been on the whole not only a movement from ignorance to knowledge, from collective impotence to collective power, from poverty of life to richness of life, but also in some profound sense a pilgrimage from lower to higher. And it will follow, in spite of constant lapses and false routes, which have to be corrected, that the road of progress is in the main a road onward in the same general direction; that the better order which a reformer wishes to substitute for the present order must be a fuller realization of the spirit of the existing order itself. This belief does not rule out changes which many people would call extreme or revolutionary; to the eye of the historian most revolutions are little more than a ruffling of the surface of life. But it does mean that a change which violates the consciences of men, a change which aims at less justice and more violence, at more hatred and less friendliness, at more cruelty and less freedom, has the probabilities heavily against its ultimate success.

The instinct of the average man is apt to be shrewdly right on this point. We do instinctively judge men and movements, not by the amount of suffering or bloodshed they cause, but by the quality of human behaviour which they represent. For a general to cause a thousand deaths by an unsuccessful attack is a much slighter disturbance of the World Order than if, for example, he were to cause one innocent man to be condemned to death by forging false documents. The first would be a disaster and perhaps deserving of blame; the second would imply a shattering of the very foundations on which the World Order rests.

We seem to be led to a profound and almost a complacent conservatism, but I think there has been one flaw in this justification of ordinary organized societies. It is the same as lurked in Pliny's arguments above, justifying *Roma Dea* to the rebellious Christian or Jew. It justifies them so far as they really represent, however imperfectly, the World Order; so far as they *are* organizations for justice and freedom. That is, the argument applies only to the action of the organized society within its own borders, and utterly fails to touch the relation of the state or society to those outside. On the inside a state is an organization for good government and mutual help; and it has a machinery, elaborate and well thought out, by which it can improve its powers and correct its errors. And only in cases of extreme failure are its own members its enemies. But towards other states or societies it is something utterly different; just as a tigress to her own cubs is a clever and delightful mother, but to strangers nothing of the kind. Seen from the outside, a state is mainly a fighting power, organized for the use of force. It is represented by diplomacy in its better moments and by war in its worse. And towards subject societies, if it has them, its relation is ambiguous; in favourable conditions, they are members of the whole and in accord with it; in unfavourable conditions, they approach more and more nearly to rebels and half-conquered enemies. The relation of empires to subject communities is, in fact, the great seed-ground for those states of mind which I have grouped under the name of Satanism.

An appalling literature of hatred is in existence, dating at least from the eighth century BC, in which unwilling subjects have sung and exulted over the downfall of the various great empires, or at least poured out the delirious, though often beautiful, visions of their long-deferred hope. The Burden of Nineveh, the Burden of Tyre, the Burden of Babylon: these are recorded in some of the finest poetry of the world. The Fall of Rome, the rise of her own vile sons against her, the plunging of the Scarlet Woman in the lake of eternal torture and the slaying of the three-quarters of mankind who bowed down to her, form one of the most eloquent and imaginative parts of the canonical Apocalypse. The cry of oppressed peoples against the Turk and the Russian is written in many languages and renewed in many centuries. What makes this sort of literature so appalling is, first, that it is inspired by hatred; and next that the hatred is at least in part just; and thirdly, the knowledge that we ourselves are now sitting in the throne once occupied by the objects of these execrations. Perhaps most of us are so accustomed to think of Babylon and Nineveh and Tyre, and even Rome, as seats of mere tyranny and corruption, that we miss the real meaning and warning of their history. These imperial cities mostly rose to empire not because of their faults, but because of their virtues; because they were strong and competent and trustworthy, and, within their borders and among their own people, were mostly models of effective justice. And we think of them as mere types of corruption! The hate they inspired among their subjects has so utterly swamped, in the memory of mankind, the benefits of their good government, or the contented and peaceful lives which they made possible to their own peoples. It is an awe-inspiring thought for us who now sit in their place.

The spirit that I have called Satanism, the spirit of unmixed hatred towards the existing World Order, the spirit which rejoices in any widespread disaster which is also a disaster to the world's rulers, is perhaps more rife today than it has been for over a thousand years. It is felt to some extent against all ordered Governments, but chiefly against all imperial Governments; and it is directed more widely and intensely against Great Britain than against any other Power. I think we may add that, while everywhere dangerous, it is capable of more profound world-wreckage by its action against us than by any other from that it is now taking. A few years ago probably the most prosperous and contented and certainly in many ways the most advanced region of the whole world was Central Europe. As a result of the War and the policy of the victors after the War, Central Europe is now an economic wreck, and large parts of it a prey to famine. A vast volume of hatred, just and unjust, partly social, partly nationalist, partly the mere reaction of intolerable misery, is rolling up there against what they call the Hungerherren, or Hunger-Lords. The millions of Russia are torn by civil war; but one side thinks of us as the people who, taking no risks ourselves, sent tanks and poison-gas to destroy masses of helpless peasants; and the other side thinks of us as the foreigners who encouraged them to make civil war and then deserted them. All through the Turkish Empire, through great parts of Persia and Afghanistan, from one end of the Moslem world to the other, there are *Mullahs*, holy men, seeing visions and uttering oracles about the downfall of another Scarlet Woman who has filled the world with the wine of her abominations, and who is our own *Roma Dea*, our British Commonwealth, whom we look upon as the great agent of peace and freedom for mankind. Scattered among our own fellow-subjects in India the same prophecies are current; they are ringing through Egypt. Men in many parts of the world—some even as close to us as Ireland—are daily giving up their lives to the sacred cause of hatred, even a hopeless hatred, against us, and the World Order which we embody. I have read lately two long memoranda about Africa, written independently by two people of great experience, but of utterly different political opinions and habits of thought; both agreed that symptoms in Africa pointed towards a movement of union among all the native races against their white governors; and both agreed that, apart from particular oppressions and grievances, the uniting forces were the two great religions, Christianity and Islam, because both religions taught a doctrine utterly at variance with the whole method and spirit of the European dominion—the doctrine that men are immortal beings and their souls equal in the sight of God.

This state of things is in part the creation of the War. In part it consists of previously latent tendencies brought out and made conspicuous by the War. In part the War has suggested to susceptible minds its own primitive method, the method of healing all wrong by killing or hitting somebody. And for us British in particular, the War has left us, or revealed us, as the supreme type and example of the determination of the white man to rule men of all other breeds, on the ground that he is their superior. Here and there peoples who have experience know that the British are better masters than most; but masters they are, and masters are apt to be hated.

There is a memorable chapter in Thucydides, beginning with the words: *Not now for the first time have I seen that it is impossible for a Democracy to govern an Empire.* It may not be impossible but it is extraordinarily difficult. It is so difficult to assert—in uncritical and unmeasured language—the sanctity of freedom at home, and systematically to modify or regulate freedom abroad. It is so difficult to make the government at home constantly more sympathetic, more humane, more scrupulous in avoiding the infliction of injustice or even inconvenience upon the governed British voters at home, and to tolerate the sort of incident that—especially in the atmosphere of war—is apt to occur in the government of voteless subjects abroad. When I read letters from friends of my own who are engaged in this work of world-government, I sometimes feel that it brings out in good men a disinterested heroism, a sort of inspired and indefatigable kindness, which is equalled by no other profession. And I think that many English people, knowing as they do the immense extent of hard work, high training and noble intention, on which our particular share in World Order is based, feel it an almost insane thing that our subjects should ever hate us. Yet we must understand if we are to govern. And it is not hard to understand. We have seen lately in Amritsar a situation arising between governors and governed so acutely hostile that a British officer, apparently a good soldier, thought it right to shoot down without warning some hundreds of unarmed men. In Mesopotamia, since the War, it is said that certain villages which did not pay their taxes, and were thought to be setting a bad example, were actually bombed from the air at night, when all the population was crowded together in the enclosures.[1] In Ceylon, in 1915, large numbers of innocent people were either shot or flogged, and many more imprisoned, owing to a panic in the Government. In Ireland prisoners have been tortured to obtain evidence and, it is alleged, innocent men murdered to suppress it. In Rhodesia a few weeks ago a boy of sixteen, who shot a native dead for fun, was let off with eight strokes of the birch.

I wish to pass no harsh judgement on the men who did any of these things. I give full value to the argument that those of us who sit at home in safety have no right to pour denunciation on the

[1] I am happy to say that the accuracy of this report about Mesopotamia is denied by the officials concerned; in particular it seems clear that the bombing was done by day, not by night. I therefore withdraw my own statement unreservedly, and have only allowed it to stand in the text because to omit it silently might not seem a sufficiently explicit withdrawal.

errors of overworked and overstrained men in crises of great peril and difficulty. I mention these incidents only to illustrate how natural it is for imperial races to be hated. The people who suffer such things as these do not excuse them, and do not forget them. The stories are repeated, and do not lose in the telling. And many a boy and girl in the East will think of the English simply and solely as the unbelievers who habitually flog and shoot good people, just as the Jews felt about the Romans, or the Manichaeans about the Orthodox. Now my own view is that all these actions in their different degrees were wrong; all were blunders; also, all were really exceptional and not typical; and, further, that no action like them, or remotely approaching them, is normally necessary for the maintenance of the Empire. I am too confirmed a Liberal to take the opposite view. But suppose we had to take it. Suppose we were convinced by argument that all these actions were wise and necessary, and that violence and injustice of this sort are part of the natural machinery by which Empire is maintained; that the rule of the white man over the coloured man, the Christian over the 'heathen', the civilized over the uncivilized, cannot be carried on except at the cost of these bloody incidents and the world-wide passion of hatred which they involve, I think the conclusion would be inevitable, not that such acts were right—for they cannot be right—but simply that humanity will not for very long endure the continuance of this form of World Order.

William Morris used to say that no man was good enough to be another man's master. If that were true of individuals, it would, as great authorities have pointed out, be much more true of nations. No nation certainly is as trustworthy as its own best men. But I do not think it is true, unless, indeed, you imply in the word 'master' some uncontrolled despotism. Surely there is something wrong in that whole conception of human life which implies that each man should be a masterless, unattached and independent being. It would be almost truer to say that no man is happy until he has a master, or at least a leader, to admire and serve and follow. That is the way in which all societies naturally organize themselves, from boys at school to political parties and social groups. As far as I can see, it is the only principle on which brotherhood can be based among beings who differ so widely as human beings do in intellect, in will power or in strength. I do not think it is true that no nation is good enough in this qualified sense to be another's master. The World Order does imply leaders and led, governors and governed; in extreme cases it does imply the use of force. It does involve, amid a great mass of other feelings, the risk of a certain amount of anger, and even hatred, from the governed against the governor. A World Order which shirked all unpopularity would be an absurdity.

I sometimes think, in comparing the ancient world with the modern, that one of the greatest distinguishing characteristics of modern civilization is an unconscious hypocrisy. The ancients shock us by their callousness; I think we should sometimes startle them by the contrast between our very human conduct and our absolutely angelic professions. If you ask me what possible remedy I see, from the point of view of the British Commonwealth, against these evils I have described, I would answer simply that we must first think carefully what our principles are, and not overstate them; next, we must sincerely carry them out. These principles are not unknown things. They have been laid down by the great men of the last century, by Cobden and Macaulay and John Stuart Mill, even to a great extent by Lord Salisbury and Gladstone. We hold our Empire as a trust for the governed, not as an estate to be exploited. We govern backward races that they may be able to govern themselves; we do not hold them down for our own profit, nor in order to use them as food for cannon. Above all, in our government and our administration of justice, we try to act without fear or favour, treating the poor man with as much respect as the rich man, the coloured man as the white, the alien as the Englishman. We have had the principles laid down again and again; they are all embodied in the Covenant of the League of Nations, which we have signed, and which is on sale everywhere for a penny.

It was a belief of the ancient Greeks that when a man had shed kindred blood he had to be purified; and until he was purified the bloodstain worked like a seed of madness within him, and his thoughts could never rest in peace or truth. The blood, I fear, is still upon the hands of all of us, and some of the madness still in our veins. The first thing we must do is to get back to our pre-war standard. Then, from that basis, we must rise higher.

The War has filled not only Russia, but most of Eastern Europe and Western Asia with the spirit that I have called Satanism; the spirit which hates the World Order wherever it exists and seeks to vent its hate without further plan. That is wrong. But this spirit would not have got abroad; it would not have broken loose and grown like seed and spread like pestilence, had not the World Order itself betrayed itself and been false to its principles, and acted towards enemies and subjects in ways which seem to them what the ways of Nero or Domitian seemed to St John on Patmos. I do not know whether it is possible for a nation to repent. Penitence in a nation, as a rule, means nothing but giving a majority to a different political party. But I think it is possible for individual human beings, even for millions of them. I see few signs so far of a change of heart in the public action of any nation in the world; few signs of any rise in the standard of public life, and a great many signs of its lowering. Some actions of great blindness and wickedness, the sort of actions which leave one wondering whether modern civilization has any spiritual content at all to differentiate us from savages, have been done, not during the War, but since the War was over. Yet I am convinced that, though it has not yet prevailed in places of power, there is a real desire for change of heart in the minds of millions. This desire is an enthusiasm, and is exposed to all the dangers of enthusiasm. It is often ignorant; it is touched with folly and misplaced passion and injustice. It is even exploited by interested persons. These are serious faults, and must be guarded against; but I believe the desire for a change of heart is a genuine longing, and, furthermore, I believe firmly that unless the World Order is affected by this change of heart, the World Order is doomed. Unless it abstains utterly from war and the causes of war, the next great war will destroy it. Unless it can seek earnestly the spirit of brotherhood and sobriety at home, Bolshevism will destroy it. Unless it can keep its rule over subject peoples quite free from the spirit of commercial exploitation and the spirit of slavery, and make it like the rule of a good citizen over his fellows, it will be shattered by the widespread hatred of those whom it rules.

The present World Order, if it survives the present economic crisis, has a wonderful opportunity, such an opportunity as has never been granted to any previous order in the history of recorded time. Our material wealth, our organization, our store of knowledge, our engines of locomotion and destruction, are utterly unprecedented, and surpass even our own understanding. Furthermore, on the whole, we know what we ought to do. We have, what no previous Empire or collection of ruling states ever had, clear schemes set before us of the road ahead which will lead out of these dangers into regions of safety; the League of Nations, with the spirit which it implies; the reconcilement and economic reintegration of European society; and the system of Mandate for the administration of backward territories. We have the power, and we know the course. Almost every element necessary to success has been put into the hands of those now governing the world except, as an old Stoic would say, the things that we must provide ourselves. We have been given everything, except, it would seem, the resolute and sincere will. Just at present that seems lacking; the peoples blame their rulers for the lack of it, and the rulers explain that they dare not offend their peoples. It may be recovered. We have had it in the past in abundance, and we probably have the material for it even now. If not, if for any reason the great democracies permanently prefer to follow low motives and to be governed by inferior men, it looks as if not the British Empire only, but the whole World Order established by the end of the War and summarized roughly in the League of Nations, may pass from history under the same fatal sentence as the great empires of the past—that the world which it ruled hated it and risked all to compass its overthrow.